Successful school leadership

Linking with learning and achievement

Christopher Day, Pam Sammons,
Ken Leithwood, David Hopkins, Qing Gu,
Eleanor Brown and Elpida Ahtaridou

Open University Press

Open University Press
McGraw-Hill Education
McGraw-Hill House
Shoppenhangers Road
Maidenhead
Berkshire
England
SL6 2QL

email: enquiries@openup.co.uk
world wide web: www.openup.co.uk

and Two Penn Plaza, New York, NY 10121-2289, USA

First published 2011

A catalogue record of this book is available from the British Library

ISBN-13: 978-0-33-524243-6 (pb) 978-0-33-524244-3 (hb)
ISBN-10: 0-33-524243-X (pb) 0-33-524244-8 (hb)
eISBN: 978-0-33-524245-0

Library of Congress Cataloging-in-Publication Data
CIP data applied for

Typeset by RefineCatch Limited, Bungay, Suffolk
Printed in Great Britain by CPI Antony Rowe, Chippenham and Eastbourne

Fictitious names of companies, products, people, characters and/or data that may be used herein (in case studies or in examples) are not intended to represent any real individual, company, product or event.

The *McGraw·Hill* Companies

Successful school leadership

Contents

Figures

Tables

x TABLES

Appendices

Contributors

Christopher Day is Professor Emeritus at the School of Education in the University of Nottingham. Prior to this he worked as a teacher, lecturer and local authority schools adviser. He is editor of *Teachers and Teaching: Theory and Practice* and co-editor of the *Educational Action Research* journal. He has recently directed a nine-country European research project on successful principalship in schools in challenging urban contexts; a national project on school leadership and pupil outcomes; and a national project on effective classroom teaching. He is currently directing a 14-country project on successful school principalship. His books on teachers' and leaders' work, lives and effectiveness have been published in several languages and include *The New Lives of Teachers* (2010, Routledge); *Teachers Matter* (2007, Open University Press); *Successful Principalship: International Perspectives* (2007, Springer); *A Passion for Teaching* (2004, Falmer); *International Handbook of the Continuing Professional Development of Teachers* (2004, Open University Press) and *Leading Schools in Times of Change* (2000, Open University Press).

Pam Sammons is a Professor of Education at the Department of Education, University of Oxford and a Senior Research Fellow of Jesus College, Oxford. Previously she was a Professor at the University of Nottingham (2004–09) and a member of its Teaching and Leadership Research Centre. She spent 11 years at the Institute of Education, University of London (1993–2004) where she was a Professor of Education and Co-ordinating Director of its International School Effectiveness and Improvement Centre. She has been involved in educational research for nearly 30 years with a special focus on school effectiveness and improvement, school leadership, pre-school influences and promoting equity in education. She has a strong interest in educational policy reform and evaluation. She has conducted many studies of primary and secondary schools and their influence on pupils. She has special expertise in longitudinal and mixed-methods research designs. Her recent publications include: 'The Contribution of Mixed Methods to Recent Research on Educational Effectiveness', in Tashakkori and Teddlie (eds) *Handbook of Mixed Methods Research* (2010, Sage) and 'Equity and Educational Effectiveness', in *International Encyclopedia of Education* (2010, Elsevier).

Ken Leithwood is Professor Emeritus of Educational Leadership and Policy at OISE/University of Toronto. His research and writing are about school leadership, educational policy and organizational change. He has published more than 80 referred journal articles, and authored or edited more than three dozen books. For example, he is the senior editor of both the first and second *International Handbooks on Educational Leadership and Administration* (1996, 2003, Kluwer) and co-editor of the *International Handbook of Educational Policy* (2007, Kluwer). His most recent books include *Distributed Leadership According to the Evidence* (2009, Routledge), *Leadership with Teachers' Emotions in Mind* (2008, Corwin), *Making Schools Smarter* (2006, Corwin, third edition) and *Teaching for Deep Understanding* (2006, Corwin). Professor Leithwood is the recipient of many awards for his work, such as the University of Toronto's *Impact on Public Policy* award, and is a *Fellow of the Royal Society of Canada*. He currently serves as a special advisor to the Ontario Ministry of Education's Leadership Branch.

David Hopkins is Professor Emeritus at the Institute of Education, University of London, where until recently he held the inaugural HSBC iNet Chair in International Leadership. He is a Trustee of Outward Bound, holds visiting professorships at the Catholic University of Santiago, the Chinese University of Hong Kong and the Universities of Edinburgh, Melbourne and Wales, and consults internationally on school reform. Between 2002 and 2005 he served three Secretary of States as the Chief Adviser on School Standards at the Department for Education and Skills. Previously, he was Chair of the Leicester City Partnership Board and Dean of the Faculty of Education at the University of Nottingham. Before that again he was a Tutor at the University of Cambridge Institute of Education, a secondary school teacher and outward bound instructor. David is also an international mountain guide, who still climbs regularly in the Alps and Himalayas. His recent books, *Every School a Great School* (2007) and *System Leadership in Practice* (2009) are published by the Open University Press.

Qing Gu is an Associate Professor in the School of Education, University of Nottingham, UK. She is a member of the Executive Committee of the British Association for International and Comparative Education (BAICE), a member of the *Compare* editorial board, and Reviews Editor of the *International Journal of Educational Development*. Her research interests are teacher professional development, school leadership and improvement, and intercultural learning. Since she joined the University of Nottingham on completion of her PhD (Birmingham) in 2004, Dr Qing Gu has contributed to the success of a range of international and national research projects as director, co-director and lead researcher, including an ESRC project on international students' experiences in UK higher education, a British Academy project on the impact of study abroad experiences on the returnees' work and lives, a HEFCE project on university–school partnerships and two government-funded large-scale research projects on teachers' work and lives and school leadership. She is also co-director of two ESRC seminar series. She is the author of *Teacher Development: Knowledge and Context* (2007, Continuum), and co-author of *Teachers Matter* (2007, Open University Press), *New Lives of Teachers* (2010, Routledge) and an original paper on mixed-methods research published in *Educational Researcher* in 2008.

Eleanor Brown is a Research Associate and PhD student in the School of Education, University of Nottingham, UK. She has a long-standing interest in education, beginning her career teaching English as a foreign language in Spain and Costa Rica. Since completing a Master's degree in Diplomacy and International Relations in 2006, she has worked as a qualitative researcher on a number of projects including: The Impact of School Leadership on Pupil Outcomes (DCSF), School–University Partnerships (HEFCE), Effective Classroom Practice (ESRC), Cultural Diplomacy (British Council) and Peace Education (British Academy). She has co-authored several articles and reports including: *10 Strong Claims about Successful School Leadership* (2010, National College for Leadership of Schools and Children's Services), 'Education, Citizenship and the New Public Diplomacy in the UK: What Is the Relationship?' (*Citizenship, Social and Economics Education*, 2009), and 'Developing a Culture of Peace via Global Citizenship Education' (*Peace Review*, 2008). She is currently working on an ESRC-funded PhD examining the role of NGOs in global peace education and social change, a comparative study of Britain and Spain.

Elpida Ahtaridou is a Principal Researcher at LSN. Prior to joining LSN, she was a Researcher at the London Centre for Leadership in Learning (LCLL) at the Institute of Education (IoE). Before that Elpida worked as a Lecturer in Education Studies at the University of Central Lancashire (UCLAN) and as a Lecturer in Teacher Training Post-Compulsory Education at the University of Plymouth. Elpida has project managed and participated in a number of international and national research projects including the 'Evaluation of the Policy Impact of PISA', 'Reflections on the Performance of the Mexican Education System', and the 'Analytic Review of School Leadership in England' for the OECD. Her most recent publications include 'System Leadership: A Response to the Challenges Facing Urban Schools in England' in the *International Handbook of Research on Urban Education* (forthcoming, with D. Hopkins) and 'School Leadership in England: Contemporary Challenges, Innovative Responses and Future Trends' (2009, with D. Hopkins and R. Higham).

Foreword

This book builds upon the results of an empirical three-year national research project *The Impact of Leadership on Pupil Outcomes* (IMPACT), which was commissioned by the Department for Children, Schools and Families (DCSF) in conjunction with the National College of School Leadership (NCSL) in England. The project is the largest and most extensive study of contemporary leadership to be conducted in England to date. Its sampling methods and innovative mixed-methods design enabled it to examine the work of heads and other school leaders in a range of primary and secondary schools nationally and, in particular, the impact of the heads upon pupil outcomes. All these schools were recognized as having achieved success in terms of improvement in pupil attainment measures and were highly effective in value-added terms over at least a three-year consecutive period.

Of the few empirical research projects internationally in this area the most notable have been the work of Silins and Mulford (2002) in Australia, which explored connections between leadership and organizational learning; the review of literature by Hallinger and Heck (1996); the best-evidence synthesis reported by Robinson, Hohepa and Lloyd (2009) in New Zealand; and the research by Leithwood, Jantzi and Steinback (2009) in North America. However, none of these investigated leadership exclusively in primary and secondary schools that had demonstrated sustained pupil achievement gains.

Our research sought to test and refine existing models of school leadership as far as they can demonstrate an impact on pupil outcomes. It was hypothesized that while such models were common across contexts in their general form, they would likely be highly adaptable and contingent in their specific enactment. The results demonstrated that heads in more effective schools are successful in improving pupil outcomes through who they are – their values, virtues, dispositions, attributes and competences – the strategies they use, and the specific combination and timely implementation and management of these strategies in response to the unique contexts in which they work. Change which leads to improvement is clearly not a linear process.

The aims of the IMPACT study were:

a) to establish how much variation in pupil outcomes (as measured by, for example, achievement, engagement, involvement, motivation) is accounted for by variation in the types, qualities, strategies, skills and contexts of school leadership, in particular those of heads as 'leaders of leaders'; and

b) to determine the relative strengths of the direct and indirect influences of school leadership, especially that of the head, upon teachers and upon pupils' outcomes.

The study thus sought to:

a) collect and analyse attainment, attendance and behavioural data at a national level in order to explore the relationship between leadership and pupil outcomes;

b) collect evidence to identify and describe variations in effective leadership practice (types, qualities, strategies and skills) with a view to relating these changes to variations in conditions for pupil, teacher and organizational learning and outcomes;

c) explore to what extent variations in pupil outcomes are accounted for by variations in types, qualities, strategies, skills and contexts of leadership;

d) identify which influences significantly moderate the effects of leadership practice on a range of both short- and long-term pupil outcomes;

e) identify which influences significantly mediate the effects of leadership practice on a range of both short- and long-term pupil outcomes; and

f) provide robust, reliable data on a) to b) which would inform the work of the Department for Education and Skills (DCSF), the National College for School Leadership (NCSL), local authorities (LAs), and schools.

Statistical analyses of national data sets on pupils' attainment identified three groups of schools which had made sustained improvements in academic outcomes but from different starting points: Low Start, Moderate Start and High Start. Responses to questionnaires sent to a large national sample of heads and key staff in schools which had made such consistent improvements, combined with 20 detailed case studies of primary and secondary schools, enabled the identification of direct and indirect relationships between the work of effective heads, changes in school and classroom processes and conditions for improvements in pupil outcomes.

Although the IMPACT project focused on schools that were identified as having significantly raised pupil attainment levels over a relatively short three-year period, many of the schools continued to maintain or further improve their results in subsequent years. The ability to continue to improve or to sustain effectiveness over longer periods is the result of heads' applications of strong educational values and combinations and accumulations of context-sensitive strategies within and across school development phases, and an indicator that improvement has become embedded in the school's work and culture.

The project resulted in ten strong, evidence-based claims about successful school leadership:

- Headteachers are the main source of leadership in their schools.
- There are eight key dimensions of successful leadership.
- Headteachers' values are key components in their success.
- Successful heads use the same basic leadership practices but there is no single model for achieving success.
- Differences in context affect the nature, direction and pace of leadership actions.
- Heads contribute to student learning and achievement through a combination and accumulation of strategies and actions.
- There are three broad phases of leadership success.
- Heads grow and secure success by layering leadership strategies and actions.
- Successful heads distribute leadership progressively.
- The successful distribution of leadership depends on the establishment of trust.

While the chapters in this book do not address these claims directly, we return to them in our final chapter.[1]

There are four implications for policy:

- The first is to emphasize that neither 'top-down' nor 'bottom-up' change works just by itself; they have to be in balance – in creative tension. The balance between the two at any one time will depend on the head's diagnosis of the development phase of the school and policy context and their prioritizing and layering of strategic actions.
- Second, in creating new landscapes of schooling, policy makers need to understand the limitations of their role and to focus their energies increasingly on creating the conditions in which professionalism can thrive. This implies horizontal and lateral ways of working with assumptions and governance arrangements very different from what we know now.
- Third, leaders themselves and those responsible for leadership training and development standards need increasingly to focus their efforts on enhancing leaders' values, their diagnostic abilities and the interpersonal and strategic acumen, which enables them to combine,

---

[1] The ten claims have been reported elsewhere in summary form (Day et al., 2010).

accumulate and apply different combinations of strategies which are context-specific in ways which lead to improved pupil outcomes. Such diagnostic abilities, values, qualities, strategies and skills are illustrated in this book. It should be no surprise to realize that much of this is still relatively unknown territory.

- Finally, it is becoming clear that a sense of agency, commitment, resilience, trust, collaboration, the progressive distribution of leadership and moral purpose are at the forefront of leadership innovation.

The research reported in the book should, therefore, be seen not only in the context of the UK government's sustained and persistent initiatives to raise school standards through a range of reforms but in the context of school reform efforts internationally. There needs to be a greater focus in the introduction and management of systems-wide reform upon improving understandings of school leadership in all its forms and contexts and, based upon these, the development of a range of strategies for leadership recruitment, selection, training and development. All of these strategies must explicitly connect the quality of school leadership with the quality of student learning and achievement.

Acknowledgements

We would wish to acknowledge four groups of colleagues who were part of the project research team for various periods and who made important contributions to the development of the original IMPACT project: first, the work of our research colleagues Alison Kington, Clare Penlington, Alma Harris, Palak Mehta and James Ko; second, the contributions made by the Project Steering Group, especially the critical friendships of Graham Hanscomb and Martin Young; third, the project secretary Martina Daykin and Hayley McCalla, the person whose patience, humour and technical skills enabled this book to be assembled. Our final words of appreciation are reserved for the heads and staff of the 20 case study schools who gave generously of their time so that knowledge about associations between who heads are and what they do to grow and sustain improvement in the education of children and young people in their schools might be increased. It is these and all the skilful, committed and resilient professionals in schools throughout the world to whom this book is dedicated.

PART 1
Contexts for success

1 Leaders and contexts
What previous research tells us about the relationship

The genesis of this book was a large-scale, three-year research project carried out in England entitled 'The Impact of School Leadership on Pupil Outcomes' (IMPACT). Like a great deal of other research on leadership, one primary aim of the project was to discover what it is that successful school leaders do – their 'practices' – and why these are effective in promoting school improvement. Several subsequent chapters summarize what we learned about this matter. But this first chapter is not about leadership practices; it is about how the contexts in which leaders work influences (or ought to influence) such practices. One of the central claims appearing throughout this book is that: (a) there is a core set of practices that almost all successful leaders use, but (b) to have their desired effect, these practices must be enacted in ways that are sensitively appropriate to the contexts in which leaders find themselves.

Leadership success, in other words, depends significantly on leaders' values and qualities, and on the skill with which leaders understand the underlying causes of the problems they encounter and respond to those problems in ways that are productive *in context*, not in general. Contexts, from this perspective, are unavoidable elements of the problems leaders need to solve if they are to improve their organizations. Failure to understand and respond suitably to one's context is a formula for inadequate solution finding and weak leadership. Indeed, Kelly and Shaw argue that such inadequacies are common. 'Many schools', they claim, 'don't solve problems, they adopt solutions' (2010: 50).

Ironically, the contexts in which most school leaders find themselves also make adopting solutions a pretty attractive 'modus operandi'. For example, if the adopted solution doesn't work, someone else is to blame. Furthermore, many of those at a higher pay grade than yours are urging you to adopt their solutions – perhaps even holding you accountable for such adoption – since they invented many of the solutions to begin with and need confirmation of their efforts. But adopting solutions is even more seductive for school leaders because it is low cost, cognitively speaking. The famously hectic, fast-paced nature of school leaders' work makes low cost, if not essential, then at least very seductive. School leaders rarely have more than several minutes to think about any single challenge before going on to the next (e.g., Kmetz, 1982). Indeed, evidence suggests that principals are confronted with about 150 distinct problems to solve in the course of a typical day (Leithwood and Steinbach, 1995), which explains why 'running on automatic pilot' is how most school leaders make it through their days.

Interacting with different individuals and groups in different contexts to get problems solved and responding (rather than reacting) to a range of external local and national guidelines and policies is what all successful school leaders do well. Because the contexts are so complicated and intense much of the time, selecting those features of the individual, group, school or policy contexts that warrant explicit problem solving by the school leader is a key leadership capacity. Do some features of the context matter more than others? If so, how do they matter? These are the questions explored in this chapter.

The significant place of context in general leadership theory

Educational leadership research has not yet done justice to the importance of the ability to lead and manage contexts, and the problems and dilemmas which they create, in explaining leadership success. The most practical consequence of this neglect has been failure to adequately prepare leaders for the unique challenges they will face if they are to be successful in those contexts. However, a number of well-tested general leadership theories acknowledge, often in quite different ways, the importance of leaders' contexts. A sample of four such theories illustrate this claim. While these theories are rarely reflected in studies of educational leadership, they demonstrate just how critical general leadership theorists consider context to be in accounting for leadership success. They also illustrate the wide range of contexts that have been considered relevant for leaders' attention.

The first illustrative theory is Yukl's (1994) Multiple Linkage model. This model asserts a prominent role for 'situational variables' which influence many potential mediators of leadership influence independently of anything leaders do; for example, while teacher motivation is a critical mediator of heads' leadership, the high levels of commitment many teachers bring to their work with students significantly discounts the negative influence on their motivation of otherwise demotivating heads' behaviour. Examples of situational variables which Yukl has found consequential for leaders' consideration are size of the work group, organizations' policies and procedures, and the prior training and experience of organizational members.

A second example is *leader-member exchange theory* (LMX) (e.g., Graen and Uhl-Bien, 1995). This theory asserts the likelihood of quite different leader–follower relations depending on leaders' perceptions of followers' attitudes, capacities and responsibilities. Variation in teacher attributes, the context for leadership in this theory, means, for example, that a successful head will interact quite differently with the 'newly minted' teacher struggling to teach reading to her class of students who mostly have English as a second language (ESL) than she will with the veteran teacher who routinely offers workshops to colleagues in her network or LA (local authority) or school district on teaching ESL students. A recent study of leadership distribution (Anderson, 2010) found that teacher expertise was the most significant criterion for principals in their decisions about such distribution. So teacher experience and expertise are key contextual variables when school leadership is viewed through an LMX lens.

Information processing perspectives on leadership (e.g., Lord and Maher, 1993) are arguably the most context-sensitive of all the approaches to understanding how and why leaders adapt to the contexts in which they find themselves. From these perspectives, leaders shape their actions in response to both internal and external contexts. Internal contexts include their own understandings (e.g., knowledge about effective teaching and learning), dispositions (e.g., sense of self-efficacy) and characteristics (e,g., gender and other physical attributes). Leaders' understandings and dispositions strongly influence their interpretation of the challenges they face and what would be a useful response to those challenges, implicating leader experience, again, as an important contextual variable. Leaders' characteristics, in contrast, influence how others respond to what the leader does, a response which in part depends on the nature of the leadership 'prototypes' (internalized models of ideal leaders) possessed by colleagues and/or followers and judgements by those colleagues about how well the leader matches their prototypes. Leadership, according to this perspective, is attributed to a person by those who then volunteer to be followers, pointing to the experiences with, and understandings about, leadership on the part of one's school colleagues as a key contextual variable.

Cross-cultural leadership theory provides a final example of contextually sensitive approaches to leadership. The norms, values and taken-for-granted understandings widely shared within national cultures define the meaning of context for this line of theory. By far the largest effort of its kind, the GLOBE project (e.g., House et al., 2004), for example, has examined the relationship between six dimensions of national culture (e.g., assertiveness, future orientation, uncertainty avoidance, power distance) and the preference for different leadership practices (e.g., charismatic, team-oriented, participative) across 62 countries. Results suggest significant differences among national cultures in the dominant prototypes of successful leadership. For example, people from country cultures which value high 'power distance' (see Hofstede, 2001, for more on this dimension of culture) are much more accepting of non-participative forms of leader decision making. Although cross-cultural leadership research highlights elements of context not directly relevant to the study on which this book is based, it does provide further support for claims that a host of contextual variables are likely to exercise significant effects on the success leaders experience in their efforts to increase the productivity of their organizations.

Research on school leaders' contexts

In 1996, Hallinger and his colleagues concluded that 'researchers have given inadequate attention to the influence that the organizational context exerts on educational administrators' (Hallinger et al., 1996: 529), even though it seems self-evident that the 'school's environment offers both constraints and resources that shape the situation in which the principal will lead' (p. 532). In the years since that assessment, the amount of research at least touching on school leaders' contexts has grown considerably. For example, in preparation for writing this chapter, we examined the past decade's issues of six of the most prominent academic journals publishing educational leadership research.[1] Adopting a liberal definition of what counts as research on leaders' contexts, we were able to locate a corpus of 60 original studies.

While 60 studies seems substantial, it is clear from our reading of this research that approaches to the study of context have been relatively eclectic, making the accumulation of knowledge complicated. At one extreme, claims have been made about context being almost all that matters for leaders without the provision of systematic evidence to justify such a claim; some case study approaches to better understanding successful leadership are the most common sources of this claim (e.g., Gordon and Patterson, 2006). A very different position on leadership contexts has emerged from quantitative studies of educational leadership which sometimes treat contextual variables as something to be 'controlled for' or 'partialled out' of explanations for leader effects. Such an approach essentially dismisses context as a substantive problem to be addressed by leaders. However, in the educational effectiveness literature there are a growing number of studies that seek to study the role of school context, especially schools in disadvantaged or challenging communities (Muijs et al., 2004; Harris et al., 2006).

Notwithstanding such approaches, the significant amount of recently published research does help to inform us about the consequences of leaders' contexts for what leaders do and the impact of those practices. But these studies conceptualize leadership contexts in two quite different ways.

---

[1] *Educational Administration Quarterly, Journal of Educational Administration, Journal of School Leadership, Educational Leadership and Management, School Effectiveness and School Improvement*, and the *International Journal of Leadership in Education*.

One set of studies conceives of contexts as *antecedents* of leadership practices. Underlying this conception is the (usually implicit) assumption that leaders, more or less explicitly, think about the circumstances in which they are working and tailor what they do accordingly. This assumption, consistent with both 'contingent' and 'styles' leadership theory (Northouse, 2007), imagines leaders possessing large repertoires of practices which they are able to flexibly match and enact in ways that are well suited to the needs, challenges and opportunities facing their organizations at specific points in time.

The second set of studies conceptualizes contexts as *moderators* of leaders' effects on organizational outcomes. Moderators either dampen or magnify the impact on organizational outcomes of the same set of leadership practices. This conception of contexts is consistent with models of leadership claiming that some sets of leadership practices are likely to be more effective than others in most contexts. Both instructional and transformational leadership theories are examples of such models (e.g., Hallinger, 2003; Leithwood and Jantzi, 2006). But the implicit assumption in studies of contexts as moderators is that when leaders behave in similar ways across different contexts, their contribution to organizational outcomes may turn out to be more or less useful depending on the settings in which they are exercised. This section of the chapter reviews a sample of the research on educational leaders' contexts sometimes treated as antecedents and sometimes as moderators. A total of 12 contextual variables (some belonging to larger categories) are identified and the nature of their influence on what leaders do is described.

School characteristics

School size

Considerable evidence suggests that while smaller schools are generally more productive for student learning (Leithwood and Jantzi, 2009), they are exceptionally challenging for their leaders, expecially when these schools are also in rural areas. As Clarke and Wildy's (2004) study points out, for example, leaders of small schools often have teaching as well as administrative duties, may find themselves located in very conservative communities, have greater influence on their schools because they are a larger proportion of the staff, but are awarded less influence in their districts or LAs than leaders of large schools.

School level

Differences in the contexts found in primary (elementary), middle and secondary schools have consistently different effects on the practices of their leaders. For example, Seashore Louis and Wahlstrom (in press) found that elementary, as compared with middle and secondary schools, experienced higher levels of both shared and instructional leadership with significant impacts on student learning. A teacher in middle and high schools would be: 'less likely to trust their principals, to report that he or she actively involves parents and teachers in decisions, and is active as an instructional leader in the building. At the secondary level, high schools have a higher "leadership deficit" than middle schools.' Of course, the effects of school size and school level are often difficult to separate because of systematic differences in the size of elementary and secondary schools in most jurisdictions. Typically smaller primary (elementary) schools, this evidence suggests, should enjoy more successful leadership practices on average.

Subject matter

Spillane's (2005) study of leadership in a sample of Chicago elementary schools was concerned with school leaders' beliefs and practices about improving their students' literacy as compared with numeracy capacities. These differences were marked. As Spillane explains:

> Regardless of their position, most leaders' visions for instructional improvement involved integrating literacy throughout the day rather than treating it as a stand-alone subject. Further, leaders understood literacy as an overarching measure of student and school progress. In contrast, leaders constructed their responsibilities with respect to mathematics as getting teachers to follow the curriculum in order that students would do well on standardized tests. Mathematics was a priority mainly because of district policy.
>
> (Spillane, 2005: 389)

Leaders in this study also looked to quite different resources for their school improvement efforts. For improving literacy, these leaders typically looked to the expertise of teachers and teacher leaders within their own schools, whereas expertise for improving mathematics was thought to come primarily from external sources.

Academic emphasis

A growing body of research has begun to point to a cultural variable, academic emphasis, as a critical school-level influence on student learning. This research (e.g., Ma and Klinger, 2000; McGuigan and Hoy, 2006) indicates that increases in a school's academic climate are positively related to increased maths and reading achievement, the size of the relationship competing with socio-economic status (SES) in its explanatory power (Goddard, Sweetland and Hoy, 2000).

Some of this evidence also suggests that it is an influential mediator of leadership effects on students. De Maeyer et al.'s (2006) research is one source of such evidence. Carried out in 47 Flemish secondary schools, this study examined the effects on student learning of 'integrated leadership', a concept of leadership proposed by Marks and Printy (2003) which combines elements of instructional and transformational leadership. De Maeyer et al. found that 'integrated' leadership had a greater indirect influence on reading proficiency in schools with higher levels of academic emphasis.

Teacher characteristics

Collective teacher efficacy (CTE)

This shared teacher disposition is conceptualized as the level of confidence a group of teachers feels about their ability to organize and implement whatever educational initiatives are required for students to reach high standards of achievement. The effect of efficacy (or collective confidence) on teacher perform-ance is indirect through the persistence it engenders in the face of initial failure and the opportunities it creates for a confident group to learn its way forward, rather than giving up. High levels of collective teacher efficacy are associated with considerably improved experiences for students (e.g., Goddard et al., 2000).

In highly efficacious schools, teachers accept responsibility for their students' learning. Learning difficulties are not assumed to be an inevitable by-product of low SES, lack of ability or family background. Among many other positive consequences, CTE creates high expectations for students and encourages teachers to set challenging benchmarks for themselves, engage in high levels of planning and organization, and devote more classroom time to academic learning (Tschannen-Moran and Barr, 2004).

When teachers feel highly efficacious, those in leadership roles are able to tackle more ambitious improvement initiatives and spend less effort convincing their teaching colleagues of the need for change, and can expect teachers to provide considerable leadership themselves.

Trust in colleagues, students and parents

This form of relational trust includes a belief or expectation on the part of most teachers that their colleagues, students and parents support the school's goals for student learning, and will reliably work toward achieving those goals. Transparency, competence, benevolence and reliability are among the quali-ties persuading others that a person is trustworthy. Evidence suggests that teacher trust is critical to the success of schools, and nurturing trusting rela-tionships with students and parents is a key element in improving student learning (e.g., Lee and Croninger, 1994; Bryk and Schneider, 2003).

In schools with low levels of trust, leaders face uphill battles in their improvement efforts. Trust is commonly thought of as the lubricant that keeps organizations running smoothly. When organizational members and stakeholders lack trust in one another, their willingness to collaborate is much diminished and the initiative allowed those in leadership roles significantly restrained. Recent evidence, including our own (see Chapter 9), points to principal leadership as a critical contributor to trust among teachers, parents and students (e.g., Tschannen-Moran, 2001; Bryk and Schneider, 2003).

Leader characteristics

Length of experience

This variable combines both length of experience in one's school and overall years as a school leader. As a central tendency, school leaders face a steep learning curve in the early parts of their work but become increasingly confident in their abilities over time. For example, Weindling and Dimmock (2006) found that newly appointed heads in England found themselves grappling with difficulties arising from the legacy of the leadership style and practices of the previous head, the need to communicate and consult with staff, the public image of the school, and possible weaknesses in some members of the senior leadership team. This initial set of challenges for new heads was followed by efforts to make relatively superficial (often organizational) changes in their schools, moving on to a focus on more fundamental improvement to the quality of teaching and learning. If heads stayed in the same school for an extended period of time (e.g., eight or more years), they were likely to spend time consolidating their earlier changes before entering a period of potential complacency. The heads in the study reported in this book, however, did not conform to this pattern, but rather continued to demonstrate their passion for continuing improvement. Leaders who moved on to another school in Weindling and Dimmock's (2006) research, however, were likely to revisit many of the earlier stages, although sometimes moving through them more quickly the second or third time.

Race

Although based on the study of a single school in the USA, Brooks and colleagues' (2007) analysis, within and across groups of black and white secondary school leaders, points to substantial race-related differences in leaders' values and norms. Black leaders in this study viewed themselves as crucial role models for black students waging an 'uphill battle' against the negative influence of popular culture on the aspirations of their students.

These leaders also viewed themselves as advocates for their students, actively seeking out scholarships and other opportunities that would contribute to student success. They recruited black teachers to this largely African-American school and 'mentored promising black teachers into formal leadership positions' (Brooks and Jean-Marie, 2007: 761). White teachers in the school, on the other hand, appeared to hold limiting stereotypes of their students' potential and the challenges presented to them by their family circumstances.

These stereotypes did not seem to be informed by any direct evidence (it is not clear from this study whether black leaders' responses to white students were also based on stereotypes). Relationships between the two sets of leaders were restrained, largely avoiding any direct discussion of racial issues facing the school. This study suggests that, in the face of significant racial diversity, leaders are challenged to discard their stereotypes and explicitly work to understand unfamiliar cultures.

District/regional context

The work leaders undertake in their schools is typically influenced quite directly by the larger organizational context in which their schools are located. Local authorities in England and school districts in North America will be the most common examples of such contexts for many readers. Among the most pervasive new initiatives by districts in North America (strongly promoted by national accountability policies) is the demand that school leaders and their staffs become more evidence-based in their decision making; and local authorities in England are charged by the national government with ensuring that their standards for teaching, learning, and pupils' well-being and attainment are met.

Studies of school responses to this widespread initiative help to illustrate the increasingly interdependent nature of school and LA/district leadership if major changes in schools' standard-operating procedures are to materialize. For example, Wohlstetter and colleagues (2008) found that school leaders and their staffs require not only considerable support from their districts, but also sufficient autonomy to make decisions that reflect the authentic needs of their schools. The extent to which school leaders use systematic evidence in their decisions is also influenced by the data-use practices modelled by LA/district leaders. District or LA leaders also are the primary sources school leaders look to for help in building their data-related capacities.

National context

Investments in education

Leaders face widely different challenges arising from the levels of investments their countries make in education. Taking an extreme example, Bush and Oduro report that 'in 1990 expenditure per student in OECD countries was

40 times that of countries in sub-Saharan Africa' (2006: 361). For school leaders in such countries, these levels of investment translate into poorly trained and motivated teachers, crowded and decaying facilities, lack of basic educational resources and, in extreme circumstances, even lack of water or latrines. Under such conditions, inordinate amounts of a school leader's efforts are consumed with basic operational and administrative tasks, dramatically eroding time for improving teaching and learning.

Policies

Since the mid-1990s, national education policies have had an increasingly strong influence on the work of school leaders. In England, for example, implementing the National Curriculum and the Primary Strategies (Weindling and Dimmock, 2006) and the 'Every Child Matters' (ECM) agenda has been a substantial part of the work of school leaders, in much the same way as the No Child Left Behind (Evans, 2009) legislation in the USA.

National policies such as these significantly restrict the autonomy of school leaders and their staffs, forcing attention in schools to the consideration and implementation of government-defined priorities. The influence of such national policies on the work of school leaders is a function of the mechanisms for ensuring accountability that are part of them. In countries with such policies, a significant part of the visioning and direction-setting functions associated with successful leadership has migrated to central levels.

Characteristics of students and their families

The final context examined in this chapter is a large handful of conditions or features experienced by students and their families including, for example, national or ethnic culture, religion, parental education and expectations, language spoken in the home, number of parents in the home, parents' employment status and especially family income. Although each of these features may have demonstrably independent effects, more often than not they 'travel' in clusters. In a great deal of the research aiming to explain variation in student achievement across school, a sample of these features are aggregated to represent the family's SES.

Schools serving low-SES families often find themselves in an 'iron circle' that begins with the family's impoverished economic conditions and poor formal qualifications. These conditions may be a consequence of unemployment; cultural, racial and linguistic diversity; recent immigration; high mobility; family breakups and the like. These conditions often give rise to such family risk factors as erratic parenting skills, poor parental supervision, low family income, poverty, isolation, family violence, abuse, neglect, and parental conflict. Low SES families are, also, more likely to have low expectations for their children's performance at school.

Impoverished economic conditions increase the chances that families will be struggling to survive in communities living in high-density housing and that their members will be suffering from malnutrition, other health problems and substance abuse. These are community risk factors, as are high turnover of residences, and lack of facilities and services for young people.

Students from diverse, minority and economically deprived family backgrounds have traditionally been much less successful in school than have their majority, middle-class peers. The immense literatures on urban schooling, social justice and equity are some of the most visible indicators of just how concerned educators, policy makers and academics are about increasing the success rates of these students. But the size of these literatures and the extended time over which they have developed also suggest how intractable the problem has proven to be. Relatively recent calls to 'turn schools around' and 'narrow the achievement gap' are simply contemporary expressions of these long-standing concerns.

Beginning with the now-famous evidence reported by James Coleman and his colleagues (1966), study after study suggest that family SES explains from a third to a half of the difference in student achievement across schools (Lytton and Pyryt, 1998). Socio-economic status is highly related also to violence, dropping out of school, entry to post-secondary education and levels of both adult employment and income. Most measures of SES are relatively immune to change by schools. But there are other characteristics of families which schools and their leaders should consider alterable. Walberg (1984), referring to these characteristics as family 'educational culture', identified the assumptions, norms and beliefs held by the family about intellectual work in general and school work in particular. Family educational culture manifests itself in family work habits, academic guidance and support provided to children, and stimulation to think about issues in the larger environment. Other components of family culture include academic and occupational aspirations and expectations of parents or guardians for their children, the provision of adequate health and nutritional conditions, and physical settings in the home conducive to academic work.

Differences in the family-related conditions of students have created some of the most persistent challenges faced by leaders and their teacher colleagues in efforts to provide more equitable outcomes for all of their students. These circumstances are also associated with forms of leadership often different from the leadership found in schools serving middle-class students. Hallinger, Brickman and Davis found that 'principals in higher-SES schools exercised more active instructional leadership . . . than their counterparts in school serving students of lower SES' (1996: 542). This finding is consistent with most research on this issue prior to (e.g., Goldring, 1990) and following this study. Seashore Louis and Wahlstrom's (in press) study, for example, found that:

As student poverty and diversity increase, teachers' experience of shared and instructional leadership from the principal decreases. In addition, teachers in lower income and higher diversity schools also report that teachers' leadership around collective responsibility for student learning is lower, and that teachers are less likely to share norms around teaching and instruction. In other words, both principal and teacher leadership that focuses on improving student learning is less.

(Seashore Louis and Wahlstrom, in press)

Evidence reported by Goldring and her colleagues (2008) diverges from this general conclusion, however. This well-designed study distinguished two clusters of principals, those attending to many different factors in their school more or less simultaneously (eclectic leaders) and those with a narrower focus on teaching and learning and/or student-related issues. Contextual factors proved to be a big part of the explanation for differences in how these two groups of leaders behaved. Eclectic leaders were located in schools with higher academic emphasis, higher student engagement and fewer disadvantaged students. Most were also leading medium-sized elementary schools. Eclectic leadership, it is reasonable to conclude, may be quite functional under such circumstances; the job is to ensure that the school maintains its good practices and that all stakeholders remain committed to the school's mission. Leaders with a narrower focus typically faced more challenging problems. These problems required deeper engagement in addressing the most pressing challenges facing their school improvement efforts, particularly though not exclusively in their early years of headship, as the research reported in this book shows.

Conclusion

This chapter began with the claim that leadership success is heavily dependent on the qualities and skills through which leaders understand the underlying causes of the problems they encounter and respond to those problems in ways that are productive *in context* – not *in general*. Contexts, we argued, are unavoidable elements of the problems leaders need to solve if they are to improve their organizations. We further argued that failure to understand and respond suitably to one's context is a formula for inadequate solution finding and weak leadership. So a central goal for the chapter was to illustrate the range of contexts that might need to be understood as part of successful leadership problem solving – a sensitizing goal.

Our review of evidence has been linear, to this point, however; we have reviewed one context at a time. But no leader has the luxury of doing anything so simple. Consider, for example, the general problem of a school head helping teachers adapt their pedagogy to better meet the needs of a growing population of economically deprived children now entering their school. Pedagogical practices well suited to an earlier, largely middle-class population of students become a liability in the face of this quite different group of students. The general solution to this problem, executed more or less collaboratively with one's teachers, is something like this:

1   Collect information about the forms of pedagogy that have proved to be successful with disadvantaged students.
2   Collect information about forms of pedagogy that are typically practised in your school.
3   Identify similarities and differences between the typical practices used in your school and the practices that have proved to be successful with disadvantaged students.
4   Provide professional development for staff aimed at helping them understand the changes that are needed in their pedagogy and acquiring the skills needed to make those changes.
5   Monitor the implementation of those changes in teachers' classrooms, identifying additional supports that teachers need in order to change.
6   Assess the effects of these changed pedagogical practices on students' learning and engagement and refine your solution in response to this assessment.

While this general solution seems useful as a framework for what school leaders might do in the face of this problem, does it matter how this solution is enacted by a leader:

*   *if the school is in a policy context featuring annual high-stakes tests for students or not?* The effects of the changes in teachers' pedagogy have to be visible in the test results very quickly.
*   *if the school is a primary or secondary school?* Getting a good estimate of teachers' existing practices is more challenging for leaders who may have very little familiarity with the specialized forms of instruction enacted in some secondary school disciplines.
*   *if the school is serving a socio-economically highly disadvantaged community?* The effects of changes in pupil behaviour, attendance and engagement in class have to be visible in the early stages of new headship.
*   *if the students' families are Eastern European, Asian, African, Mexican or Vietnamese?* Cultural, ethnic and religious traditions strongly influence the intellectual and emotional starting points for student learning.
*   *if the students' first language is English or Urdu?* If the first language of students is not the language of instruction, a whole other layer

of second language instruction will have to be introduced to the school.

- *if the school is in England or Thailand?* The Western leadership practices expected in England not only allow for, but assume, considerable initiative from those in formal school leadership roles. Expectations of leaders in Thailand are much more community- or family-like in nature.
- *if the school serves 200 students or 1500 students?* It is clearly more complicated to collect and make sense of the current pedagogical practices of 60 as compared with 12 teachers.
- *if the school leader is highly trusted and long serving or is new to the school and has not yet developed a trusting relationship with staff?* Leaders who are highly trusted and well known to their staffs are awarded much more latitude in their decision making by their staffs than are leaders who have yet to develop such trust.

Each of these unique features of the leader's context does matter; some features matter a great deal. Yet this would seem to support the view of context that we disparaged in the introduction to this chapter (the 'context-is-all-that-matters' view). But that is not our conclusion, nor is it the position adopted in the rest of the book.

The problem with the context-is-all-that-matters position is that there is nothing for leaders to build on as they immerse themselves in problem solving; under such conditions, the cognitive cost of problem solving would be exorbitant. And this is what creates an important role for those leadership practices extolled in the more fully tested models of successful leadership. Research often guided by these models does justify the claim that some practices are very useful across contexts (Day and Leithwood, 2007). This is true of both the instructional and transformational models alluded to above, for example, not to mention models of 'authentic' and 'integrated' leadership (Marks and Printy, 2003; Avolio and Gardner, 2005), among others. Our argument throughout the book, therefore, is that there is a knowable set of core leadership practices used by almost all successful leaders (described more fully in Chapter 6). These practices provide the foundation for context-sensitive problem solving when enacted in ways that are appropriate for those contexts. However, as the chapters in this book will demonstrate, these core practices are only the starting points for leadership action, not the end. Moreover, the empirical research findings reported in this book demonstrate unequivocally that the application of leadership practices themselves need to be accompanied by timely and sustained possession of certain leadership virtues, qualities and dispositions.

2 What all successful leaders do in most contexts

The previous chapter ended with the claim that successful leadership depends significantly on the sensitivity of leaders' practices to the many features of the school and wider contexts that make a difference to the quality of schooling for children. We also claimed, however, that leaders exercise such sensitivity by building on a foundation of 'core' leadership practices which, evidence suggests, are useful in most circumstances. Leaders' sensitivity manifests itself in adaptations, combinations and accumulations of these core practices to contexts that matter, as well as sometimes enacting other 'purpose-built' practices.

These claims emerged from an extensive review of evidence about different aspects of school leadership which we carried out prior to beginning data collection for the study on which this book is based (Leithwood et al., 2006b). The second chapter of that initial review of evidence, entitled 'The Nature of Successful Leadership Practices', provided a detailed description of the core leadership practices, and these practices became an important part of the framework, guiding especially the quantitative portion of our research project, which employed a survey approach (discussed in more detail in Chapter 3). We 'tested' the extent to which successful leaders in our study sample enacted those practices and how those practices interacted with other elements of the school organization to influence school improvement and pupil learning.

Results of our study support our claim that the practices identified in our initial review of evidence are central to what successful leaders do. So this chapter provides a summarized description of those practices, as they appeared in our initial review, and adds the relatively small amount of evidence reported by others since we completed that review.

The four categories of core leadership practices

The core leadership practices summarized in the following sections of this chapter 'fit' into four categories, each category representing an important goal for leaders to accomplish if they are to successfully help improve their schools. These categories (slightly re-titled from their original) are 'Setting directions', 'Developing people', 'Refining and aligning the organization', and 'Improving the teaching and learning programme'. Associated with each of these categories are from three to five specific leadership behaviours or practices, 14 in total.

Justification for our claims about the value of these practices initially was based on our own analyses of original empirical research, along with such previous systematic reviews of relevant evidence by ourselves and others as, for example, Yukl (1994), Hallinger (2003), Waters et al. (2003), Leithwood and Jantzi (2005) and Leithwood and Riehl (2005). Some of these reviews included whatever leadership practices were measured by the available research, some were based on evidence collected in non-school contexts, and some had their roots in theories or 'models' of either instructional or transformational leadership. The body of evidence related to our claims about the four sets of leadership practices is by now quite large, with approximately four dozen published studies and more than 180 unpublished studies conducted in school and local authority/district contexts since about 1990. By most social science standards, this body of evidence should be considered relatively large and is growing quickly in its methodological sophistication. Amount and quality of evidence aside, however, the way one makes sense of this evidence is also an important issue. Our approach is represented in the four core leadership categories which, we believe, are warranted on both theoretical and empirical grounds.

As we argued in our initial review, simply listing specific leadership practices can be pretty meaningless unless there is some underlying idea holding them together. The great advantage of leadership theories, for example, is that theories possess conceptual glue which help to explain how and why things work as they do and so build understanding. The glue that holds the categories of core leadership practices together can be found in an explanation of why each category is important to exercise if leaders are to have a substantial and positive impact on their schools.

The extent to which educational policies and other reform efforts improve what students learn finally depends on their consequences for who teachers are and what teachers do. What teachers do, according to a particularly useful model for explaining workplace performance (O'Day, 1996; Rowan, 1996), is a function of their motivations and abilities, and the situations in which they work. The relationship among these variables can be represented in this deceptively simple formula:

$$Pj = f(Mj, Aj, Sj)$$

in which:

- P stands for a teacher's performance;
- M stands for the teacher's motivation (in Yukl's (1994) Multiple Linkage model of managerial effectiveness, M includes the effort to engage in a high level of performance as well as demonstrating a high degree of personal responsibility and commitment to the organization's goals);
- A stands for the teacher's abilities, professional knowledge and skills (in Yukl's model, such performance also includes their understanding of their job responsibilities); and
- S represents their work settings – the features of their school and classroom.

Relationships among the variables in this model are considered to be interdependent. This means two things. It means that each variable has an effect on the remaining two (for example, aspects of teachers' work environments are significant influences on their motivations). It also means that changes in all three variables need to happen in concert or performance will not change much. For example, neither high ability and low motivation, nor high motivation and low ability foster high levels of teacher performance; neither does high ability and high motivation in a dysfunctional work environment. Furthermore, a dysfunctional work setting will likely depress initially high levels of both ability and motivation.

The implications for leadership practices of this account of workplace performance are twofold. First, leaders will need to engage in practices with the potential to improve all elements in the formula – teachers' and other staff members' abilities and motivations, and the settings in which they work. Second, although not directly related to the purposes of this chapter, leaders will need to engage in those practices more or less simultaneously. The overall function of successful leaders, according to this formulation, is to improve the condition of all three variables, since they are interdependent. How each of the four categories is related to such improvement is explained in subsequent sections of the chapter.

A second type of theoretical justification for the four categories is that they are closely related to how others have tried to make sense of evidence about successful school leadership practices. For example, Hallinger's (2003) model of instructional leadership includes three categories of practices (encompassing ten more specific behaviours):

- *Defining the school's mission*, which includes framing and then communicating the school's goals (part of our 'Setting directions' category);
- *Managing the instructional programme*, which includes supervising and evaluating instruction, co-ordinating the curriculum, and monitoring

student progress (included in our 'Improving the teaching and learning programme' category); and

- *Promoting a positive school learning climate*, which encompasses protecting instructional time, promoting professional development, maintaining high visibility, providing incentives for teachers, and providing incentives for learning (specific practices distributed across our 'Developing people' and 'Refining and aligning the organization' categories).

A more recent example of such sensemaking is the 'best evidence synthesis' of school leadership effects research by Robinson, Hohepa and Lloyd (2009). These researchers proposed a five-fold classification of successful school leadership practices, as follows:

- *Establishing goals and expectations*, part of our 'Setting directions' category;
- *Resourcing strategically*, a significant part of 'Refining and aligning the organization';
- *Planning, co-ordinating, and evaluating teaching and the curriculum*, much of which we have included in 'Improving the teaching and learning programme';
- *Promoting and participating in teacher learning and development*, our 'Developing people' category; and
- *Ensuring an orderly and supportive environment*, also part of 'Refining and aligning the organization'.

What about empirical justification for the four categories? Such a justification depends on evidence demonstrating the value of the practices as a whole. The most recent such evidence is provided by two reviews of unpublished empirical dissertation evidence, the second of which is a quantitative meta-analysis (Leithwood and Sun, 2009, 2010). These were reviews of approximately five dozen studies of the effects of the four categories of leadership practices (as well as the individual practices within each category) on three types of 'outcomes', including school conditions, teacher attitudes, dispositions and practices, and student outcomes. Using an 'effect size'[1] statistic ('d') to report results, the four categories of practices, as a whole, had a relatively large effect (d = .57) on a range of teacher 'outcomes' associated with school improvement: for example,

---

[1] An effect size (ES) is any of several measures of association or of the strength of a relation and is often thought of as a measure of practical significance. This statistic allows us to judge the *importance* of a result. It also allows us to directly *compare* the results of several studies which report evidence in quite different ways. It is common for effect sizes in the .20 range to be interpreted as small, in the .50 range to be interpreted as moderate, and .70 or more to be interpreted as strong.

job satisfaction, sense of community, trust in leader, organizational citizenship behaviour, teacher efficacy and teacher motivation. The four categories of leadership practices as a whole also had a moderately strong effect (.44) on a wide range of school conditions influencing the implementation of change including, for example, teacher cohesion, improved teaching, school culture and shared decision making. These reviews of evidence found, on average, a small but significant effect on student learning – but with effects ranging from insignificant to moderately large, depending on the teacher, school and classroom conditions mediating that influence.

Three quite recent individual studies add further empirical support for the value of our four-fold classification of successful leadership practices. Leithwood, Harris and Strauss (2010) report significant contributions of the four sets of practices to school turnaround success and explain how different phases of the turnaround process call for modifications in how each set of practices is enacted. Finnigan and Stewart (2009) also reported evidence pointing to the value of the four sets of practices for leaders working to turn around underperforming schools. Finally, with a focus on leadership practices which influence improvements in classroom instruction, Supovitz et al. found that 'principals are the most important actor in student learning . . . in part because of their indirect influence on teacher instruction through collaboration and communication around instruction between peer teachers' (2010: 46). In addition, 'principals . . . focus on instruction, foster community and trust, and clearly communicate school mission and goals' (p. 43); these practices cross all four of our categories. The next four sections of the chapter provide a brief description and justification for each of the four categories.[2]

Setting directions

This category of practices carries the bulk of the effort to motivate leaders' colleagues (Hallinger and Heck, 1998). It is about the establishment of 'moral purpose' (Fullan, 2003; Hargreaves and Fink, 2006) as a basic stimulant for one's work. Most theories of motivation argue that people are motivated to accomplish personally important goals for themselves. For example, such goals are one of four sources of motivation in Bandura's theory of human motivation (1986).

Hallinger's (2003) review of evidence concerning instructional leadership found that mission-building activities on the part of principals are the most influential set of leadership practices, and the synthesis of evidence by Robinson, Hohepa and Lloyd (2009) reported a medium effect size of .42 for

---

[2] These sections are adapted from Leithwood et al. (2006), Chapter 2.

practices they associated with *Establishing goals and expectations*. From her review of leadership that influences classroom practice, for example, Printy (2010) concluded that:

> Principals who develop compelling missions and goals, establish cultures of collaboration and trust and encourage instructional improvement, draw teachers together to engage in joint work to improve teaching and learning.
>
> (Printy, 2010: 115)

Three more specific sets of practices are included in this category, all of which are aimed at bringing a focus to both the individual and collective work of staff in the school or district. Undertaken skilfully, these practices are one of the main sources of motivation and inspiration for the work of staff.

Building a shared vision

Building and communicating compelling visions of the organization's future is a fundamental task included in both transformational and charismatic leadership models. Bass's (1985) 'inspirational motivation' is encompassed in this practice, a dimension that Podsakoff defines as leadership behaviour 'aimed at identifying new opportunities for his or her unit ... and developing, articulating, and inspiring others with his or her vision of the future' (1990: 112). Substantial recent evidence supports the value of this practice in schools. For example, Silins and Mulford (2002) found positive and significant effects of a shared and monitored mission, while Harris and Chapman's small-scale qualitative study of effective leadership in schools facing challenging circumstances reported that:

> Of central importance ... was the cooperation and alignment of others to [the leader's] set of values and vision ... Through a variety of symbolic gestures and actions, they were successful at realigning both staff and pupils to their particular vision.
>
> (Harris and Chapman, 2002: 6)

As another example of school-based evidence, Supovitz et al.'s (2010) study of principals' leadership influence on teachers' instructional practices found that 'clearly communicating the school mission and goals' was significantly associated with reports by teachers of making a greater degree of changes in their teaching and learning practices. And in a turnaround school context, Finnigan and Stewart (2009) found that the most successful turnaround leaders in their sample:

> Articulated a vision that involved reading as a core component. Additionally [they] strengthened their vision and direction through a

clear articulation of their high expectations for school staff. Finally, the principals targeted attention and resources not to just meeting the accountability requirements . . . but on improving the school organization.

(Finnigan and Stewart, 2009: 595)

Locke (2002) has argued that formulating a vision for the organization is one of eight core tasks for senior leaders and a key mechanism for achieving integration or alignment of activities within the organization; that is, '. . . tying all the processes together so that they are not only consistent with one another but actively support one another' (Locke, 2002: 3). After Locke (2002), we include as part of vision building the establishment of core organizational values. Core values specify the means by which the vision is to be accomplished.

Fostering the acceptance of group goals

While visions can be inspiring, action typically requires some agreement on the more immediate goals to be accomplished in order to move toward the vision. Building on such theory, this set of practices aims not only to identify important goals for the organization, but to do so in such a way that individual members come to include the organization's goals among their own. Unless this happens, the organization's goals have no motivational value. So leaders can productively spend a lot of time on this set of practices. Giving short shrift or failing to revisit and reinforce through everyday practices misses the point entirely. This set of practices includes leader behaviours 'aimed at promoting cooperation among [teachers] and getting them to work together toward a common goal' (Podsakoff et al., 1990: 112).

In local authority/district and school settings, strategic and improvement planning processes are among the more explicit contexts in which these behaviours are manifest. One of the 11 effective managerial behaviours included in Yukl's Multiple Linkage model, 'planning and organizing', encompasses a portion of these practices. Planning and organizing include 'Determining long-range objectives and strategies' and 'identifying necessary steps to carry out a project or activity' (1994: 130).

High performance expectations

This set of leadership practices is included as part of 'Setting directions' because it is closely aligned with goals. While high performance expectations do not define the substance of organizational goals, they demonstrate, as Podsakoff explains, 'the leader's expectations of excellence, quality, and/or high performance' (Podsakoff et al., 1990: 112) in the achievement of those goals. Demonstrating such expectations is a central behaviour in virtually all conceptions of transformational and charismatic leadership. Sun's (2010) meta-analysis of school-based evidence found that, among other practices in this direction-setting category, *holding high performance expectations* contributed significantly to many school conditions associated with improvement.

Developing people

The three sets of practices in this category make a significant contribution to staff motivation. Their primary aim, however, is capacity building – building not only the knowledge and skills staff need to accomplish organizational goals but also the dispositions to persist in applying that knowledge and skill (Harris and Chapman, 2002). Individual teacher efficacy is arguably the most critical of these dispositions and it is a third source of motivation in Bandura's (1986) model. People are motivated by what they are good at. And *mastery experiences*, according to Bandura, are the most powerful sources of efficacy. So building capacity leading to a sense of mastery is highly motivational, as well. In our research we found that it was not only individual, but also collective efficacy which enabled the school's improvement journey to progress.

Providing individualized support/consideration

Bass and Avolio include, as part of this dimension, 'knowing your followers' needs and raising them to more mature levels . . . [sometimes through] the use of delegation to provide opportunities for each follower to self-actualize and to attain higher standards of moral development' (1994: 64). This set of behaviours, claim Podsakoff et al. (1990), should communicate the leader's respect for his or her colleagues and concerns about their personal feelings and needs. This is a set of practices common to all of the two-dimensional models of leadership (Ohio State, Contingency theory and Situational Leadership theory) which include task orientation and *consideration for people*.

Encompassed by this set of practices are the 'supporting', and 'recognizing and rewarding' managerial behaviours associated with Yukl's (1994) Multiple Linkage model, as well as Hallinger's (2003) model of instructional leadership and the Waters et al. (2003) meta-analysis. This set of leadership behaviours has attracted more leadership research outside of schools since the 1960s than any other. Finnigan and Stewart (2009), for example, provide new evidence suggesting that successful turnaround school leaders:

> targeted resources (including instructional resources) toward their vision and provided support to teachers in their efforts to improve . . . [In these schools] the principal was viewed as someone who listened to the complaints of parents and teachers but also identified solutions

to their problems . . . and teachers at [these] schools reported positive communication and feeling supported through the evaluation process because they were given feedback about how to improve curriculum and instruction.

(Finnigan and Stewart, 2009: 508–9)

Intellectual stimulation

Behaviours included in this dimension include encouraging colleagues to take intellectual risks, re-examine assumptions, look at their work from different perspectives, rethink how it can be performed (Podsakoff et al., 1990; Avolio, 1994), and otherwise 'induc[e] . . . employees to appreciate, dissect, ponder and discover what they would not otherwise discern' (Lowe, Kroeck, and Sivasubramaniam, 1996: 415–16). Waters, Marzano and McNulty (Waters et al., 2003; Marzano et al., 2005) include 'challenging the status quo' among the practices contributing to leader effects on students.

This is where the leader's role in professional development is found to be a key role, especially for leaders of schools in challenging circumstances (Gray, 2000). But it recognizes the many informal, as well as formal, ways such development occurs. It also reflects our current understandings of learning as constructed, social and situated. All models of transformational and charismatic leadership include this set of practices. A considerable amount of the educational literature assumes such practices on the part of school leaders, most notably the literature on 'instructional' leadership which places school leaders at the centre of teaching and learning improvement efforts in their schools (e.g., Hallinger, 2003; Stein and Spillane, 2005).

One of the most dramatic results of Robinson, Hohepa and Lloyd's (2009) synthesis of research was the very strong effect on student achievement (ES = .84) of leaders' efforts to promote the learning of their teachers, especially when leaders participated in that learning with their teachers. Such behaviour straddles this set of leader behaviours, as well as the next.

Providing an appropriate model

This category entails 'leading by example', a general set of practices associated with models of 'authentic leadership' (Avolio and Gardner, 2005), demonstrating transparent decision making, confidence, optimism, hope, resiliency, and consistency between words and deeds. Locke (2002) claims that core values are established by modelling core values in one's own practices. Both Hallinger (2003) and Waters et al. (2003) note the contribution to leader effects of maintaining high visibility in the school, a visibility associated with high-quality interactions with both staff and students. Harris and Chapman found that their successful heads 'modelled behaviour that they considered desirable to achieve the school goals' (2002: 6).

Also encompassed by this dimension is Bass's 'idealized influence', a partial replacement for his original 'charisma' dimension: Avolio (1994) claims that leaders exercise idealized influence when they serve as role models with the appropriate behaviours and attitudes that are required to build trust and respect in followers. Such modelling on the part of leaders 'sets an example for employees to follow that is consistent with the values the leader espouses' (Podsakoff et al., 1990: 112). The qualitative effects of this are shown in our case studies of schools in Chapters 7 and 8 of this book.

Sun's (2010) meta-analysis reported that, by itself, *modelling valued practices* had a medium-strength effect (ES = .54) on important school conditions and, along with *providing intellectual stimulation* and *individual support*, significantly influenced the majority of teacher attitudes and dispositions related to school improvement (ES = .50 in both cases).

Refining and aligning the organization

This is the 'S', situation or working conditions, variable in our equation for predicting levels of performance described earlier. There is little to be gained by increasing people's motivation and capacity if working conditions will not allow their effective application. In Bandura's (1986) model, beliefs about the situation are a fourth source of motivation; people are motivated when they believe the circumstances in which they find themselves are conducive to accomplishing the goals they hold to be personally important. The three practices included in this category are about establishing the conditions of work which will allow staff to make the most of their motivations and capacities.

Sun's (2010) meta-analysis of practices included in the category 'Refining and aligning the organization', reported moderate but significant effects on the majority of teacher attitudes and dispositions. Especially *building collaborative cultures* and *strengthening school cultures* made moderately strong contributions (.42 to .47) to most consequential school conditions. Two of the five dimensions of leadership practice associated with this category in Robinson, Hohepa and Lloyd (2009), *resourcing strategically* and *ensuring an orderly environment*, had small to medium effects on student learning (.31 and .27 respectively).

Building collaborative cultures

A large body of evidence has accumulated since Little's (1982) early research which unambiguously supports the importance of collaborative cultures in schools as central to school improvement, the development of professional

learning communities and the improvement of student lea
and Kruse, 1998; Rosenholtz, 1989). Additional evidence cle
leaders are able to build more collaborative cultures and sugge͟ᵥᵤ _
that accomplish this goal (e.g. Waters et al., 2003; Horn and Little, 2Uιᵥ,
For leaders of schools in challenging circumstances, creating more positive
collaborative and achievement-oriented cultures is a key task (Sammons,
Thomas and Mortimore, 1997; West, Ainscow, and Stanford, 2005). Printy's
review of evidence supports this claim, indicating that 'Strong collaborative
relationships oriented to improvement appear to be a necessary requisite
for quality teaching' (2010: 113). We will show in Chapter 9 of this book how
this is connected, also, to organizational democracy, trust and the consciously
progressive distribution of leadership.

Connolly and James (2006) claim that the success of collaborative activity
is determined by the capacity and motivation of collaborators along with
opportunities for them to collaborate. Success also depends on understanding
and, where appropriate, changing the legacy of prior conditions. For example,
a history of working together will sometimes build trust, making further
collaboration easier. It is increasingly recognized that trust is a key element in
encouraging collaboration and that individuals are more likely to trust those
with whom they have established good relationships (Louis and Kruse, 1995;
Bryk and Schneider, 2002). Participative leadership theory and leader–member
exchange theory are concerned with the nature and quality of collaboration in
organizations and how to manage it productively.

Leaders contribute to productive collaborative activity in their schools by
being skilled conveners of that work. They nurture mutual respect and trust
among those involved in collaborating, ensure the shared determination of
group processes and outcomes, help develop clarity about goals and roles for
collaboration, encourage a willingness to compromise among collaborators,
foster open and fluent communication among collaborators, and provide
adequate and consistent resources in support of collaborative work (Mattessich
and Monsey, 1992; Connolly and James, 2006).

Restructuring and redefining roles and responsibilities

This is a leadership function or behaviour common to virtually all conceptions
of management and leadership practice. Organizational culture and structure
are two sides of the same coin. Developing and sustaining collaborative cultures
depend on putting in place complementary structures, typically something
requiring leadership initiative. Practices associated with such initiatives
include creating common planning times for teachers, and establishing team
and group structures for problem solving (e.g., Hadfield, 2003). Hallinger
and Heck (1998) identify this variable as a key mediator of leaders' effects on
students. Restructuring also includes distributing leadership for selected tasks

and increasing teacher involvement in decision making (Reeves, 2000), although, as we will show in later chapters, this takes time and the wise application of context-sensitive judgement.

Successful turnaround principals in Finnigan and Stewart's research 'quickly appeared to be successful at not only developing a positive and collaborative school climate and culture but also providing teachers with the resources they needed' (2009: 600). They also created solid blocks of time for teachers to collaborate and insisted on such collaboration, thus making continuing teacher isolation not an option. One criticism of this and much other reported research, however, is that it is not able to look at the extent to which this is sustained over time. Chapter 8 of this book provides empirical evidence of how such collaboration was sustained over time in the case study schools.

Building productive relationships with families and communities

Shifting the attention of school staffs from an exclusively inside-the-school focus to one which embraces a meaningful role for parents and a close relationship with the larger community was identified during the 1990s as the biggest change in expectations for those in formal school leadership roles (e.g., Goldring and Rallis, 1993). More recently, Muijs, Harris, Chapman, Stoll and Russ (2004) have identified this core practice as important for improving schools in challenging circumstances, and our research provides further affirmation. Attention to this focus has been encouraged by evidence of the contribution of family educational cultures to student achievement in schools (e.g., Coleman, 1966; Finn, 1989), the increase in public accountability of schools to their communities through the widespread implementation of school-based management (Murphy and Beck, 1995), and the growing need for schools to actively manage public perceptions of their legitimacy (e.g., Mintrop, 2004).

Connecting the school to its wider environment

School leaders spend significant amounts of time in contact with people outside of their schools seeking information and advice, staying in tune with policy changes, anticipating new pressures and trends likely to have an influence on their schools and the like. Meetings, informal conversations, phone calls, email exchanges and Internet searches are examples of opportunities for accomplishing these purposes. The extensive number of network learning projects facilitated by the National College of School Leadership in England provided especially powerful opportunities for connecting one's school to at least its wider educational environment (Jackson, 2002), although once the funding subsidy and associated external human resource support for this ended, in 2006, there are considerable doubts as to the extent to which many of these networks were able to be sustained.

In addition, in spite of the considerable time spent by school leaders on this function, we are unaware of any research, to date, that has inquired about its contribution to improving pupil learning and/or the quality of the school organization. The evaluation of network learning communities in England, for example, suggested little positive impact on pupil attainment (Sammons, Mujtaba and Earl, 2007). However, research has been conducted about the effects of this practice in non-school organizations. Referring to it as 'networking', Yukl includes it in his Multiple Linkage model of leadership as one of 11 critical managerial practices. He describes this practice as 'Socializing informally, developing contacts with people who are a source of information and support, and maintaining contacts through periodic interaction, including visits, telephone calls, correspondence, and attendance at meetings and social events' (1994: 69).

Improving the teaching and learning programme

This category of leadership practices straddles several others, particularly the 'Developing people' and 'Refining and aligning the organization' categories. It is included in response to evidence that leadership practices which specifically focus on the core technology of teaching are likely to have a greater effect on school improvement than those that are more indirect (e.g., Marks and Printy, 2003; Robinson, Hohepa and Lloyd, 2009; Printy, 2010).

Evidence about the effects of this set of practices is still mixed, however. Surprisingly, Hallinger's (2003) review suggested that those leadership practices which involve close association with the classroom and supervision of what happens in the classroom appear to have the least effect on students. On the other hand, when managerial behaviours have been included in other recent research on school leadership effects, they have explained almost as much as did leadership behaviours (e.g., Leithwood and Jantzi, 1999). Furthermore, the research synthesis carried out by Robinson and her colleagues (2009) reported a moderate effect of related practices on student achievement (ES = .42). So they are important, as a class: especially those that create stability, strengthen the infrastructure, and provide timely and informative feedback to teachers about their work.

Staffing the programme

Although not touched on by Hallinger (2003) or Waters et al. (2003), this has been shown to be a key function of leaders engaged in school improvement. Finding teachers with the interest and capacity to further the school's efforts is the goal of this activity. Recruiting and retaining staff are a primary task for those who lead schools in challenging circumstances (Gray, 2000) and are evidenced in the case study schools in our IMPACT research.

Providing teaching support

This set of practices, included in both Hallinger (2003) and Waters et al. (2003), includes 'supervising and evaluating instruction', co-ordinating the curriculum, and providing resources in support of curriculum, instruction and assessment activity. West et al. (2005) indicate that, for leaders of schools in challenging contexts, focusing on teaching and learning is essential. This includes controlling behaviour, boosting self-esteem, and talking and listening to pupils. It also may include urging pupils and teachers to put a strong emphasis on pupil achievement. Such an 'academic climate' makes significant contributions to achievement (De Maeyer et al., 2006; Sammons, Thomas and Mortimore, 1997). Our own quantitative research findings, reported in Part 2 of this book, confirm this and shows that controlling behaviour and engaging pupils are key prerequisites to influencing the quality of pupil outcomes, particularly in schools in challenging circumstances.

Monitoring school activity

Waters et al. (2003) analysed associated leadership effects on students with leader monitoring and evaluating functions, especially those which focused on student progress. The purposeful use of data is reported by West et al. (2005) to be a central explanation for effective leadership in failing schools (see also Reynolds, Stringfield and Muijs, n.d.). Hallinger's (2003) model includes a set of practices labelled 'monitoring student progress'. Monitoring operations and environment is one of Yukl's (1994) 11 effective managerial practices; and Gray et al. (1999) report that tracking student progress is a key task for leaders of schools in challenging circumstances.

Buffering staff from distractions to their work

A long line of research has reported the value to organizational effectiveness of leaders preventing staff from being pulled in directions incompatible with agreed goals. This buffering function acknowledges the open nature of schools and the constant bombardment of staff by expectations from parents, the media, special interest groups and the government. Internal buffering is also helpful, especially buffering teachers from excessive pupil disciplinary activity. Successful turnaround principals in Finnigan and Stewart's study 'buffered teachers from the demands of district administrators and the account-ability policy in general' (2009: 603). They also 'conducted ongoing moni-toring of implementation and performance outcomes and thus focused the attention of the school staff on student achievement and other types of data' (p. 604).

Conclusion

To this point we have discussed in a disembodied way leadership practices. But who, you might ask, delivers them? Who (or what) are the desirable sources of these practices? While heads or principals are always key sources, growing evidence points to multiple other sources of leadership as something to be encouraged in many circumstances. In studies to date, for example, these sources have been administrators other than principals (Finnigan and Stewart, 2009), teachers (Supovitz et al., 2010), parents (Hallinger and Heck, 2009) and teams of teachers (Leithwood and Mascall, 2008). Or such distribution has been described as simply 'shared' (Wahlstrom and Louis, 2008) or 'collaborative' (Hallinger and Heck, 2010). The bulk of evidence, in sum, suggests that distributing leadership practices is relatively effective in most circumstances although, as we noted in our IMPACT results, the early stages of turning around an underperforming school is not one of them. A more nuanced treatment of distributed leadership is developed in later chapters of the book.

Finally, our four broad categories of leadership practices – and 14 more specific practices – capture the evidence about what effective leadership is in most contexts. These core practices, which are further evidenced in Chapter 6, provide a powerful source of guidance for practising leaders. However, leaders do not do all of these things all of the time; you don't have to create a shared vision every day. And the way you go about each set of practices will certainly vary by context. If your school has been labelled as 'failing', you are likely to do more selling of your vision to staff initially than developing it collaboratively – and you are likely to be more autocratic than democratic in the early days so you can get on with your 'turnaround' mission. So what is contingent about leadership is not the basic or core practices but the way they are enacted. It is the enactment that must be sensitive to context, not the core practices themselves. Parts 2 and 3 of this book provide powerful evidence of the ways heads of effective and improving schools in England go about this and the values, qualities and skills which they exercise in the process.

PART 2
Leadership actions and pupil outcomes

3 Models of leadership and pupil outcomes

Introduction

In this chapter we describe the mixed-methods approach adopted in the IMPACT study of school leadership and pupil outcomes. We argue that a combination of qualitative and quantitative research approaches is needed to provide a synergistic understanding of leadership and the way it relates to changes in pupil outcomes over time.

The chapter discusses how we identified a sample of academically effective and improved schools for our study. It describes the way two questionnaire surveys of head teachers and key staff were developed, informed by existing research and literature (discussed earlier in Chapters 1 and 2). It also provides details of analyses we used to study the various data sets on pupil attainment, and on staff and head teachers' responses to our surveys, and how we sought to model the direct and indirect effects of leadership on pupil outcomes using statistical approaches. In later chapters of this book we move on to present case study results that extend, enrich and contextualize the findings through in-depth study of individual schools (see Chapters 7–9).

From the survey analyses we identified a range of constructs that provide a basis for a model of school leadership strategies and actions. These include strategies such as 'Setting directions', 'Refining and aligning the organization' and 'Developing people' as well as the creation of 'Leadership trust'. We show how such constructs were identified and were related to other important features of school and classroom processes, such as the senior leadership team's influence on learning and teaching, and the creation of professional ways of working that we term 'Teachers' Collaborative Culture'. We go on to investigate important intermediate pupil outcomes including pupil motivation and a positive learning culture, improved school conditions, and high academic standards, and show that these, in turn, are linked with and predict changes in pupil behaviour and attendance, and ultimately changes in a school performance measured in terms of pupils' academic outcomes.

The chapter also presents and discusses a new statistical model that helps to illuminate the complex associative and potentially causal relationships that underpin significant improvements in schools' academic outcomes and sustained effectiveness for a large sample of English primary and secondary schools (Sammons et al, 2011).

Research aims and objectives

The overall aim of the study was:

> To identify and map empirically grounded direct and indirect causal and associative relationships between effective leadership and pupil outcomes.

In particular, through our quantitative analyses we sought:

(a) to establish how much variation in pupils' academic outcomes (measured by national assessments and public examination results) is accounted for by variation in the types, qualities, strategies, skills and contexts of school leadership, in particular those of head teachers as 'leaders of leaders'; and

(b) to determine the relative strengths of the direct and indirect influences of school leadership, especially that of the head, upon teachers and upon pupils' outcomes.

In later chapters we go on to examine these issues further through our 20 in-depth case studies of primary and secondary schools, which provide rich and more nuanced accounts by various stakeholders of their school's leadership and improvement journeys.

Mixed-methods design

Large-scale studies of complex social and educational phenomena increasingly adopt a mixed-methods approach to research design (Tashakkori and Teddlie, 2003; Day et al., 2008; Teddlie and Sammons, 2010). This research study brought together an experienced team with complementary and diverse research careers and areas of expertise (qualitative and quantitative) from different perspectives and in different contexts, both UK and international.

The choice of a mixed-methods research design was influenced by the review of literature conducted at the beginning of the study. The initial review of the literature appeared in both a detailed (Leithwood, Day, Sammons,

Harris and Hopkins, 2006) and summary form (Leithwood, Harris and Hopkins, 2008). The summary version was organized around seven claims justified by varying amounts of fairly robust empirical evidence that we have discussed in more detail in Chapter 1. The literature review informed our research design and particularly the development of the questionnaire surveys and initial rounds of case study interviews that focused on measuring features of schools and their leadership and enhancing our understanding of the role of heads in schools' improvement processes.

The research was divided into three related but overlapping phases. These three phases illustrate the mixed-methods approach to the research design, where both the qualitative and quantitative components are given equal weight. In addition, the findings from different phases contributed to the development of the research instruments through an iterative process of analysis, hypothesis generation, testing, integration and, ultimately, synthesis.

Figure 3.1 provides a schematic illustration of the different phases and strands of the research and their sequencing, and indicates the process by which we sought to integrate the various sources of evidence to address our aims.

The use of mixed-methods increased the possibilities of identifying various patterns of association and possible causal connections between variation in different indicators of school performance (as measured by national data on pupil attainment and other survey outcomes) and measures of school and departmental processes, and the way these are linked with different features of

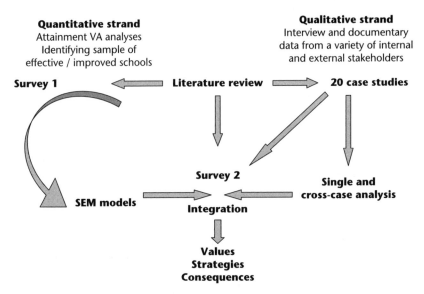

Figure 3.1   Research design: integrating evidence about effective/improved schools

leadership practices. By incorporating both extensive quantitative and rich qualitative evidence from participants about their perceptions, experiences and interpretations of leadership practices and school with independently collected data on school performance based on changes in pupil outcomes and measures of school organization and processes over three years, it was possible to conduct analyses in parallel and to allow evidence from one source to extend or to challenge evidence from another source.

At certain points in the research process we analysed the quantitative evidence (attainment data and questionnaire surveys) separately and independently from the in-depth analyses of case study data collected for a smaller sample of schools. At other stages we deliberately chose to allow one source to inform the other. This process of dialogue was enhanced by various meetings (whole team and both mixed- and single-method subgroups).

The sequencing of the study was an important feature that facilitated the integration of evidence and attempts at synthesis and meta-inferences.

The quantitative strand of the project involved four components.

1   An analysis of national data sets on over 15 000 primary and 3500 secondary schools' performance was conducted to identify schools that were effective in promoting pupil progress and improving their overall academic results over a consecutive three-year period. The analyses were based on relevant published national attainment and examination data and key indicators including value added (VA) measures that investigate pupil progress and raw performance indicators for individual schools. These included the percentage of pupils achieving performance benchmarks such as level 4 at age 11, the end Key Stage 2 in primary, or the percentage achieving 5A*–C grades at GCSE at age 16, the end of Key Stage 4 in secondary school.

2   An initial Phase 1 survey of heads and key staff in a sample of such effective and improving schools was used to explore various features of school organization and processes identified as likely to be relevant in our literature review, including leadership. The survey questions asked heads and key staff to report on the extent of change in different features of school activity and practice over the last three years of their leadership in the school. This period was chosen to coincide with the years for which the analysis of improvement in pupil attainment had taken place. (Some examples of the survey questions are shown in Appendix 3.1.)

3   A second follow-up Phase 2 questionnaire survey of heads and key staff was conducted one year later to explore in more detail particular strategies and actions that were perceived to relate to improvement (informed by the interim results of the analyses of the first survey and case study findings).

4   A questionnaire survey of pupils in 20 case study schools in two successive years provided additional data on pupils' views and perceptions of teaching and learning, leadership and school culture and climate.

The qualitative strand of the research involved in-depth case studies based on three visits a year over two years in 20 highly effective and improved schools, ten each from the primary and secondary phases of education. These involved detailed interviews with head teachers and a range of key staff and stakeholders to provide authentic accounts of the processes of improvement as they perceived and experienced them in the context of the leadership of their particular institutions. In addition, the case studies involved observation of features of practice specifically identified by staff in these schools as important in accounting for their improvement. The case study sites were selected to represent schools in different sectors and contexts, including different levels of advantage and disadvantage, and ethnic diversity of student intake. Proportionately more effective and improved schools from disadvantaged contexts were included in the case study component of the research to reflect the policy interest in England during the mid-1990s to 2007 period that focused on raising standards in schools facing challenging circumstances.

Interviews with heads and key staff prompted them to speak about those issues which were most significant to them in relation to the research aims and objectives, and also covered aspects identified as potentially important in the literature review. Interviews with other colleagues in the school provide further insights outside the formal school leadership into perceptions of the nature and impact of the practice and effectiveness of participating heads in the role of school (and departmental) leadership, including the involvement of the senior leadership team (SLT) and middle managers (e.g. Key Stage leaders and heads of departments) and leadership distribution. Thus the case studies, although primarily qualitative in nature, also had a mixed-methods component.

The sampling strategy: analyses of schools' performance using pupil attainment and effectiveness measures

England is unique in the availability of a range of national assessment data sets collected annually and analysed centrally by DCSF (Department for Children, Schools and Families, now renamed the Department for Education) and other bodies including the Fischer Family Trust (FFT) and LAs. At the time the study was being initiated, the DCSF was still perfecting its approach to developing contextualized value added (CVA) performance indicators for schools. These were not at that stage available for the three years (2003 to 2005) that form the focus of this research. However, the FFT had available analyses of national pupil data sets at the school level involving raw pupil-level data (unadjusted for pupil background) and both simple (control only for pupil prior attainment) and contextualized measures of school performance (based on control for individual-level prior attainment and pupil background characteristics). In school effectiveness research, value added measures, particularly contextual value added (CVA) measures, are widely recognized (Sammons, Thomas and Mortimore, 1997; Teddlie and Reynolds, 2000; Luyten and Sammons, 2010) as providing fairer measures of school performance because they take into account important differences between schools, in the characteristics of the pupil intakes they serve, that have been shown to predict later pupil attainment. The role of pupil background is one of increasing policy interest, in England and elsewhere (for example, to the Narrowing the Gaps agenda in England), and practitioners are also very aware of the importance of pupil context and intake, and their impact on schools' work and the day-to-day challenges teachers face in their classrooms.

Multi-level models (based on hierarchical regression and pupil-level data) have been used to develop value added measures over several decades (Goldstein, 1995), and the DCSF has recognized the benefits of CVA indicators in its publication of schools' results in achievement and attainment tables in England.

The survey sampling was based on the analysis of value added and pupil attainment data provided by the FFT. The FFT used contextual value added multi-level analyses to provide statistical estimates (residuals) of individual school effects for the three years 2003 to 2005, for all primary and secondary schools in England. The analyses identified schools that were more academically effective, and that had shown sustained improvement across three years, for further study (Gu, Sammons and Mehta, 2008).

Approximately a third of primary (34 per cent) and of secondary (37 per cent) schools for which national data were available over the three-year period were identified as fitting our sampling criteria, being classified as more effective or improved in terms of changes in pupil attainment measured by their national assessment or examination results, and in terms of value added indicators of pupil progress. It should be noted that English schools have recorded substantial rises in national assessment and examination results during the period 1996 to 2008 and also improvements in performance in international assessments such as TIMMS, and this is likely to reflect the impact of the strong policy drive to raise standards and support the improvement of weaker schools (Sammons, 2008). Our sampling frame allowed the project to focus on the leadership features and processes of such successful schools in line with our research aims and questions, and thus the results can be interpreted in terms of processes and approaches that characterize academically more effective and improving schools in their context.

Nationally, a greater proportion of schools in England are in Free School Meal (FSM) Band 1 (0–8 per cent of pupils eligible for FSM) and Band

2 (9–20 per cent eligible) than in FSM Band 3 (21–35 per cent eligible) and Band 4 (36 per cent or more eligible), and this is the case for both primary and secondary schools. The FSM measure is an indicator of low family income and of social disadvantage in the pupil intake. We sought to over-sample schools from areas of higher disadvantage (Bands FSM3 and 4) in order to achieve a more balanced (less skewed towards low disadvantage) sample of schools in relation to level of disadvantage of pupil uptake, particularly in the case of primary schools where the larger numbers allowed us to over-sample disadvantaged schools in the ratio 3:2. Pupils in schools from more disadvantaged areas tend to start from a lower attainment level, and thus such a sample allowed us to include a sizeable number of schools that had seen pupil progress and attainment improve from very low levels and explore in greater depth the impact of leadership on the improvement of pupil outcomes in schools in challenging circumstances, a topic of particular interest to policy makers in many countries.

Three school improvement groups

Three subgroups of schools were identified based on analyses of attainment and value added trends over three years:

- those improving from low to moderate or low to high in attainment and identified as highly effective in national value added analyses;
- those improving from moderate to higher moderate or high in attainment and identified as highly effective in value added; and
- those with stable high attainment and highly effective in value added.

Proportionately more schools responding to the survey were in the low to moderate/high group: those that had made rapid recent improvement over three years from a low base.

We hypothesized that schools which (a) make rapid improvement over the short term and (b) were originally in a low attainment group were likely to have different leadership profiles from those in the stable high effectiveness category. We labelled the low to moderate or low to high group as *the Low Start Group*, the moderate to higher moderate or high group as *the Moderate Start Group*, and the stable high and high to higher group as *the High Start Group*. We explored associations between the improvement groupings and a range of influences relating to heads' years of experience in total and in their current schools, the number of heads in the previous ten years, school education sector and school socio-economic contexts, and survey results (see Gu, Sammons and Mehta, 2008, for details). In Chapter 5 we present further details of the survey findings for these three groups of schools, which differed in their improvement trajectories.

Questionnaire survey

A questionnaire survey was conducted with forms for head teachers and key staff with leadership roles (2 per school at primary level; 5 per school at secondary) to explore these stakeholders' perceptions of features of leadership and school processes. The survey adopted a number of scales comprising sets of complete items identified as potentially important in the initial literature review (Leithwood et al., 2004, 2006a). In addition, it included specific items that focused on heads' and key staff's perceptions of change in different areas of their school's work, and in other kinds of pupil outcomes (non-academic areas such as engagement, motivation, behaviour and attendance) over the previous three years. The head teacher survey covered six areas:

- leadership practice
- leaders' internal states
- leadership distribution
- leadership influence
- school conditions
- classroom conditions

The key staff survey was designed to closely mirror that of the heads so that comparisons could be made between the two groups in terms of perceptions of these same six areas. Table 3.1 shows the sample response rate. This rate was

Table 3.1 Phase 1 survey response rate

	Sample size surveyed (N)	Returned heads questionnaires (N)	Response rate (%)
Heads			
Primary	1550	378	24
Secondary	1140	362	32
Key staff at school level			
Primary	1550	409 (schools)	26
Secondary	1140	393 (schools)	34
Key staff at questionnaire level			
Primary	3100	608	20
Secondary	5700	1,167	20

Table 3.2 Number of secondary schools in the sample by school context (FSM Band) and secondary school improvement group

Improvement groups	School context (FSM Band)					
	FSM 1 & 2	(%)	FSM 3 & 4	(%)	Total	(%)
Low Start	83	(49.7)	84	(50.3)	167	(100)
Moderate Start	63	(82.9)	13	(17.1)	76	(100)
High Start	109	(94.8)	6	(5.2)	115	(100)
Total	255	(71)	103	(29)	358	(100)

higher for head teachers of secondary schools, which were followed up in more detail to ensure roughly equal numbers of responses from schools in each sector. Although not high, the response rate is very typical of that achieved by surveys of schools in England in recent years.

Overall, nearly two-thirds (65.6 per cent) of primary schools in the Low Start Group, compared with under one in 10 (8 per cent) of the High Start Group served more disadvantaged pupil intakes, defined as FSM Bands 3 and 4. For secondary survey responses the pattern was broadly similar. Here, around a half (50.3 per cent) of schools in the Low Start Group were from high-disadvantage contexts (FSM Bands 3 and 4), while only around one in 20 (5.2 per cent) of the High Start Group were from Bands 3 and 4. This emphasizes the strong link between low attainment and pupil intake characteristics evident in many educational effectiveness studies (Teddlie and Reynolds, 2000). However, in our sample, all schools, including the Low Start Group, had shown substantial improvement in raw results and were identified as highly effective in value added multi-level analyses that controlled for both pupil prior attainment and background characteristics (Table 3.2 illustrates patterns for the secondary sample).

Analysis strategies

We used a range of approaches for the analysis of the various data sets available from both the qualitative and quantitative strands, and to facilitate the integration of evidence and development of conclusions. The range of data types, their accumulation over a two-year period and the sample sizes included in the project provided a powerful variety of data analyses that were applied progressively over the stages of the project. Figure 3.2 summarizes the sampling strategy adopted in the project and the sequencing of activity.

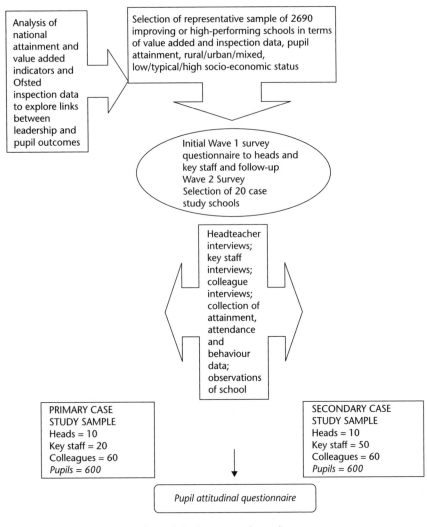

Figure 3.2 Summary of sampling

Survey responses

As noted above, the literature review informed both the development of the initial Phase 1 survey of heads and staff in our sample of effective and improved schools and the initial interviews used with the purposive sample of 20 of these survey schools chosen for in-depth case study.

A range of statistical techniques were used to analyse the questionnaire survey data. In our Interim Report (Day et al., 2008) we presented the results of the initial descriptive analyses of the Phase 1 survey data. We made comparisons between heads' and key staff's responses to explore the extent of similarity or difference in views and perceptions. In addition, we examined the data according to a range of variables of particular interest to policy makers and practitioners. The variables used for comparisons included school sector (primary or secondary) and school context (based on school FSM Band), comparing schools with more disadvantaged pupil intakes (FSM Bands 3 and 4) and those with less disadvantaged intakes (FSM Bands 1 and 2). We also examined other potential sources of influence, including the head's total years of experience and the head's time in their current post. Our analyses reported on the extent of statistically significant differences in head teacher and key staff responses in schools with different levels of socio-economic disadvantage.

A particular focus of interest, given the design of the study, was to explore similarities and differences in survey responses between the three school improvement groups identified in the sample. Further analyses examined the leadership characteristics and practices in schools with different effectiveness and improvement profiles (Gu, Sammons and Mehta, 2008). These analyses allowed the project team to explore the patterns of association between school contexts measured by attainment profiles as well as in terms of social disadvantage and survey results. Analyses of open-ended questions in the survey also identified the three most important actions or strategies taken by heads in the previous three years that they felt had been most influential in promoting school improvement. These strategies were classified and examined by school improvement group and school FSM context. It was hypothesized that school organizational history and context would influence school leaders' approaches to promote and sustain improvement. This is an important feature of the study and was addressed initially by analysis of the survey results and later in more depth via individual school profiles and the development of 'lines of success' which illustrated heads' roles in different phases of their schools' improvement journeys in the case studies (Day et al., 2009, 2010).

Identifying underlying dimensions

Further analysis of the Phase 1 survey data was used to test the extent to which the features of leadership practices identified as important in the literature review could be confirmed using data from our sample of effective and improved schools in England. Both principal components and confirmatory factor analysis (CFA)[1] were adopted to explore the underlying structure of the head teacher and key staff Phase 1 questionnaire survey data.

Developing hypothesized causal models

In addition, these quantitatively derived dimensions were related to hypothesized models of the proposed links between different features of leadership practice and measures of pupil outcomes. Structural equation modelling (SEM) was adopted to develop hypothetical causal models that are intended to represent the patterns of underlying interrelationships between a range of dependent and independent variables that measure different features of leadership, school and classroom processes and their relationships to a dependent variable of interest, in this case measured change in pupil attainment outcomes over three years.

Model building enables 'the systematic study of underlying concepts in a particular research context and the consideration of the relationships between them' (Silins and Mulford, 2002: 581). In this study our focus was on those schools that were successful (defined by assessment and examination measures of improved pupil performance-based outcomes over three years) in England and the relationship between leadership practices and school processes that were hypothesized as likely to promote improvements in pupils' measured attainments.

In developing the SEM models we were influenced by previous leadership research, especially that of Silins and Mulford (2004), that had examined links between schools' organizational learning and indicators of pupil outcomes based on pupil perceptions and self-report in their LOSLO (leadership for organizational learning and improved student outcomes project) study of leadership and organizational learning. In a later development their study modelled relationships with academic attainment at a particular time point, though measured only by completion of high school (Mulford, 2007). Their approach fitted well with our conceptualizations of leadership as an influence on both individual and organizational change and learning that is likely to operate on pupil outcomes via its more direct impact on culture organization, staff motivation, commitment and practices. which themselves affect teaching and learning in the classroom.

Our IMPACT study of leadership and pupil outcomes is the first use of SEM of the impact of head teachers on changes in school performance using

---

[1] Confirmatory factor analysis is a statistical technique that explores underlying dimensions and helps us to summarize the survey data. In the study this helped to establish whether the items that were included in the survey to measure theoretical scales derived from the literature are empirically confirmed in our English sample of more effective schools.

pupil attainment data for schools in England. By focusing on predicting *change* in attainment over time, our models can be seen as dynamic rather than cross-sectional (in contrast to the LOSLO study) because they seek to identify the factors that *predict*, directly and indirectly, improvement in academic results for a large sample of more effective and improved schools.

Models were developed separately for primary and secondary schools to establish whether the relative influence of school leadership on pupil outcomes showed similar patterns between the two sectors, and to identify any features specific to one sector (see also Chapter 4).

In addition, the discussion in team meetings of the emerging quantitative SEM models, together with these cross-case study interview data, facilitated further quantitative and qualitative analyses. Our study thus can be seen to approximate to a longitudinal, concurrent mixed-methods approach with multiple points of dialogue and integration of evidence from the two strands during the research period (Tashakkori and Teddlie, 2003).

Overview of quantitative results

Actions identified by heads as most important in promoting school improvement

The initial analyses of the Phase 1 survey made comparisons of head teacher and key staff responses according to key variables of interest, particularly by school improvement group, school disadvantage context (FSM Band) and sector (primary and secondary). In this chapter we provide only a brief summary of selected findings arising from the exploration of underlying dimensions of practice and the development of causal models using SEM. First, however, the actions and strategies that head teachers reported as being important in their school's improvement process are discussed, because our study of these helped to inform our modelling strategy and provided further evidence for triangulation.

Additional data collected from the surveys included a request for details of the three actions/strategies identified by heads as most influential in improved pupil academic outcomes *during the previous three years*. Given their schools were in different phases of improvement (See Chapter 7), these data have limited value in terms of their generalizability. These written data were analysed to establish which strategies and combinations of actions were perceived to have been most important and most frequently adopted by schools. The coding and analysis of these actions/strategies provide a background for the more in-depth probing and discussion of approaches adopted by schools in the 20 case studies and reported elsewhere (Day et al., 2009).

These results were categorized based on inductive analysis of the range of actions and areas cited (see Appendices 3.2 and 3.3). In some cases actions could be said to fall into more than one category: for example, 'Use of performance data to set high expectations' was considered to fall into both the category 'Encouraging the use of data and research' and the category 'Demonstrating high expectations for staff'. These data were then used to produce figures for the number of responses in each category (a total of the number of times the action/area was mentioned) and the number of cases (a total of all heads who mentioned the area, regardless of how frequently they mentioned it).

The most frequently cited actions/strategies by primary heads were:

- improved assessment procedures (28.1 per cent)
- encouraging the use of data and research (27.9 per cent)
- teaching policies and programmes (26.0 per cent)
- strategic allocation of resources (20.4 per cent)
- changes to pupil target setting (20.2 per cent)
- providing and allocating resources (19.4 per cent)
- promoting leadership development and CPD (15.9 per cent)

Similarly, actions/strategies most frequently cited by secondary heads were:

- encouraging the use of data and research (34.0 per cent)
- teaching policies and programmes (27.7 per cent)
- school culture (21.1 per cent)
- providing and allocating resources (19.5 per cent)
- improved assessment procedures (18.6 per cent)
- monitoring of departments and teachers (15.9 per cent)
- promoting leadership development and CPD (15.1 per cent)

The responses were further grouped according to the major categories of leadership practices identified as important in the literature survey, namely 'Setting directions', 'Developing people', 'Refining and aligning the organization', 'Improving teaching practices' and 'Academic emphasis'. Overall, for primary heads, actions and strategies relating to the category 'Improving teaching practices' were cited most commonly (a total of 359 representing 28.4 per cent of the 1263 actions/strategies listed), followed by those who promoted their school's 'Academic emphasis' (cited 251 times or 19.9 per cent of the total). Responses relating to the category 'Refining and aligning the organization' reached 209 (16.6 per cent), followed by those concerned with 'Setting directions' (122, 9.7 per cent) and 'Developing people' (119, 9.4 per cent).

Examples of written comments related to the strategy of using data and of curriculum change to raise attainment included:

- giving specific data to individuals and teams to help inform planning and target setting

- pupil tracking, target setting and mentoring scheme
- improve/change curriculum on offer at Key Stage 4

Examples of written survey comments related to actions/strategies linked with staff development included:

- managing some teachers' learning
- building a learning network
- focus on the role of the middle leader
- development of a culture of research and innovation
- development of a learning toolkit for staff

For secondary heads a similar pattern to that identified for primary heads was found when individual actions/strategies were further grouped into larger categories. Overall, actions related to 'Improving teaching practices' received the largest number of mentions (258 out of the total 1168 responses made, 22.1 per cent), followed by a reference to actions related to promoting the school's 'Academic emphasis': these featured in 188 responses (16.1 per cent). Actions relevant to 'Refining and aligning the organization' were noted 179 times (15.3 per cent of total actions/strategies cited), followed by those connected to 'Setting directions' (115, 11.5 per cent) and 'Developing people' (98, 8.4 per cent).

These results draw attention to the role of the head teacher as an instructional (teaching and learning) leader as conceptualized by Hallinger (2005), who argued that leadership must be viewed as a process of mutual influence whereby instructional leaders influence the quality of school outcomes through shaping the school mission and the alignment of school structures and culture. This in turn promotes a focus on continuous improvement and high expectations centred on raising the quality of teaching and learning.

In the next part of this chapter we move on to discuss the process of modelling the statistical associations between various dimensions of leadership activity measured by the survey items and changes in pupil outcomes. Our models investigate the relationships among constructs related to leadership, those related to school processes and teachers' work, and changes in various school conditions and pupil outcomes. The models explain, in particular, the extent that these predict improvement in pupil attainment across three years.

Investigating the relationships between leadership, school processes and changes in pupil outcomes: developing the structural equation models (SEM)

Exploratory factor analysis (EFA) followed by confirmatory factor analysis (CFA) were used to test the existence of hypothesized underlying dimensions identified as important in the literature review and measured by groups of survey items. Further SEM tested the proposed structural relations (i.e., through path analysis) between these and changes in key indicators of pupil attainment at the school level. Coefficients measured the strength of the net predictive link between two factors, taking into account all the relationships between other factors included in the model.

Four features (theoretical dimensions) that measure leadership practice were identified in the literature review:

- Setting directions;
- Developing people;
- Refining and aligning the organization; and
- Managing the teaching and learning programme.

A good 'fit' CFA model was identified for the primary head sample, in that the hypothesized model was consistent with the questionnaire data. Four dimensions (latent variables) of the measure of leadership practice for the primary sample were confirmed:

- 'Setting directions';
- 'Developing people';
- 'Refining and aligning the organization (external strategies)'; and
- 'Use of data'.

These can be seen as a subset of activities/actions that help define the original leadership practice (where the use of data measure is deemed to be part of the broader construct of managing the teaching and learning programme).

Table 3.3 lists the questionnaire items that identify these four dimensions for the primary head teacher sample.

We hypothesized that 'Setting directions' would precede and influence actions related to 'Refining and aligning the organization', 'Developing people' and a focus on 'Use of data' (as explored later in the SEM analysis). It can therefore be seen as a 'prime' feature of leadership. The results confirmed that *there are a number of distinctive shared, core leadership practices adopted by the improved and effective primary schools in this sample, irrespective of school context.* The three dimensions of leadership practice – 'Setting directions', 'Developing people' and 'Refining and aligning the organization (external strategies)' – can be viewed as core practices in this sample and are likely to be generalizable to the wider population of such primary schools. However, there were differences in relation to 'Use of data'. This was a stronger feature of disadvantaged schools and those in the Low Start Improvement Group (a topic we will discuss further in Chapter 5).

Table 3.3   The questionnaire items that underpin the four-factor CFA model on leadership practice (primary heads)

Dimensions	Questionnaire items			
Setting directions	1d. demonstrating high expectations for staff's work with pupils	1e. demonstrating high expectations for pupil behaviour	1f. demonstrating high expectations for pupil achievement	1g. working collaboratively with the governing body
Developing people	2b. encouraging staff to consider new ideas for their teaching	2e. promoting leadership development among teachers	2f. promoting a range of CPD experiences among all staff	2g. encouraging staff to think of learning beyond the academic curriculum
Refining and aligning the organization (external strategies)	3c. encouraging parents in school's improvement efforts	3d. increasing dialogue about school improvement between pupils and adults	3f. buidling community support for the school's improvement efforts	3l. working in collaboration with other schools
Use of data	4g. encouraging staff to use data in their work	4h. encouraging all staff to use data in planning for individual pupil needs		

A broadly similar but five-factor model of leadership practice was identified for the secondary head sample:

1   Setting directions
2   Developing people
3   Refining and aligning the organization (internal strategies)
4   Use of data
5   Use of classroom observation

Table 3.4 lists the survey items that identify this five-factor model of secondary leadership practice. The results reveal that the leadership dimension we term 'Use of classroom observation', as described by items in the questionnaire survey, was a more important feature for the improvement and effectiveness of secondary schools than it was for primary schools in the sample. This may reflect either the important role of departments and heads of departments within secondary schools (Harris et al., 1995; Sammons et al., 1997), that

Table 3.4 The questionnaire items that underpin the five-factor CFA model on leadership practice (secondary heads)

Dimensions	Questionnaire items			
Setting directions	1d. demonstrating high expectations for staff's work with pupils	1e. demonstrating high expectations for pupil behaviour	1f. demonstrating high expectations for pupil achievement	1g. working collaboratively with the governing body
Developing people	2b. encouraging staff to consider new ideas for their teaching	2e. promoting leadership development among teachers	2f. promoting a range of CPD experiences among all staff	2g. encouraging staff to think of learning beyond the academic curriculum
Refining and aligning the organization (internal strategies)	3a. encouraging collaborative work among staff	3e improving internal review procedures	3h. allocating resources strategically based on pupil needs	3j. structuring the organization to facilitate work
Use of data	4g. encouraging staff to use data in their work	4h. encouraging all staff to use data in planning for individual pupil needs		
Use of observation	4b. regularly observing classroom activities	4c. after observing classroom activities, working with teachers to improve their teaching	4d. using coaching and mentoring to improve quality of teaching	

secondary schools emphasized this more over the three-year period, or that this was a longer-standing practice in primary schools and thus embedded in the organizational culture.

Figure 3.3 illustrates that the five dimensions of secondary leaders' practice were also statistically significantly correlated, in line with results found for the primary sample. The dimension 'Refining and aligning the organization (internal restructuring)' shows a stronger link with 'Developing people' than other factors, suggesting that head teachers in more effective or improved secondary schools who implement changes in one of these areas tend to bring about change in other areas also. Case study data in other chapters goes on to explore the qualitative evidence that illuminates and extends understandings

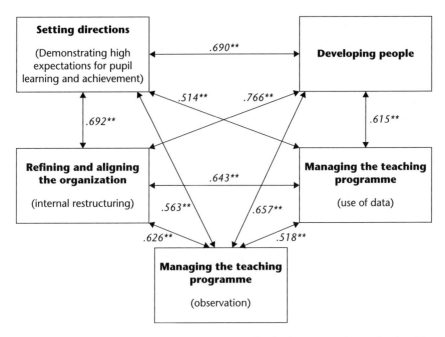

Figure 3.3   Correlations between five dimensions of leadership practice (secondary heads)

** Statistically significant $p < 0.001$.

of these statistical patterns of association identified from our questionnaire results.

We examined the mean factor scores for the five dimensions in relation to leaders' practices for the secondary sample. In contrast to the primary sample, where the dimension 'Developing people' showed the highest mean score, the score for 'Setting directions' was the highest for the secondary sample. The result suggests that 'Setting directions' is a feature of leadership activity accorded a higher priority by secondary than primary head teachers, and this may reflect the greater organizational complexity and size of secondary schools.

In contrast to results for the primary sample, statistically significant differences were found in secondary heads' perceptions in relation to some of the five dimensions on leadership practice between schools in different FSM bands, different school improvement groups and different sizes. This extends the explorations conducted at item level (Silins and Mulford, 2004; Gu, Sammons and Mehta, 2008).

Statistically significant differences were found relating to the four dimensions of:

- 'Setting directions';
- 'Refining and aligning the organization (internal strategies)';
- 'Observation'; and
- 'Use of data'.

The mean factor scores for the Low Start school improvement group were higher than those for the other two school improvement groups, indicating the greatest level of reported change in all four of these dimensions of leaders' practices over the previous three years (2003–05). This suggests that level of leadership activity and emphasis may need to be greater to act as a catalyst for improvement in secondary schools that have a low starting base in terms of pupil attainment. In Chapter 5 we go on to discuss the findings related to our three school improvement groups in more depth.

Improvement in school conditions

We do not present all the details of the results of our survey analyses of different dimensions related to school processes and teachers' work in this book (the interested reader can find these in the full report, Day et al., 2009). Nonetheless, one example of the findings in relation to the change in school conditions is illustrated in Tables 3.5 and 3.6, before discussion of the overall model that predicts improvements in overall school performance as measured by changes

Table 3.5 Heads' perceptions of the extent of items-related change in school conditions over three years (primary)

Questionnaire item	Extent of change				
	No change (%)	A little (%)	Some (%)	A lot (%)	Total* (%)
Enhanced commitment and enthusiasm of staff	54 (14.4)	50 (13.3)	121 (32.2)	151 (40.2)	376 (100.1)
Promoted an orderly and secure working environment	79 (21)	47 (12.5)	85 (22.5)	166 (44)	377 (100)
Enhanced local reputation	64 (17.1)	65 (17.3)	125 (33.3)	121 (32.3)	375 (100)
Improved pupil behaviour and discipline as a result of a whole school approach	78 (20.7)	55 (14.6)	107 (28.5)	136 (36.2)	376 (100)

* Because of rounding, percentages might not add up to 100.

Table 3.6 Heads' perceptions of change in school conditions over three years (secondary)

Questionnaire item	Extent of change				
	No change (%)	A little (%)	Some (%)	A lot (%)	Total* (%)
Enhanced commitment	32	49	150	130	361
and enthusiasm of staff	(8.9)	(13.6)	(41.6)	(36)	(100.1)
Promoted an orderly and	41	58	137	125	361
secure working environment	(11.4)	(16.1)	(38)	(34.6)	(100.1)
Enhanced local reputation	44	53	107	156	360
	(12.2)	(14.7)	(29.7)	(43.3)	(99.9)
Improved pupil behaviour	44	70	127	119	360
and discipline as a result of	(12.2)	(19.4)	(35.3)	(33.1)	(100)
a whole school approach					

* Because of rounding, percentages might not add up to 100.

in pupil attainment outcomes across three school years. First, the results are shown in terms of the extent of change that had occurred. There are strong similarities between the two sectors, although secondary heads were more likely to place more emphasis on enhancing their school's local reputation. The results from the key staff survey were in line with those found for head teachers. We illustrate the findings from the head teacher survey in Tables 3.5 and 3.6.

We used CFA to examine the associations between the items related to changes in school condition in more detail. A three-factor model was identified for secondary schools. This points to the extent of changes in the behavioural climate in school conditions and positive change (reductions) in specific types of poor pupil behaviour over the previous three years. The results are shown in Table 3.7.

A similar CFA was conducted on the items related to changes in school conditions for the primary head teacher survey (Table 3.8). It distinguished four rather than three factors. The primary scale on improvement in pupil behaviour ('PupMisBe') is identical to that of the secondary scale. However, the two primary scales on improvement in school conditions ('ImpSchoCo') and pupil attendance ('PupAtten') vary somewhat. For example, an improved homework policy emerged as one of the items for the primary sample, but for secondary schools the item 'enhanced commitment and enthusiasm of staff' featured more strongly in the factor on improved school conditions. In addition, the primary CFA model has an additional scale on the extent of change or improvement in terms of reduction in staff mobility and absence ('StaffAbs').

Table 3.7 The questionnaire items that underpin the three-factor CFA model of improvements in school conditions (secondary heads)

Dimensions	Questionnaire items		
Improvement of school conditions (ImpSchoCo)	12f. school experienced: enhanced commitment and enthusiasm of staff	12g. promoted an orderly and secure working environment	12h. improved pupil behaviour and discipline as a result of a whole school approach
Improvement in pupil behaviour (PupMisBe)	13f. changes in physical conflict among pupils	13i. reduction in physical abuse of teachers	13j. reduction in verbal abuse of teachers
Improvement in pupil attendance (PupAtten)	13a. changes in pupils' lateness to lessons	13b. pupils' lateness to school	13d. pupils missing class

Table 3.8 The questionnaire items that underpin the four-factor CFA model of improvement in school conditions (primary heads)

Dimensions	Questionnaire items		
Reduction in staff mobility and absence (StaffAbs)	12a. reduction in staff mobility	12b. reduction in staff absence	
Improvement of conditions (ImpSchoCo)	12d. school experienced improved homework policies and practices	12f. promoted an orderly and secure working environment	12g. improved pupil behaviour and discipline as a result of a whole school approach
Improvement in pupil behaviour (PubMisBe)	13f. changes in physical conflict among pupils	13i. physical abuse of teachers	13j. verbal abuse of teachers
Improvement in pupil attendance (PupAtten)	13a. changes in pupils' lateness to lessons	13e. pupils' mobility/turnover	13d. pupils missing class

Due to these differences it was decided to analyse the primary and secondary head teacher survey data separately and to construct separate models (SEM) to predict changes in pupil attainment outcomes for the purpose of making comparisons across the two sectors.

A structural model of leadership practice in effective or improved secondary schools

Theoretical relationships between the various dimensions of leadership practices and school processes were first postulated by the researchers, based on their knowledge of related fields and empirical research in the area of study, including the emerging case study findings and the literature review. The hypothesized structure was then tested statistically with survey data from the secondary head sample.

We created a full SEM model (shown in Appendix 3.4) of head teachers' perceptions of leadership practices and relationships with change (improvement) in pupil academic outcomes over three years (2003–05). This was based on survey data from secondary head teachers linked with measures of school performance constructed from data on student attainment in national GCSE examinations. The strength of the loadings indicates the nature and strength of the relationships between 19 dimensions that emerged from the analyses of the data set. Four levels of relationships were identified, predicting change in pupil attainment outcomes.

Level 1

Level 1 comprises the three main dimensions of leadership: 'Setting directions', 'Refining and aligning the organization' and 'Head trust' plus three other dimensions – 'Developing people', 'Use of data' and 'Use of observation' – that are linked with the first two.

There is a strong positive correlation between the first two constructs ($r = 0.70$) 'Setting directions' and 'Refining and aligning the organization', both relating to *change* in the practice of leadership over the three-year period of 2003–05. However, no significant links were found between either of these two constructs and the separate construct of 'Head trust', suggesting that these two key aspects of leadership practices by the head may have differing roles in improving school performance and pupil outcomes. As will be discussed later, the head teacher's impact on change in pupil academic outcomes seems to operate through their influences on different groups of people in the school and on a range of intermediate outcomes relating to improvement in dimensions we term teacher collaborative culture, pupil motivation, behaviour and attendance. The positive consequences of school leaders' high relational trust for school organization and for pupils have been discussed in detail in Robinson's work (Robinson, 2007; Robinson, Lloyd and Rowe, 2008). She argues that trust in schools is a core resource for improvement. In addition to the three key dimensions of leadership, there are another three dimensions at this level: 'Use of data', 'Developing people' and 'Use of observation'. These three dimensions, together with 'Setting directions' and 'Refining and aligning the organization', form a structural model *of change in leadership practice and activities* over three years. There appear to be no direct or indirect relationships between this structural model and the independent construct 'Head trust' (though see Chapter 9 for further discussion of the qualitative data). We also identified links between these measures of leadership practice and the dimensions of distributed leadership (described below). This leadership practice model can be seen as at the core of head teachers' strategic thinking and planning to effect improvement, while the 'Head trust' factor reflects relationships and the emotional functioning of the organization. These matters are discussed further in the case study chapters in Part 3 of the book, particularly Chapters 7, 8 and 9.

Level 2

Level 2 comprises four dimensions in relation to leadership distribution in the school: 'Distributed leadership', 'Leadership by staff', 'SLT collaboration' and the 'SLT's impact on learning and teaching'.

Our results reveal that the dimension 'Head trust' has a direct moderate effect on the dimension 'SLT collaboration' and also direct but relatively weaker effects on the other dimensions 'Leadership by staff', 'SLT's impact on leaning and teaching', and 'Distributed leadership'. The two dimensions 'Refining and aligning the organization' and 'Setting directions' also are found to have an indirect and positive impact on 'Distributed leadership' through 'Developing people'. The effect of change in the extent of 'Developing people' over three years on 'Distributed leadership' is by contrast weak and negative. This may be because where more attention is required for 'Developing people'. the conditions may not yet be seen as appropriate for greater 'Distributed leadership'. In Chapter 7, the time lines of improvement in the case study schools illustrate the various phases of school improvement.

As the SEM results for secondary schools suggest, the leadership practices of the head and of the SLT (Levels 1 and 2 dimensions) appear to influence, directly or indirectly, the improvement of different aspects of school culture and conditions (Level 3 variables), which then indirectly impact on the change in pupil academic outcomes through improvements in several important intermediate outcomes (Level 4 variables). We outline these relationships below.

Level 3

Level 3 comprises four dimensions related to improved school and classroom processes which seem to function as mediating *factors* in this structural model: 'Teacher collaborative culture', 'Assessment for learning', 'Improvement in school conditions', and 'External collaborations and learning opportunities'.

Level 4

Level 4 comprises four dimensions that relate to improvements in intermediate pupil outcomes: 'High academic standards', 'Pupil motivation and learning culture', 'Change in pupil behaviour', and 'Change in pupil attendance'. These constructs are shown to be important *intermediate outcomes* which have either direct or indirect effects on the extent of changes in pupil academic outcomes over three years.

It is also evident that some dimensions in our model have direct effects on constructs at more than one level. For example, in addition to its impact on Level 2 variables, the dimension 'Head trust' also has a direct moderate positive impact on 'Teacher collaborative culture' (Level 3). 'Refining and aligning the organization' also has a direct moderate impact on 'Improvement in school conditions' (Level 3). This dimension also indirectly promotes positive change in pupil academic attainment outcomes through change in pupil behaviour (Level 4).

It is also interesting to note that the dimension 'Teacher collaborative culture' has a direct moderate impact on improvement in 'Pupil motivation and learning culture' over three years. This, in turn, has an indirect effect on change in the 'Pupil academic outcomes' measure through the impact on two other dimensions related to intermediate student outcomes 'Improvement in pupil attendance' and 'Improvement in pupil behaviour'.

In addition, three constructs were found to have small direct positive impacts on change in 'Pupil academic outcomes'. These were the dimensions 'SLT's impact on learning and teaching', 'Leadership by staff' and 'Improvement in pupil behaviour'.

We constructed a similar SEM to predict changes in primary schools' academic performance in English and in mathematics (measured by change in the percentage of pupils reaching Level 4 in assessments at the end of KS2 over three years). The models were found to be in broad accord with those reported for secondary schools (for further details, see Day et al. 2009). They again point to the way SEM can help to uncover the interrelationships among different features of leadership activities and practices, and other indicators of school organization and culture, and show how leadership activities shape school and classroom processes and, indirectly, pupil outcomes. We illustrate these models briefly in Chapter 4, when discussing primary and secondary sector differences.

Conclusions

This chapter has briefly summarized the research design of our leadership and pupil outcomes IMPACT study. It has explained the importance of the mixed-methods design and the sampling strategy we adopted to study improving and effective schools and highlighted some of the questionnaire survey findings in academically effective and improving schools in England that provided data on heads' and key staff's perspectives. Full details of the project findings are presented in detailed reports (Day et al., 2007, 2009). In later chapters of the book we draw together both the qualitative case study and quantitative results to increase our understanding of the associative and causal direct and indirect effects of leaders on their school improvement journeys leading to improved pupil outcomes.

The current research study is, we believe, the first of its kind to focus explicitly on studying leadership and pupil outcomes in a large sample of schools identified as more academically effective and improved. We built on earlier innovative quantitative research such as that by Silins and Mulford (2004) and Mulford (2008) that explored leadership effects on a range of non-cognitive pupil outcomes and on an indicator of attainment using SEM approaches. Our study differs, however, because we did not adopt a cross-sectional approach examining attainment at a specific time point but rather chose an explicit focus in predicting change in school attainment over time, based on improvement in pupil outcomes. Thus our SEM can be seen to fit a dynamic rather than a static theory of educational effectiveness (Creemers and Kyriakides, 2008). This has advantages because we have been able to examine schools in three different improvement groups depending on their initial starting point in terms of pupil attainment (low, moderate or high) as well as using SEM to predict change in outcomes across all schools in the sample.

Our findings provide new evidence that demonstrates the nature of the links between various dimensions and practices of heads and changes in school processes and, ultimately, pupil outcomes. This chapter has sought to illustrate the existence of moderately strong direct effects of leadership on a range of important dimensions of school and classroom processes and pointed to modest but statistically significant indirect links between changes in school conditions that lead to improvements in students' academic outcomes at the school level for a large sample of improved and effective schools.

Robinson et al'.s (2009) report of the results of a 'best evidence' meta-analysis of 27 studies of school leadership effects noted variation in these effects depending on the type of leadership practice being examined. Results of Robinson's review indicated approximately the same level of effect as typically reported in earlier studies – small (.11) to medium (.42) effect sizes, although in a few instances surprisingly large effect sizes were reported. The variation between individual studies found by Robinson is marked, indicating the potential problem of the influence of outlier studies based on small numbers conducted in the USA only and at an earlier time period. Our own research investigated in more detail different dimensions of leadership linked with strategies and actions. The results of this strand suggest that some leadership effects on various school and classroom processes are moderately strong. The effects on improvements in pupils' outcomes operate, however, indirectly, as might be expected given the role of leaders, especially the head teacher, in schools. A range of research in the school effectiveness tradition has drawn attention to the relative strength of teacher compared with school effects (Scheerens and Bosker, 1997; Teddlie and Reynolds, 2000; Creemers and Kyriakides, 2008). It follows that school and leadership effects would be expected to operate most closely on academic outcomes via their effects on teachers, and teaching quality and on promoting a favourable school climate and culture that emphasize high expectations and academic outcomes. Our study highlights, in particular, the importance of promoting an orderly and favourable behavioural climate and positive change in pupil behaviour and attendance as intermediate outcomes that themselves promote improvement in school attainment levels. It also highlights the direct links between head-teacher actions to refine and align the organization and improvement in school conditions.

While the direct effects of school leadership are generally found to be weak (as noted in our review of literature in Chapter 2), these effects should be interpreted in relation to the size of the effects of other school variables, which are generally found to have relatively small effects in comparison with teacher effects (Creemers and Kyriakides, 2008). However, through consistency in approach and a clear focus, we suggest that 'synergistic effects' may be promoted through the combination and accumulation of various relatively small effects in the same direction that promote better teaching and learning and an improved culture, especially in relation to pupil behaviour and attendance and other pupil outcomes such as motivation and engagement as illustrated in our models. The case study chapters provide further rich illustrations and evidence of such interactions (see especially Chapters 7 and 8).

Our results differ somewhat from those reported by Kruger, Witziers and Sleegers (2007), who investigated the impact of school leadership on school-level factors. Their study also used a SEM to test and validate a causal model. They found no direct or indirect effects of educational leadership on their outcome (identified as student commitment) in a secondary analysis of data on secondary schools and leadership in the Netherlands. A major difference is that they did not study attainment or improvement in attainment and thus direct comparisons with our findings are not possible. Nonetheless, their models do indicate significant relationships between leadership and quality of the school organization that are in accord with our findings. More comparative research on leadership effects in a range of different countries and investigating a greater variety of student outcomes is needed to test the generalizability of the present findings in other contexts (Pashiardis, 2003; Braukmann and Pashiardis, 2009). Recent multi-level longitudinal research by Kythreotis, Pashiardis and Kyriakides (2010) in Cyprus examined changes in the attainments of one age group of primary students. It examined the relationships among three dimensions they termed school leadership, school culture and student achievement, and suggested evidence of some small possible direct effects of school leadership. This work, however, did not examine change in school performance (i.e. school improvement) over three years as has been reported here.

We also acknowledge limitations in our study. Because we focus on predicting change in student outcomes and explore the factors associated with this, our results are particularly relevant to enhancing understanding about the processes of school improvement and the role of leadership in improving schools. We do not cover the full range of schools and so our findings cannot tell us about leadership practices in schools where pupil attainment results are only as might be predicted by intake, or where they are by contrast declining or ineffective. Moreover, in the quantitative models, we rely on head teacher and key staff survey data to provide measures based on perceptions of leadership, of change in processes including school conditions and of intermediate pupil outcomes that we relate to independent measures of change in measured pupil attainment at the school level across a three-year period. The strength of our mixed-methods design, however, incorporating rich data from 20 case study schools, further extends the scope and rigour of the research and provides additional evidence relevant to our understanding of the ways leaders can promote better pupil outcomes in more academically effective and improved schools (Day et al., 2009). In subsequent chapters we highlight these.

4 Similarities and differences between primary and secondary leaders
A badly neglected distinction in leadership research

Introduction

In this chapter we bring together the empirical evidence from our study, focusing particularly on the quantitative evidence from the two national surveys of heads and key staff, in order to investigate some of the similarities and differences in leadership between primary and secondary schools in our sample. The discussion will focus upon leaders' professional values, their characteristics and practices, the 'distribution of leadership', the major challenges that heads felt they faced in the first year of their headship in their current schools, and models of leadership impact on improvement in pupil outcomes. Our evidence suggests that differences in school size, curriculum, organizational structures, conditions and culture, as well as heads' values, qualities and educational ideals contribute to some distinctive as well as similar practices in primary and secondary schools (Day et al., 2009). These have implications for the forms, content and configuration of training and development programmes and raise issues of transferability of leaders between the sectors.

We focus here on primary and secondary school differences because they have received relatively little attention in the extant literature, as can be seen in the review in Chapter 2. Although much has been written over the years about leadership in primary and secondary schools, this has primarily focused upon issues, tensions and challenges which tend to be identified as unique to primary or secondary schools and/or as being shared by both school sectors (e.g. Davies, 1987; Wallace and Huckman, 1999; Southworth, 2008; Woods et al., 2009; Cameron, 2010; Highfield, 2010). This may be related to educational researchers' own methodological, moral and ideological interests. It may, also, be related to the availability of research funding which may, at least in part, influence the robustness of the data collected and thus the validity that the research evidence may lend to the theory and knowledge of school sector distinctions. The breadth and depth of the quantitative and qualitative evidence that we gathered in our study, however, enabled us to compare and contrast leadership practices and identify similarities and sector differences in the leadership of effective and improved schools in England. In this way we are able to make additional contributions to current knowledge and understanding of school leadership and its impact on the learning outcomes of pupils in primary and secondary school phases.

Professional values

Our research demonstrates that heads in more effective schools are successful in improving pupil outcomes through who they are as well as what they do. Their professional values, ethics and educational ideals are integral to what they do, why they do it and how they adapt their practices to the unique features of the policy, organizational and human context in which they work. Evidence in our research also suggests that successful heads strategically translate their values, beliefs and ethics into their visions, purposes, strategies and practices, and that these are widely communicated, clearly understood and supported by staff, students and the external community. In other words, the organizational values and practices of more effective and improving schools essentially reflect the professional values of those who lead them.

Primary and secondary heads in our research demonstrated similar professional values. In the Phase 2 survey (see Day et al., 2009 for details), five categories of leadership values that were perceived by heads were identified as having had a significant impact on a range of areas that promoted their schools' improvement:

- moral/ethical responsibility: success for all (including mention of priority given to the Every Child Matters agenda and promoting Equal Opportunities)
- promoting and modelling respect and trust (honesty, integrity, encouragement) and encouraging autonomy
- passion and commitment: faith, religious values and promoting the enjoyment of teaching and learning
- professionalism: modelling high standards of personal and professional practice
- raising standards: promoting continuous school improvement and achieving a high-quality education for all pupils

Heads in both sectors reported that their professional values had had an important influence on the school's direction, how people were developed in the school, leadership of teaching and learning, the organization of the school, and staff and pupil relationships. Primary heads also emphasized the strong impact of their professional values on their teachers' commitment to their schools, and key staff responses endorsed this view.

Case study evidence also reveals the importance of values in terms of a sense of purpose:

> Now it's a culture of 'we can do' and 'the children can do' and there's no such word as 'can't'. Everyone's involved in evaluation and expectations.
>
> (Primary Deputy Head)

Headship characteristics and practices in relation to school sector

In Chapter 2 we showed that educational leadership studies have identified four broad categories of basic leadership practices: 'Setting directions', 'Developing people', 'Refining and aligning the organization' and 'Managing the teaching and learning programme' (Hallinger and Heck, 1999; Hallinger, 2001; Leithwood et al., 2006b; Leithwood and Day, 2007; Day et al., 2009). Evidence presented in Chapter 6 largely confirms findings of previous studies that, despite differences in school contexts, almost all successful primary and secondary heads draw on the same repertoire of basic leadership practices (Leithwood et al., 2006a; see also Waters et al., 2003; Marzano et al., 2005). However, our research also adds to the existing knowledge by pointing to some important school sector differences in specific sets of practices.

Setting directions

One of the central functions of building vision and setting directions is to engage individual members of the school organization so that the organizational goals have motivational value at both the micro (individual) and meso (school) levels (Leithwood et al., 2006a). Leithwood and Day (2007) argue that this category of leadership practices accounts for the largest proportion of leadership effects. The significance of this leadership practice to improving pupil outcomes was also highly rated by the majority of the primary and secondary heads in our research, particularly in terms of demonstrating high performance expectations.

Similarities in leadership actions and their perceived impact on pupil outcomes

There was a consensus among the primary and secondary heads in terms of the 'most important' leadership actions which had led to improved pupil outcomes. The main focus of leadership actions cited was linked to:

- standards and quality enhancement and school improvement and development planning
- enhancing teacher quality/CPD and research and development
- reculturing (in relation to school vision and directions)

The following quotations from case studies illustrate how heads' core values and vision were strategically played out in daily interactions, organizational structures, and roles and responsibilities of the staff and students.

> We did a whole day on vision and values with the whole staff, both teaching and non-teaching, and that really helped. Now we've got the vision and values. The school was in special measures and you either sort it out or it closes.
>
> (Primary Head)

> I had the aspiration that we'd do the best for every youngster, but I think what I'm now seeing is that the aspirations are so much higher than we would ever expect, that the youngsters will achieve far more than we did expect 14 years ago. I think aspirations have stayed the same, philosophically, but in a practical sense we're expecting more from students.
>
> (Secondary Head)

In both school sectors, the setting of high expectations for staff and students was also a central strategy in developing the teaching and learning programmes. Thus, not surprisingly, this category of leadership practices was perceived by both primary and secondary heads and their staff to have had a strong positive impact on *the climate and culture of the school* as well as on *the school's approach to learning* and *the leadership of teaching and learning*.

> I think she has a very strong vision of exacting how she wants things to be. She will have an idea and she will be very driven and enthusiastic about a change. So she is very positive and encouraging like that.
>
> (Primary Teacher)

He is a visionary. Part of his role is to initiate change and for people to then bring that change into being.

(Secondary Assistant Head)

Differences in perceptions of impact

However, our survey results pointed also to the existence of some sector differences in heads' perceptions of their priorities for positive change. Primary heads were more likely to report that their strategies and actions had a significant impact on *pupil engagement in learning* and *the way teachers teach*, while secondary heads were more likely to report a significant impact on measured outcomes in terms of *pupil attainment and progress*. In addition, primary heads tended to place a greater emphasis upon the positive impact of their leadership actions on *parental involvement in pupil learning* than their secondary peers. Of course, this may also reflect the greater opportunities for contact with parents in primary schools and their smaller scale.

Developing people

Similarities in leadership actions

Understanding and developing people are seen as 'central to the ways in which successful leaders integrate the functional and the personal' (Leithwood et al., 2006b: 6). Results of the surveys, together with findings of the case studies, provide additional evidence which supports this observation of Leithwood and his colleagues. For the majority of the primary and secondary heads, a high priority on developing people and on creating positive relationships made a significant contribution to building a collective repertoire of knowledge and skills, a collective sense of efficacy and a collective sense of direction within their schools – all of which were fundamental to the work of improving pupil outcomes. Thus, as might be expected, creating professional learning opportunities and shaping school cultures which nurtured staff and teachers' professional development, offered intellectual stimulation and promoted capacity building were high on the agenda of the successful heads in this research.

In the Phase 1 survey, we investigated three specific practices in this category: 'Continuing professional development (CPD)', 'Developing care and trust' and 'Modelling professional practice'. We found that the majority of the primary (N = 226, 60 per cent) and secondary (N = 217, 60 per cent) heads reported a moderate or substantial increase over the previous three years in relation to strategies for promoting a range of CPD experiences among all staff. For a minority of primary heads (N = 58, 16 per cent) and a similar proportion of secondary heads (N = 54, 15 per cent), 'very significant' increases were implemented in their schools to promote professional development opportunities for their staff. Evidence from the case studies also shows that staff were encouraged to participate in a range of professional training and development opportunities in both sectors. These were viewed as being fundamental to improving teaching and learning quality.

> It's a shared vision. We in the SLT know where we're going and we put a lot of effort into the CPD, looking at the training needs of the staff, sharing that information. All senior managers, on a rolling programme, monitor their subject areas. We reflect on what we're doing, not just by ourselves. We involve staff in evaluations. We'll evaluate any new resources we buy, any intervention strategies are evaluated and if they're not effective, we discontinue them. If they're effective, we increase them.
>
> (Primary Deputy Head)

> And INSET is such in this school there is a philosophy that you do not need to go anywhere else to be trained – we get a lot of rubbish from outside. The idea is that everything you need to know we can teach you here, there is someone here that can show you how to do it. So, I guess that there is a certain level of expertise that has been fostered, nurtured, identified and developed and obviously that has filtered its way down.
>
> (Secondary Head of Department)

Approximately three-quarters of primary and secondary heads reported various degrees of increase in their leadership practices which focused on developing care and trust in their schools. Among them, 15 per cent of primary heads (N = 58) and 14 per cent of secondary heads (N = 51) indicated 'very significant' changes in this area. Similarly, close to three-quarters of heads in both sectors reported moderate or significant increase in modelling high levels of professional practice in their schools. Most importantly, for both the primary and the secondary sample, less experienced heads were more likely to report change in these areas in their schools over the last three years, indicating that developing people is an important area of focus when heads first take up post in a school. We go on to discuss the importance of trust in more detail in Chapter 9.

Case study evidence again illustrates this focus on creating a caring and high-trust environment.

> I think the fact that it is a small school and that the staff are very close and work together and go to each other with ideas and share problems

and the fact that we are a small school and have the opportunity to work so closely with each other.

(Primary Teacher)

Teachers really care and understand the students.

(Secondary Pupil)

Differences in leadership actions

There was little evidence in our research which pointed to significant sector differences in heads' efforts to understand and develop people in their schools. This reconfirms the importance of this core leadership practice as an important means of promoting improved pupil outcomes in both school sectors, and in schools in all phases of improvement (see Chapter 7 for details). It also suggests that, for both primary and secondary schools, there is a key set of leadership actions and strategies which motivates members of the school organization and develops their sense of efficaciousness – both individually and collectively; this is despite the difference in contexts between school sectors.

Refining and aligning the organization

Successful heads improve or establish new conditions of work, cultural norms and organizational infrastructure – which enable staff to make the most of their motivations and capacities and accomplish the goals they hold to be personally and organizationally important (Foster and St. Hilaire, 2004; Leithwood and Day, 2007). In line with findings from the literature review (Leithwood et al., 2006a), the research also identified that building collaborative cultures, establishing productive relations with parents and the community, restructuring and reculturing the organization, and connecting the school to its wider environment were key specific practices within and across different phases of school development in both sectors.

Similarities in leadership actions

For both primary and secondary heads, *broadening participation in and communication about change needed to promote improvement* was reported to be a key leadership strategy designed to promote improvement. For example, various degrees of increase in efforts to engage parents and build community support in school improvement were reported by the majority of the primary and secondary heads. In total 44 per cent (N = 166) of primary heads and 42 per cent (N = 149) of secondary heads reported an increased intensity in the actions they had taken to engage parents in their schools' improvement over the previous three years, with a substantial minority indicating 'a lot' or 'very significant' change in this area (35 per cent of primary, 28 per cent of secondary heads). Around a quarter of all primary and secondary heads surveyed reported a substantial increase in efforts to build community support for school improvement over the previous three years.

Case study interviews illustrate this emphasis on parents and the community:

> We are very much there for families as well. We are always there if they need to come and talk to us. We are very flexible if they suddenly ring up. We have had parents coming in with being up to their eyeballs in something or they are so worried that they just need somebody to talk to, and we see ourselves as the support for them as well as for the children. The principal is very good in that we have a lot of communication with parents: we have their parents evenings and we have an open-door policy where they can just come in and help and stay the morning as well if they want, that's just fine. I think that's why we can see more than just the children's academic learning, we can see the whole picture.
>
> (Primary Teacher)

> Parents' time, there's one every day of the week at different times. Tomorrow it starts at 7.15 till 8.00 in the morning and it's a chance for parents to come up, if they've got any concerns whatsoever, without an appointment.
>
> (Secondary Assistant Head)

Differences in leadership actions and their impact on pupil outcomes

Secondary heads reported a stronger emphasis in their actions to restructure the organization and in enhancing personal and professional relationships in terms of *encouragement, empowerment and trust* than was the case for primary heads. For example, although more than half of primary heads (N = 204, 54 per cent) reported 'a lot' or 'very significant' change in practice relating to improving internal review procedures during the previous three years, more significant change in this area was reported by secondary heads. Over 70 per cent of secondary heads reported a substantial amount of change (N = 251, 71 per cent) in improving internal review procedures, with almost a third who felt that the amount of change in practice in their schools was 'very significant' (N = 105, 30 per cent) over the previous three years (the equivalent figure was only N = 43, 11 per cent for primary heads). This is likely to reflect, at least in part, the larger size and more complex structure of secondary schools.

In terms of impact, although both primary and secondary heads felt that the most significant impact of restructuring was on the *climate and culture of the school* (primary: N = 87, 54 per cent; secondary: N = 75, 56 per cent), secondary heads again focused on the impact of this on *pupil progress* to a greater extent than primary heads, who emphasized more the *school's approach to learning* and *the engagement of pupils in learning.*

Managing the teaching and learning programme

There is compelling evidence in educational research which points to the importance of this category of leadership practices in fostering organizational stability, strengthening the school's infrastructure and, through these, creating productive working conditions for teachers which impact positively on pupils' motivation and engagement in learning (Reynolds, 1998; Hallinger, 2003; Leithwood and Jantzi, 2000; Leithwood et al., 2006a). Our research provides additional evidence which indicates that heads in both sectors, as part of their improvement strategies, use a variety of strategies to enhance the quality of teaching and learning, and to develop the curriculum.

Similarities in leadership actions

Heads emphasized their actions to restructure and reculture organizations in which *care and trust* and *high-achievement-focused school cultures* were predominant features and complemented their actions to develop and motivate staff and enhance capacity building in their schools. The following quotations illustrate these findings from the case studies:

> All the time I think the school is very caring and they make sure the school is behaving good.
>
> (Primary Pupil)

> Teachers can't do it by themselves. Pupils can't do it. They say we can't do that without you. There's got to be mutual respect and it took time. Now you go to any classroom and there's purposeful teaching taking place and respect.
>
> (Secondary Assistant Head)

Another key feature of this category of leadership practice was that of *placing a high priority and consistent emphasis upon improving classroom teaching across the school.* More than half of heads surveyed (57 per cent primary and 55 per cent secondary) reported substantial change in relation to getting teachers to consider new ideas for their teaching. Nearly all key staff respondents agreed that their head encouraged them to consider new ideas for their teaching (98 per cent primary key staff and 93 per cent secondary key staff).

Incorporating evidence in the research literature into their decision making to inform practice was also rated by most primary and secondary heads as important, and different leadership practices had been used to promote this (primary: N = 253; 67 per cent; secondary: N = 229, 65 per cent).

Again, the case study evidence reveals the attention given to promoting leadership of learning:

> Trying to change the mindset of every teacher to say that every teacher is a manager and a leader; everybody is, within their own classroom.
> (Primary Head)

> I think [the head teacher] gives you the freedom to experiment – obviously not to go completely overboard and mess it all up – but he's very positive, very supportive and he will listen to you. Then obviously [the head teacher] has an overview of that but he allows you to get on with your role.
> (Secondary Head of Department)

Leadership actions aimed at *getting staff to change and improve their teaching practice* were noted as a key preoccupation for heads in our research. Areas of leadership practice that had changed significantly included a greater focus on the provision of relevant professional development and the use of classroom observations to identify personal targets for staff development. For example, 39 per cent of primary heads and 42 per cent of secondary heads reported substantial increases in support for staff to improve their teaching practice. A total of 60 per cent of primary and secondary heads surveyed reported moderate or substantial increases in the promotion of CPD for staff. This was corroborated by many key staff responses, with 52 per cent agreeing that their head promoted CPD for staff.

> I think it's crucial that the people in front of the children are motivated, that the school is committed to CPD, the caring ethos, that people are valued – I think that's crucial, that it's all levels.
> (Primary Deputy Head)

> So I show techniques on whiteboards. I also observe lessons and suggest improvements etc. and work with the heads of departments in areas that they specify and in which they might want some specific help.
> (Secondary Head of Department)

Allocating and distributing personnel and resources appropriately so as to foster student achievement was also a focus for a significant number of heads and other leaders in the schools. In the Phase 1 survey, 87 per cent of primary heads and 90 per cent of secondary heads reported a very significant increase in the way that they utilized support staff skills to benefit pupil learning over the previous three years. Also, over 70 per cent of primary and secondary heads reported a moderate or significant change in the ways they allocated resources, based on pupil needs.

Heads and staff in both primary and secondary schools were *using increasingly detailed analyses of student progress and achievement data to inform their teaching*, as we have identified in Chapter 3. For example, participants across all 20 case study schools commented that they relied upon a close analysis of pupil achievement data to inform changes in teaching and leadership practice in the school.

> I think that we are much more on top of tracking children. I think that is key. We are much more organized, so to speak, as a whole school on how we track children. Children do not fall by the wayside. We follow them through. We track them every term throughout the school and as soon as we pick up that they are not making the progress, we think of different ways of addressing that. So it's not left from one year to the next to the next to the next. So I think in the past that did happen much more.
>
> (Primary Key Stage Co-ordinator)

> The third factor is that when I came here, data were already being used extensively. It wasn't quite being used to enhance performance. It was used to identify all sorts of things. Nothing was put in place to follow it through. So I worked hard to make sure that there were interventions taking place. There was follow-up. There was mentoring, and we can show . . . we are recognized as being a school, now, that works with data very effectively.
>
> (Secondary Deputy Head)

In the Phase 1 survey, one-quarter of the heads (25 per cent primary heads and 24 per cent secondary heads) reported a *very significant* increase in their practice of using pupil achievement data as part of their decisions about change. Such extensive use of pupil achievement data to inform practice was supported by almost all the key staff in the same survey (90 per cent).

Differences in leadership actions and their impact on pupil outcomes

The survey results also pointed to some sector differences. In secondary schools a stronger school-wide focus over the recent period was made on *the use of assessment data to identify pupil needs*. Approximately one in three reported 'very significant' change in practice in this area in contrast to only one in five of the primary heads who did so. This suggests that a greater emphasis on using performance data was seen as a particular lever for improvement in the secondary sector. In addition, the emphasis on the use of performance data was particularly evident for those in more disadvantaged secondary schools (FSM bands 3 and 4), indicating that the use of data had played a particularly urgent role in their improvement efforts.

Promoting curriculum change was another example of successful leaders' behaviours. For example, heads and other leaders had promoted change in the curriculum and in teaching approaches and practice in order to sustain the quality of teaching and learning over time. However, the extent of change tended to be more substantial in primary than in secondary schools. A total of 56 per cent of primary heads, in contrast to 38 per cent of secondary heads, reported a substantial increase in their practice of broadening opportunities for student learning beyond the traditional academic curriculum. This did not, however, lead to a lower emphasis on raising academic attainment.

Secondary heads (N = 90, 70 per cent) were much more likely than primary heads (N = 66, 43 per cent) to emphasize increases in their leadership actions relating to *enhancing teacher quality/CPD*, which directly targeted improvement on pupil outcomes and the overall quality of teaching and learning in their schools. In comparison, primary heads perceived that their actions which related to improving teaching and learning had had a stronger impact on the way teachers teach, the school's approach to learning and the overall quality of teaching and learning. Again, secondary heads particularly emphasized the intended impact of their actions on pupil progress while primary heads focused upon the impact on pupil engagement in learning.

Major challenges faced by heads in their first year of headship

Approximately a half of primary and secondary heads indicated that they had faced major challenges in their first year in their current school. These were most commonly related to poor pupil outcomes or poor teaching, particularly those in the Low Start and Moderate Start school improvement groups in both sectors (see more detailed discussion on school improvement groups in Chapter 5).

Poor pupil attainment followed by poor pupil behaviour, then poor pupil progress (value added) were the most frequently noted challenges for primary heads, while, for secondary heads, poor pupil behaviour was reported to have been the number one challenge followed by poor pupil motivation or engagement with learning, then poor pupil attainment. Poor quality teaching (primaries) and coasting or complacent staff (secondaries) were also in the top five most frequently noted major challenges. In addition, poor quality buildings or facilities had been a major challenge for many secondary heads in the first years of leadership in their current school. Improvements in school buildings (due to the government's policy of investing in school buildings), were seen to have had a major positive impact in many schools during the period of our study.

Leadership distribution: shared responsibility for decision making

Robinson (2008) has argued that the nature of distributed leadership encompasses two main concepts:

- distributed leadership as task distribution; and
- distributed leadership as distributed influence processes.

The former has its roots in the theorization of leadership as the performance of particular tasks (e.g. Spillane, 2006), while the latter emerges from the view that leadership is 'an influence process that changes how others think or act with respect to the content of the influence' (Robinson, 2008: 246). The original design of the surveys in our research was influenced by the first conceptualization and thus primarily concerned with patterns of distribution of the leadership across the people in a range of entities in the school (see also Spillane et al., 2008) and their perceived effects on teaching and learning. However, the structural equation modelling of both secondary and primary school leadership also supports Robinson's (2008) identification of distributed leadership as an influence process. The structural models of leadership practice discussed in Chapter 3 revealed the interaction and interdependence between patterns of distribution of the leadership tasks, particularly those related to teaching and learning and pupil outcomes. Within this, leadership distribution was perceived to be an important influence on teaching and schools' change processes which affected, directly and indirectly, aspects of school culture and conditions. These then indirectly impacted on improvement in pupil academic outcomes.

Similarities in the distribution of leadership

Evidence in our research suggests that effective leadership relies upon developing an increasingly close and collaborative relationship between teachers and the senior leadership team (SLT). *Collective planning* was perceived by the majority of the primary and secondary heads as a strong feature of their school organization. The distribution of leadership tasks by them and their SLT was, however, not spontaneous, but strategic and planned.

The wider perspective is that we are a team. The children are with us for seven years and we all have an important part to play before, during and after the time in our class, and what we do as a whole school will benefit the person at the top end from the earliest stages if we all agree on a common approach, common format, and what we're doing is to benefit us all.

(Primary Deputy Head)

The focus of anything I'm trying to do is always teamwork. Everybody feels that they are part of the cogs and wheels that run behind the scenes. Often, when people feel isolated and are not part of the system, you get a lot of resistance from rogue elements. Once you've got that resistance that can often be the spanner in the works. Trying to get everybody to work towards the same goal and working as a team is one of my priorities.

(Secondary Deputy Head)

Both primary and secondary heads reported that they shared decision making with their SLTs and that members of the SLT in their schools shared a similar set of values, beliefs, attitudes and practices related to teaching and learning. They reported that the SLTs in their schools had a key role in creating and implementing a range of key activities, especially the development of policies relating to pupil behaviour and teaching, learning and attainment.

I think that it is generally that everyone feels that they have a say in the writing of the school's development plan. We had many meetings going on in the school with things that are filtered down. We have SLT meetings and then things are discussed at that level and then filtered down to team meetings, and then if people can't attend team meetings then they are asked to keep abreast in staff meetings. There's a contact for every staff meeting; if you can't attend, you go to that person, who took Minutes, and find out what went on. And I think generally the strategy is that everybody is kept informed and that is a real strength here.

(Primary School Manager)

[The deputy head] is working very well to focus on what's going on in the school and she's certainly got her finger on the pulse of what's happening at ground level. But at the same time she has also got her feelers out there with the parents and the community and she's doing a very good job in that regard. So that tension is resolved between the pair of them. They work well as a team.

(Secondary Head of Department)

Differences in the distribution of leadership

We found a considerable sector difference in the ways in which leadership tasks were distributed in schools, particularly in terms of the breadth and depth of the distribution of leadership responsibility across the schools.

Shared decision making was seen to have had a very significant or substantial impact on most pupil outcomes, particularly on pupil behaviour (89 per cent of primary heads versus 74 per cent of secondary heads), pupil engagement in learning (89 per cent of primary versus 72 per cent of secondary) and pupil affective or emotional learning (87 per cent of primary versus 66 per cent of secondary) in primary schools. Key staff reported considerable shared decision making and, again, this was most notable in primary schools and may reflect differences in size and organizational complexity as well as cultural norms.

There was also a marked contrast between the primary and secondary sectors in terms of the amount of responsibility for decision making shared with *middle managers*. Primary heads tended to work more closely with their middle managers in terms of sharing decision making than was the case for secondary heads. Primary heads were also much more likely than their secondary colleagues to report sharing decision making with groups of teachers. Of the 160 primary heads who responded to the particular question regarding leadership distribution, 40 per cent (N = 64) felt that they shared a substantial amount of responsibility for decision making with groups of teachers. In contrast, less than 20 per cent (N = 25, 18.8 per cent) of secondary heads reported that they did so. Primary heads were also more likely to report that they shared responsibility for some decision making with groups of pupils. These results suggest that successful primary heads favour a flatter management approach.

Modelling the links between leadership practices and pupil outcomes

In Chapter 3, we constructed a tentative structural model of heads' perceptions of leadership practices for secondary and primary schools respectively (see Appendix 4.1 for the primary model and 4.2 for the secondary). These help to map the interrelationships among different features of leadership activities and practices, and other indicators of school organization and culture, and also show how leadership activities shape school environment and classroom processes and, indirectly, change in pupil outcomes.

Similarities in interrelationships in SEM models

In Chapter 3 we discussed the way we adopted quantitative SEM models to investigate the relationships between leadership and improved pupil attainment outcomes using the quantitative Phase 1 survey data. The interrelationships between different constructs in this primary model are broadly in line with those between leadership practices and change in pupil outcomes identified in the secondary SEM model, suggesting that there are strong similarities across the two education sectors. A total of 20 variables were identified for the primary model, which are similar to the 19 variables identified in the secondary SEM model (see Appendix 4.2 for the secondary SEM model and Appendix 4.1 for the primary model). The strength of the loadings also suggests that the nature and strength of the relationships between the latent variables in the primary SEM model are also similar to those identified in the secondary model.

In addition, leadership practices of the head (i.e. 'Setting directions' and 'Redefining and aligning the organization') and 'Head trust in teachers' are two independent (i.e. not statistically related) constructs in both the primary and secondary SEM models. Through distributing leadership to SLT and the staff and improvement in a range of intermediate outcomes, they influence change in pupil academic outcomes over time. The interrelationships identified in both models support Robinson's second concept of distributed leadership as a distributed influence that 'recognizes the essentially social dimension of leadership' (2008: 251). The case studies in our research provide additional evidence, indicating that heads' trust in the qualities and capacity of the people whom they lead has a profound impact upon the breadth and depth of the leadership distribution in the processes of school change and improvement. These, in turn, influence different aspects of school culture and conditions for effective teaching and learning (Chapters 6 to 9 provide nuanced accounts of how trust promotes change and improvement in schools). In line with the secondary model, four levels of relationships were also identified for primary schools.

Key dimensions of heads' leadership in primary schools
Level 1 comprises three key dimensions: 'Setting directions', 'Refining and aligning the organization' and 'Head trust in teachers'. In addition, there are other dimensions at this level: 'Use of data' and 'Developing people'.

Key dimensions of leadership distribution
Level 2 comprises five dimensions in relation to leadership distribution: 'distributed leadership', 'Staff', 'SMT' (senior management team), 'SLT collaboration' and 'SLT's impact on learning and teaching'.

Key dimensions of school and classroom processes
Level 3 comprises four dimensions which function as mediating factors in this structural model: 'Teacher collaborative culture', 'Assessment for learning', 'Improvement in school conditions', and 'External collaborations and learning opportunities'.

Key dimensions of pupils' intermediate outcomes
Level 4 also comprises five dimensions: 'High academic standards', 'Change in pupil motivation and responsibility for learning', 'Reduction in staff mobility and absence', 'Change in pupil behaviour', and 'Change in pupil attendance'. These appear to reflect improvement in important intermediate outcomes which have direct or indirect effects on changes in pupil academic outcomes over three years.

Differences in interrelationships in SEM models

There are also, however, some sector differences. Evidence from the case studies suggests that these differences may be related to the difference in school size and organizational structures, conditions, culture and processes between primary and secondary schools.

In the primary SEM model, there is an additional dimension we term 'Reduction in staff mobility and absence', suggesting that improvement in staffing may have made a particularly strong impact on pupil outcomes. The primary model also has a new dimension 'Distributed leadership: SLT', pointing to the particularly strong influencing role of SLT in the daily lives of primary schools and its potential impact on change in pupil outcomes over time in our sample of effective and improved primary schools.

Additionally, the variable of 'Use of observation' is not found to be important in the primary model, unlike the secondary SEM. This is likely to mean only that this practice has not changed significantly over the three years in which heads were asked to comment. Last but not least, in contrast to the secondary model where three dimensions have direct effects on change in pupil academic outcomes (i.e. 'SLT's impact on learning and teaching', 'Staff (leadership)' and 'Change in pupil behaviour'), in the primary model 'Change in pupil motivation and responsibility for learning' is the only dimension which has directly impacted on the improvement in pupils' academic outcomes. It may be that the smaller organizational scale of primary schools means that only a smaller number of dimensions are likely to affect pupil attainment outcomes directly.

Summary and conclusions

The chapter has presented an overview of the similarities and differences in leadership between effective and improving primary and secondary schools in England. We focused our discussions upon the analysis of heads' actions and professional values, the 'distribution of leadership' and its impact, and the extent to which these actions, qualities and values were perceived to have positively impacted upon different aspects of pupil outcomes. Heads in both primary and secondary schools prioritized similar actions and strategies to understand and develop people in their schools. This suggests that there is a key set of leadership practices which motivates the staff and develops their individual and collective sense of efficacy in both sectors and thus are seen by all heads as an important means of promoting pupil outcomes.

The SEM models discussed in this chapter provide new evidence on the impact of school leadership on processes of school improvement. The findings point to some strong similarities between primary and secondary schools in the links between leadership practices and staff culture and the improvement in school conditions. For example, the dimensions of SLT collaboration and leadership provision by staff predict increases in the dimension 'Teacher collaborative culture', which in turn predicts improvement in terms of the dimension 'High academic standards' in both the primary and secondary models. In addition, there is a clear link between refining and aligning the organization and improvement in school conditions in both models. Also, heads' trust in the qualities and capacity of the staff had a significant impact upon the distribution of leadership responsibility across the school.

There are indications, however, that the way these shape pupil attainment outcomes may vary. The importance of improvement in pupil behavioural outcomes and attendance to promoting improvement in academic attainment is evident in the secondary SEM model. For primary schools, however, improvements in pupil motivation and responsibility for learning seem to be more directly linked with improvements in measured attainment. This may well reflect differences in the nature and extent of behaviour and attendance problems as barriers to attainment between the two sectors. Another aspect of interest is that the increased use of 'Assessment for learning' is predicted by reported changes in terms of increased 'Pupil motivation' and 'Responsibility for learning' in the primary model. In the secondary model, by contrast, the greater use of 'Assessment for learning' predicts a similar dimension, 'Improved positive learner motivation and learning culture'. By linking a large data set based on a questionnaire survey of leaders' perceptions and data on attainment outcomes for both a primary and secondary school sample, the study contributes to new understanding of the links between leadership and pupil outcomes in England.

In summary, both primary and secondary heads reported a strong emphasis upon the direct and significant impact of leadership practices related to 'Setting directions', 'Refining and aligning the organization', 'Developing people' and 'Managing the teaching and learning programmes' to achieve improvement in pupil outcomes. This is despite statistically and educationally significant differences in certain features of headship practices in different school phases.

Sector differences in leadership actions were perceived as a strategic response to act, and were based upon differences in size and organizational complexity as well as cultural norms. Thus, despite the overall similarity, some sector differences were found in perceptions of headship actions and their impact on pupil outcomes:

- *There were differences in heads' perceptions of leadership priorities and their impact on improvement in pupil outcomes.* Primary heads were more likely to prioritize strategies to improve pupil engagement in learning, the way teachers teach and parental involvement, while their secondary colleagues were more likely to report the significant influence of their actions on pupil outcomes in terms of both attainment and progress.
- *Heads in secondary schools placed a greater emphasis in their actions upon developing staff and enhancing personal and professional relationships in terms of encouragement, empowerment and trust than was the case for primary heads.*
- *More emphasis on specific targeted actions in relation to improving teaching had been given in the secondary sector, and this was particularly the case in schools in more disadvantaged contexts.* The use of performance data, for example, had a more urgent role to play in secondary heads' improvement efforts, particularly those leading schools in socio-economically disadvantaged communities.
- *There were important sector differences in the breadth and depth of the distribution of leadership responsibility across the school.* Such differences were found in terms of both patterns of the distribution of leadership tasks and leadership distribution as an important influence on schools' change processes in effective and improving schools, which affected, directly and indirectly, aspects of school culture and conditions and ultimately the improvement of pupil outcomes.

5 Characteristics and practices of leaders in schools which improved from different starting points

Introduction

This chapter focuses on the identification and exploration of various developmental trajectories of school improvement. It identifies three groups of schools with distinctive development trajectories in relation to their patterns of improvement in pupil attainment and progress. This is a unique feature of the research being based on data analysed for all English primary and secondary schools over the period 2003–05. The chapter also discusses findings from further analyses of questionnaire survey data of head teachers and key staff (already introduced in Chapter 3) which explored patterns of leadership practices in relation to the improvement group of the school.

The categorization of schools into three distinctive improvement and effectiveness groups was made to establish whether schools with different developmental trajectories also differed in their leadership and the strategies and actions adopted to promote improvement. Our findings revealed statistically and educationally significant differences in certain features and practices among these three school groups. The chapter explores important relationships between school context (in terms of the level of socio-economic disadvantage of pupil intakes) and the school improvement group, and between school context and the head teacher's time in post. We show that schools in disadvantaged contexts are more likely to have experienced many changes in leadership during the previous decade and that heads in such schools tend to be less experienced in leadership. In addition, for schools improving from a low start, more intensive actions and leadership emphases are used. The implications of this for the improvement of schools in challenging circumstances are explored.

Identifying academically effective and improved schools

As noted in Chapter 3, the IMPACT study conducted various analyses of national data sets on pupil intake characteristics, attainment and value added outcome measures to identify a potential sample of schools for a survey of leadership practices in improving and effective schools in England. These included analyses of national datasets from the FFT, the DCSF and Ofsted (particularly FFT and DCSF value added and attainment indicators, PLASC (pupil level annual school census) data about pupil intakes and Ofsted inspection data on leadership of head teachers and other staff). Analyses identified primary and secondary schools that had shown significantly better outcomes than other schools in terms of a range of indicators of academic achievement over a three-year period (2003–25). We also wanted to identify schools with no recorded change of leadership during the period of improvement (2003–05) under study.

In addition, the level of SES of school intakes, measured by the percentage of pupils eligible for free school meals (FSM) was analysed, because it is known that school context can be an influential factor that predicts differences in both individual pupils' attainments and school performance levels (Mortimore et al., 1988; Sammons et al., 1997). All schools for which national data were available can be divided into four bands where FSM1 is the least disadvantaged (0–8 per cent pupils eligible) and FSM4 the most disadvantaged (36 per cent+ pupils eligible) group. Three subgroups of schools were then identified based on analyses of national assessment and examination data, and value added indicators[1] identifying trends across three years. The groups were:

1   Low Start – improving from low to moderate or low to high in attainment and highly effective in value added;
2   Moderate Start – improving from moderate to higher moderate or high in attainment and highly effective in value added; and
3   High Start – stable high attainment and highly effective in value added.

Secondary sample

Analyses examined changes in the *percentage of pupils achieving five or more grades A*–C at GCSE and equivalents (5A*–C)* over three years and improvement

---

[1] Value added (VA) indicators include 'simple' VA measures and 'contextual' VA measures. Simple VA measures takes into account pupils' prior attainment in predicting later attainment and thus provide indicators based on pupils' relative progress in school over a period of years. They arise from a national median line. The value added score for each student is the difference (positive or negative) between their own "output" point score and the median (middle) output point score achieved by others with the same or similar starting point, or "input" point score' (DCSF definition). Contextual VA measures are more complex, taking into account a range of significant individual predictors derived from the Pupil Level Annual School Census (PLASC) (e.g. gender, special educational needs, pupil mobility, English as an additional language) and other datasets. The principle for contextual VA models remains the same as the 'simple' VA median line approach. The particular technique used to derive a contextual VA score is multi-level modelling.

in *value added measures* at KS4 (KS2–4, 2–3 and 3–4 simple and contextualized VA) to identify a group of improved and effective schools based on FFT indicators of improvement (see Appendix 5.1). There were 1141 schools showing significant and sustained improvement, constituting 37 per cent of the total of secondary schools in England.

A total of 839 secondary schools were identified that had shown significant and sustained improvement over three years and had had no recorded change of head teacher during that time (based on records in Edubase 2005 data) for our questionnaire survey of head teachers and key staff.

Primary sample

Similar sampling strategies were used for primary schools. Analyses examined changes in the *percentage of pupils achieving level 4 or above* in *English* and also in *mathematics*, and improvement in VA terms (both simple and contextual VA; again based on FFT indicators). In all, 5003 primary schools (34 per cent) of the total national sample had shown significant and sustained improvement in both. Due to the large numbers, we selected a stratified subsample of these, after deleting schools where there was a recorded change of head teacher, of 752 schools (approximately 15 per cent) from the total of 5003 schools that had experienced significant improvement by 2 or more improvement flags in simple and contextual value added terms between 2003 and 2005.

For both sectors we found that proportionately more schools identified as improved and effective (and thus potentially part of our sample) were in high-disadvantage contexts (FSM4) and proportionately fewer were in low-disadvantage contexts (FSM1) compared with the national distribution (Appendix 5.2). Because there are fewer high-disadvantage schools nationally, we stratified our sample to over-sample schools in high-disadvantage FSM bands 3 and 4 (60 per cent) compared with low-disadvantage schools in bands FSM1 and2 (40 per cent) in the selection of primary schools for the survey. Table 5.1 compares the final primary and secondary samples by FSM band against the national distribution of schools, and this is very similar to the distribution of the potential sample. Proportionally somewhat more of the effective and improved schools were in highly disadvantaged contexts (FSM4) than would be expected, given the national proportions of secondary schools in this category, suggesting that such schools have shown more improvement in results from 2003 to 2005 than other schools. This finding is in accord with analyses of trends in school attainment and from inspection judgements in England since 1993 (Matthews and Sammons, 2005; Sammons, 2008).

Table 5.1 Primary and secondary improving school samples by FSM Bands and national comparison

FSM band	Primary sample*		Primary national		Secondary sample*		Secondary national	
	N	%	N	%	N	%	N	%
Low disadvantage								
FSM1 (0–8%)	225	30	6150	42	316	38	1159	37
FSM2 (9–20%)	180	24	3896	27	280	33	1097	35
FSM3 (21–35%)	163	22	2359	16	124	15	520	17
High disadvantage								
FSM4 (36%+)	184	24	2267	15	119	14	339	11
Total	752	100	14672	100	839	100	3115	100

* Excluding schools where a change of HT was recoded as occurring in Edubase 2005. The primary sample schools in FSM groups 3 and 4 were over-sampled.

Leadership characteristics and practices in relation to school improvement groups

As noted earlier, three subgroups of schools were identified based on initial attainment levels in 2003 and change over three years from 2003 to 2005. Table 5.2 shows the number of head teacher responses to our question survey for the three school improvement groups. Proportionately more schools in the final sample were in the Low Start Group. This may reflect their greater interest in the research focus on school improvement and perhaps their particular awareness of having improved markedly from a low base during recent years (2003 to 2005).

We found statistically significant differences between the three improvement groupings in a range of structural factors relating to the head teachers' years of experience in total, the number of head teachers in post in the school over the previous ten years, school education sector and school socio-economic contexts. In addition, our analyses revealed other differences related to ways of working, leadership and strategies for improvement.

School socio-economic context

As might be expected, there were significant associations between the level of socio-economic disadvantage of the pupil intake (measured by FSM band) and the three school improvement groups for both the primary and secondary

Table 5.2 Responses to the head teacher survey by school improvement group

School improvement group 2003–2005	Primary schools*		Secondary schools**	
	N	%	N	%
Low Start	160	42	167	47
Moderate Start	94	25	76	21
High Start	123	33	115	32
Total	377	100	358	100

* One primary school responding did not supply a DCSF number, so could not be allocated to an improvement group.
** Four secondary schools responding did not supply a DCSF number or had changed numbers and could not be allocated to an improvement group.

samples. In both education sectors the High Start Group schools were relatively more likely to serve low-disadvantage communities (FSM 1 and 2), whereas the Low Start Group schools were more likely to serve high-disadvantage communities (FSM 3 and 4).

Nearly two-thirds (N = 105, 65.6 per cent) of primary schools in the Low Start Group, compared with under 1 in 10 (N = 10, 8 per cent) of the High Start Group, were in high-disadvantage contexts (FSM Bands 3 and 4). Similarly, over half (N = 84, 50.3 per cent) of secondary schools in the Low Start Group, compared with around 1 in 20 (N = 6, 5.2 per cent) in the High Start Group, were in high-disadvantage contexts. Although 71 per cent of schools responding to the survey were in relatively low-disadvantage contexts (FSM 1 and 2) only around a half (49.7 per cent) were in the Low Start Group. These results point to the importance of school socio-economic context in interpreting differences in school's raw performance results as measured by national tests and examinations, and their improvement trajectories over several years.

Head teachers' experience

For the secondary sample, heads with less total experience of headship tended to be more likely to lead high-disadvantage schools, but this pattern was not identified for primary schools in the sample. Only 20 per cent of secondary heads leading relatively low-disadvantage schools (FSM 1 and 2) had been a head teacher for three years or fewer, whereas proportionately almost twice as many head teachers (37 per cent) with similarly low amounts of experience of headship were leading high-disadvantage schools (FSM 3 and 4), as is seen in Table 5.3. In contrast, nearly half the heads (48.2 per cent) of FSM 1 and

Table 5.3   School SES contexts (FSM Band) and changes of head teachers* (secondary)

School context	Including yourself, how many head teachers has your current school had in the past ten years?			
	0–1 heads (%)	2 heads (%)	3–10 heads (%)	Total* (%)
FSM 1 & 2	70 (27.7)	133 (52.5)	50 (19.8)	253 (100)
FSM 3 & 4	24 (23.3)	39 (37.9)	40 (38.8)	103 (100)
Total	94 (26)	172 (48)	90 (25)	356 (99)

* Because of rounding, some percentages might not add up to 100.

2 schools that were more advantaged in their contexts had more than eight years of experience, whereas the proportion was somewhat lower at 38 per cent of FSM 3 and 4 schools which had a head teacher in post currently with a similar length of experience as a head teacher.

There were also significant differences between the three school improvement groups in the total years of experience of the head teacher. For both the primary and secondary samples, less experienced heads were proportionately more likely to be in post in schools from the Low Start Group, whereas schools in the High Start Group were relatively more likely to have an experienced head teacher in post. In total, 47 per cent of heads of the Low Start Group of primary schools had seven or fewer years of experience as a head teacher in contrast to only 25 per cent of those in the High Group of schools. At the secondary level, nearly two-thirds (62 per cent) of heads of the Low Start Group had the same amount of experience (seven years or below) as a head teacher compared with just under half (49 per cent) of those in the High Start Group. In both sectors, statistically significant differences were found between the three school improvement groups in terms of number of head teachers in post over the previous decade. Schools in the High Start Group were much less likely to have experienced several head teacher changes and the association was stronger for the secondary sample (Figure 5.1).

The number of head teachers in post in the school during the previous decade was also significantly related to school context, but only for the secondary sample. High-disadvantage secondary schools were relatively more likely to have experienced several changes of heads during the previous ten years compared with less disadvantaged schools (Table 5.3). There is national evidence in England that secondary schools in more challenging, highly disadvantaged contexts have greater difficulties in recruiting or retaining head teachers. Nonetheless, our research indicates that a change of head teacher can often be an opportunity or act as a catalyst for school improvement in those schools with low levels of performance previously struggling to improve. This

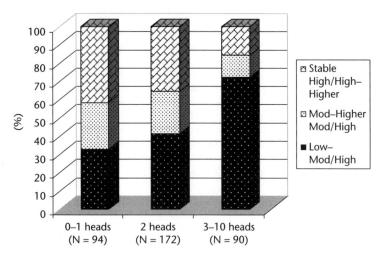

Figure 5.1 Number of heads in post over the previous decade by school and improvement group (secondary schools)

has been noted in a number of studies of improving schools and is also evident in analyses of inspection evidence in England (see Harris et al., 2006; Matthews and Sammons 2004; 2005; Muijs et al., 2004).

Our survey results provide a wealth of evidence that suggests that changing the head teacher may have contributed to the rapid improvement of schools with an initial low attainment profile (those in the Low Start Group). However, multiple changes in headship over a decade can be a symptom of a school experiencing many difficulties, and this may have inhibited the creation of a school culture focused on improvement in the past. Again, this pattern of unstable leadership can also be seen as a symptom of the challenges facing the leaders of schools with a history of difficulties as well as a possible cause of earlier poor performance. The need for further attention to be given to ways of attracting high-calibre applicants who have the qualities necessary to effect significant improvement in such schools is highlighted by this finding.

Perceived challenges facing heads in schools with different developmental trajectories

For both primary and secondary school respondents to our survey, heads from the Low Start Group were proportionately more likely than those from the other two school improvement groups to report that they had experienced three major related challenges of *poor pupil attainment, poor pupil behaviour* and *poor pupil motivation* in the first year of their headship in their current school. Three-fifths (60 per cent) of primary and secondary heads in the Low Start Group reported that they had faced all these three challenges. In contrast, close to half of those from the Moderate Start Group and only around a third or less from the High Start Group indicated that they had faced such challenges related to their pupil outcomes.

For the primary sample, over half of heads (53 per cent) in the Low Start Group, compared with close to half (47 per cent) in the Moderate Start Group and less than a third in the High Start Group (30 per cent), reported the challenge of *low engagement of parents in pupil learning*. In addition, close to half of primary heads in the Low Start Group (45 per cent) indicated that *disadvantage of intake* was a major challenge for them in the first year of their headship in their current school; in contrast, only 8 per cent of those from the Moderate Start Group and 5 per cent of those from the High Start Group reported these two problems had been the case for their schools. A similar pattern of association was also found in secondary schools relating to the prevalence of these two challenges.

However, for the primary sample only (N = 160), a statistically significant difference was found in heads' responses to the item on *difficulties in recruiting teachers*. Although only a minority, primary heads in the Low Start Group (21 per cent, N = 14) were proportionately more likely to report that they had faced this challenge compared with their peers in the other two improvement groups (Moderate Start Group: 8 per cent; High Start Group: 5 per cent).

For the secondary sample only (N = 129), heads in the Low Start Group were somewhat more likely than their peers in the other improvement groups to report that they had experienced the major challenge of *poor pupil progress* (54 per cent versus 46 per cent for the Moderate Start Group and 28 per cent for the High Start Group), a *poor reputation within local community* (42 per cent versus 29 per cent and 13 per cent respectively), *falling pupil rolls* (34 per cent versus 21 per cent and 9 per cent respectively), *high pupil mobility* (17 per cent versus 0 per cent and 7 per cent respectively) and identification of the school by inspectors as requiring *special measures/serious weaknesses* (14 per cent versus 0 per cent and 2 per cent). Moreover, also for the secondary sector only, heads in the High Start Group (N = 27, 59 per cent) were proportionately more likely to report that they had faced *coasting* or *complacent staff* in the initial phase of their headship compared with those in the other two school improvement groups (Moderate Start Group: N = 13, 54 per cent; Low Start Group: N = 18, 31 per cent). As we go on to discuss in later chapters, drawing on our case study evidence, new heads need well-developed skills of diagnoses in identifying appropriate strategies and actions that will support improvement in the light of their school's current level of performance and past developmental trajectory (see Chapters 7 and 8).

Leadership distribution

Overall there were more similarities than differences between the three improvement school groups in relation to perceptions of: the way that leadership tasks were distributed or shared within schools; the kinds of leadership practice provided by the SLT in their school, and the extent to which leadership practice in the school was reported to be provided by other people or groups. This suggests similar patterns of leadership distribution between the three improvement groups in the way leadership tasks were organized within these successful and improved schools and the provision of leadership practice by SMT/SLT in school (see Penlington et al., 2008 for further discussion based on case study evidence).

For both the primary and the secondary samples, most heads indicated that leadership tasks were delegated or distributed by the head or the SLT, and that collective planning was a strong feature of their school organization. In contrast, only a tiny minority thought leadership distribution was spontaneous or that very few other staff took on leadership tasks in their schools. (Chapter 9 provides a detailed, more nuanced, discussion of the progressive distribution of leadership.)

More collective approaches seem to characterize the work of primary schools irrespective of school improvement group. It is also likely that the different organizational scale of primary and secondary schools has an influence, with heads of department playing a more significant role in the secondary sector. These results accord with previous research that has also highlighted the important role of middle leaders in secondary schools (Sammons, Thomas and Mortimore, 1997).

The role of the SMT/SLT

For both the primary and the secondary sample, the large majority of heads strongly agreed with survey items connected with the role of the SLT, indicating that the members of the SMT/SLT in their schools 'share a similar set of values, beliefs and attitudes related to teaching and learning', 'participate in ongoing collaborative work', 'have a role in a range of activities and the development of policies relating to teaching and learning', and 'have a positive impact on standards of teaching and raising levels of pupil attainment'.

Some differences in the key staff responses were found between the improvement groups, but for the secondary sample only. Key staff from schools in the Low Start Improvement Group were the most likely to agree that members of the SLT in their school participate in 'ongoing, collaborative work' and that they 'had a role in the development of policies on lesson planning'.

This is, again, in contrast to the head teachers' responses where no significant difference was found between improvement groups. Key staff in schools that had made rapid sustained improvement in academic outcomes from a Low Start also reported greater SLT involvement in these two aspects of work, suggesting a more proactive approach to this by the head teacher and SLT in these schools. Key staff in the High Start and the Moderate Start groups also were significantly more likely to indicate a greater degree of leadership provided by heads of faculties and heads of departments, suggesting that the middle-management leadership role varied by schools' developmental trajectory improvement group. For secondary schools in the Low Start Group, active involvement of the SLT may be necessary to effect significant improvement; for other schools seeking to improve from a higher base of pupil attainment, the leadership of faculty or departmental heads may play a stronger part.

The contribution of other groups to school leadership

Primary heads in the High Start Improvement Group were somewhat more likely to report that *pupils* in their schools provided a moderate (N = 51, 42 per cent) or a substantial amount (N = 41, 33 per cent) of leadership practice, compared to those in the Low Start Group (moderate: N = 59, 37 per cent; substantially: N = 37, 23 per cent). From survey comments, pupils' involvement in leadership appears to be an area most schools are keen to develop further.

In the secondary sample, heads of schools in the Low Start Group were more likely to report that leadership practice in their schools was provided 'a great deal' or 'all the time' by:

- 'groups of teachers';
- 'individual teachers with formally assigned tasks' (e.g. KS3 co-ordinators); and
- 'the Local Authority (LA)'.

Only one in three secondary heads of the Low Start Group (N = 55, 33 per cent) indicated that their LA rarely or infrequently contributed to the provision of leadership in their schools in contrast to two-thirds of the High Start Group (N = 64, 67 per cent).

The key staff survey indicated a fairly strong degree of correspondence in general views on leadership between head teachers and other key staff. This again points to a shared understanding of the school and its organization and culture, which may be important in promoting improvement in any school, irrespective of past levels of pupil attainment. Significant differences were noted only with regards to leadership practice by the 'school improvement partners' (SIPs) and the LA. Secondary key staff from the High Start Group were the most likely to report 'infrequently' and least likely to report 'a great deal' of leadership practice by their SIPs.

When asked about the leadership practice by the LA, both primary and secondary staff in the High Start Group schools were the most likely to report 'Infrequently'. For the head teacher sample, however, a similar pattern of association relating to the LA was found only in secondary schools.

Taken together, these results indicate that external agents play a much lesser role in secondary schools with a longer history of success (the stable High Start Group of schools with a history of high effectiveness). This may reflect specific LA targeting and priorities to assist the improvement of low-attaining schools in England. Those in High Start Improvement Group may not need or wish for LA involvement, and indeed may often be acting in a supportive capacity for other schools as an SIP themselves, for example.

Changes in structures and organization

At the primary level statistically significant differences in the extent of reported change between the three school improvement groups were particularly noted in relation to building external collaborations (structure). Heads in the Low Start Group were somewhat more likely to report a moderate or a substantial amount of change in terms of *working collaboratively with the LA* (Low Start 42 per cent versus 37 per cent in the Moderate Group and 24 per cent in the High Group) and *building community support for the school's improvement efforts* (Low Start 39 per cent versus Moderate Start 28 per cent and High Start 25 per cent). In addition, we found significant associations relating to change in or restructuring the organization. Nearly two-thirds of primary heads in the Low Start Group (N = 98, 62 per cent) reported a substantial amount of change in leadership practices in relation to *improving internal review procedures* in their schools over the previous three years, whereas around half in the Moderate Group (N = 49, 52 per cent) and less than half (N = 57, 46 per cent) in the High Start Group indicated that this had occurred. These results point to the importance of the self-evaluation and review processes in supporting the improvement of schools that had low attainment levels in the past, but that were successful in raising pupil attainment.

Secondary heads in the Low Start Group schools were relatively more likely than those in the other two improvement groups to report a moderate or a substantial amount of change in leadership practice in all these areas in their schools over the previous three years. For example, in terms of structuring the organization, 79 per cent of heads of the Low Start Group of secondary schools reported a substantial amount of change in *improving internal review procedures*, compared with 61 per cent of those in the High Start

Group of schools. Likewise, over half of heads of the Low Start Group (57 per cent), compared with only around a third (34 per cent) of those in the High Start Group, reported a substantial amount of change in *ensuring wide participation in decisions about school improvement*. Another example is provided by secondary heads' responses to the extent of change in *helping clarify the reasons for their schools' improvement initiatives*, where 63 per cent of the Low Start Group reported a lot or very significant change in this aspect compared with just over half of those in the High Start Group.

Academic emphasis

Heads' responses were fairly positive for all the items relating to academic standards and expectations in their schools, and this might be expected given the study's focus on highly improved and/or highly effective schools. Primary heads showed stronger agreement about the extent of positive change in most items related to academic aspects in their school over the previous three years than their secondary counterparts. However, more secondary (N = 225, 62 per cent) than primary heads (N = 176, 47 per cent) 'agreed strongly' that the 'performance of department/subject areas was regularly monitored' and 'targets for improvement were regularly set' in their schools. Again, this suggests that these areas were especially important for improvement in the secondary context.

A large majority of key staff agreed moderately or strongly to the items relating to academic standards and expectations set in their schools. For example, when they were asked whether their schools 'set high standards for academic performance', more than 90 per cent agreed moderately or strongly. This is broadly in line with findings from the head teacher sample.

Primary heads serving schools in the Moderate Start Group (N = 79, 84 per cent) were more likely to agree moderately or strongly that 'lesson plans were regularly discussed and monitored' in their schools than those in the other two improvement groups (either the Low Start Group (N = 126, 79 per cent) or the High Start Group (N = 87, 71 per cent)). Also at the primary level, heads in the High Start Group (87 per cent) were somewhat more likely than their peers in the other two improvement groups to agree that 'pupils were regularly involved in assessment for learning' within their schools, though a majority in all groups agreed moderately or strongly with this item (the Moderate Start Group: N = 74, 79 per cent; the Low Start Group: N = 120, 75 per cent).

Heads in the Low Start Group of secondary schools were proportionately less likely to agree moderately or strongly that 'pupils respected others who had good marks/grades' (N = 99, 59 per cent) than those in the High Start Group schools (N = 88, 77 per cent).

In primary schools, key staff responses did not differ significantly by improvement group except for one item on academic standards and expectations.

Proportionately more key staff from the High Start Group (60 per cent) were likely to agree strongly that 'most pupils do achieve the goals that have been set for them' when compared with the leaders from schools in the other two improvement groups: in all, around half or 47 per cent for the Moderate Start Group and 41 per cent for the Low Start Group agreed strongly with this statement. This indicates that such heads remained aware of the need for further improvement efforts in their schools, and suggests that a continuous focus on promoting pupil achievement remains a strong priority for leaders of such schools.

However, for secondary schools, significant differences were found on most items in relation to the three groups of improving schools. Key staff from the High Start Group reported stronger agreement than their peers in the other two improvement groups when asked whether

- 'Pupils in this school can achieve the goals that have been set for them';
- 'Teachers set high standards for academic performance';
- 'The school sets high standards for academic performance'; and
- 'Pupils respect others who get good marks/grades'.

For example, 40 per cent of key staff from the High Start Group compared with only 26 per cent from the Moderate Start Group and 21 per cent from the Low Start Group agreed strongly that 'pupils in their schools can achieve the goals that have been set for them'. This points to the strong perception of continued challenges in raising standards faced by secondary schools in the Low Start Group.

Collaborative cultures and parental engagement

Both primary and secondary head teachers rated very positively all the survey items on school culture, though, again, the primary heads' views were more favourable than their secondary colleagues. In particular, almost two-thirds of primary heads (N = 233, 62 per cent) agreed strongly that there was 'ongoing collaborative planning of classroom work among teachers' in their schools, compared with just under a third of secondary heads (N = 111, 31 per cent) who reported this. In addition, only just over a third of secondary heads (N = 134, 37 per cent) agreed strongly that 'teachers and other adults in the classroom worked collaboratively', whereas twice as many primary heads (N = 291, 77 per cent) indicated that this was the case in their schools.

The majority of the key staff reported higher levels of agreement to most items relating to the culture in their schools. This is broadly in line with findings from the head teacher survey. In particular, close to 95 per cent of the key staff agreed moderately or strongly when asked whether 'teachers in their school mostly work together to improve their practice'.

School disadvantage was found to be related to different items on school culture compared with secondary head teachers' responses. Key staff in the high-disadvantage schools were relatively more likely than those from the low-disadvantage schools to agree strongly that 'the goals they are expected to accomplish with their pupils are clear to them'; that 'there is no conflict in their mind about what they are expected to do'; and that 'the school is actively involved in work with other schools or organizations'.

Taken together, these results suggests that the achievement of a common vision, or 'mindset' is likely to play a particular role in motivating and focusing the collective efforts of staff to promote improvement in pupil outcomes as a high priority in schools that are successful at raising standards in high-disadvantage contexts. These support the conclusions of earlier studies of successful schools in disadvantaged contexts (James et al., 2006; Haydn, 2001; Henchey, 2001).

For perceptions of parental engagement, both primary and secondary heads in the Low Start Group of schools had somewhat less favourable views than those in other improvement groups. Only 69 per cent of primary heads in the Low Start Group, compared with a higher figure of 86 per cent of those in the Moderate Start and High Start Groups respectively, agreed moderately or strongly that parents often visited their schools. At the secondary level, only a third (33 per cent) of head teachers in the Low Start Group, in contrast to nearly half (49 per cent) of those in the High Start Group, agreed that parents often visited the school. Key Stage managers from the High Start Group of primary schools were the most likely to agree strongly with the statement that 'parents often visit the school'. This is in line with the head teachers' responses. This also reflects a sector difference. Overall, secondary heads (N = 145, 40 per cent) were much less likely than their primary colleagues (N = 298, 79 per cent) to agree moderately or strongly that 'parents often visited the school'.

For the secondary key staff sample, higher proportions of heads of department from the High Start Group (53 per cent) were more likely to agree strongly that 'pupils feel safe in their school'. In contrast, slightly over a third (35 per cent) of those in the Low Start Group reported that they agreed strongly with this. Again, the results point to the perceived behavioural challenges still facing schools in the Low Start Group. There was much lower agreement ('agree strongly') that 'pupils felt safe in their schools' for the secondary (N = 204, 57 per cent) than the primary head teacher sample (N = 311, 82 per cent).

Perceptions of improvement in school climate and pupil outcomes

The survey explored head teacher and key staff perceptions of the extent of change in practice in their schools over the previous three years in a range of aspects related to school climate, culture and pupil behaviour and outcomes. Where change was reported, it suggested some, or in many cases considerable, improvement over the previous three years. For both the primary and the secondary sample there were many significant differences related to the three school improvement groups.

Changes in disciplinary and learning climate

Heads in the Low Start Group were more likely to report a greater degree of improvement in all aspects of pupil behaviour. In contrast, relatively less improvement was reported by those in the High Start Group schools (of course, it is highly likely that behaviour in such High Start schools was already good and not in need of change). Primary heads reported relatively less change over the previous three years than their secondary colleagues. The most marked difference was in relation to 'pupils missing class'. At the primary level 28 per cent of heads in the Low Start Group (N = 40) indicated improvement in this area compared with only 7 per cent of heads in the High Start Group. A striking 79 per cent (N = 131) of secondary heads in the Low Start Group noted improvement in this aspect of pupil behaviour (pupils missing class) over the previous three years compared with only 29 per cent of those in the High Start Group (Table 5.4).

Key staff perceptions supported those of the heads in the survey in terms of degree of improvement in non-academic areas, especially in pupil behaviour and motivation. As we have already shown in Chapters 3 and 4 in our SEM models, these pupil outcomes are more closely affected by leadership and school organization and processes, and in turn help to support changes in the overall academic performance of schools. Significant differences were found

Table 5.4 Headteachers' responses to change in 'pupils missing class' over three years by school improvement group (secondary)

Improvement groups	Extent of change in pupils missing class			
	Much worse/ worse now (%)	No change (%)	Better/much better now (%)	Total (%)
Low to Moderate/ High	3 (2)	32 (19)	131 (79)	166 (100)
Moderate to Higher Moderate/High	5 (6)	34 (45)	37 (49)	76 (100)
Stable High/High to Higher	6 (5)	74 (66)	33 (29)	113 (100)
Total	14 (4)	140 (39)	201 (57)	355 (100)

between all three improvement groups when asked about change in the discipline climate of the school in the previous three years. Key staff from the High Start Group were the most likely to report 'no change' for all items relating to discipline climate (which again is likely to reflect a good discipline climate already in place three years previously). In contrast, those from schools in the Low Start Group were the most likely to report that it is 'better now' or 'much better now' in reporting on changes over the previous three years, in line with the results for head teachers. For example, close to half of key staff from the Low Start Group reported that 'pupils' lateness to school and absenteeism' was 'much better now' (i.e. reduced). In terms of changes in 'pupils' motivation for learning', those from the Moderate Start Group (N = 75, 56 per cent) were most likely to indicate this was 'better now' compared with those from the Low Start Group (N = 119, 48 per cent).

These results support the view that there is an important association between changes in the behavioural climate of schools and improvement in pupils' academic results, particularly for Low Start schools, those making significant gains from a low base. The results are in line with the overall models outlined in Chapter 3 for all schools. They are in accord with other studies of improving schools that have had a prior history of poor performance and indicate that a strong focus on promoting better pupil behaviour and motivation is an essential part of the early work needed to raise attainment, along with a clear emphasis on improving teaching and learning (Sammons, Thomas and Mortimore, 1997; Haydn, 2001; Muijs et al., 2004; Harris et al., 2006).

Changes in overall school conditions

There was a fairly strong degree of correspondence in general views on the extent of positive change in school conditions over the previous three years between head teachers and other key staff. For both sectors, the majority of heads noted considerable improvements in a range of areas including: 'commitment and enthusiasm of staff', providing ' an orderly and secure working environment', 'enhanced local reputation' and 'improved pupil behaviour and discipline as a result of a whole school approach' (Tables 5.5 and 5.6). Secondary heads also reported some or a lot of change in terms of increasing pupil participation in education with 'more pupils going into further/higher education' (N = 230, 64 per cent). These results confirm that these successful schools were not just good at raising pupil attainment in examinations and tests but had also effected improvement in a wide range of areas and outcomes for both staff and pupils.

Secondary heads (N = 287, 79 per cent) were relatively more likely to report 'improvements in homework policies and practices' than primary heads (N = 262, 70 per cent), although this was clearly important in both sectors. More primary than secondary heads reported no change in 'staff absence' (44 per cent versus

Table 5.5 Headteachers' perceptions of change in school conditions over three years by school improvement group (primary)

Improvement groups	Extent of change				
	No change (%)	A little (%)	Some (%)	A lot (%)	Total* (%)
Enhanced commitment and enthusiasm of staff	54 (14.4)	50 (13.3)	121 (32.2)	151 (40.2)	376 (100.1)
Promoted an orderly and secure working environment	79 (21)	47 (12.5)	85 (22.5)	166 (44)	377 (100)
Enhanced local reputation	64 (17.1)	65 (17.3)	125 (33.3)	121 (32.3)	375 (100)
Improved pupil behaviour and discipline as a result of a whole school approach	78 (20.7)	55 (14.6)	107 (28.5)	136 (36.2)	376 (100)

* Because of rounding, percentages might not add up to 100.

Table 5.6 Headteachers' perceptions of change in school conditions over three years by school improvement group (secondary)

Improvement groups	Extent of change				
	No change (%)	A little (%)	Some (%)	A lot (%)	Total* (%)
Enhanced commitment and enthusiasm of staff	32 (8.9)	49 (13.6)	150 (41.6)	130 (36)	361 (100.1)
Promoted an orderly and secure working environment	41 (11.4)	58 (16.1)	137 (38)	125 (34.6)	361 (100.1)
Enhanced local reputation	44 (12.2)	53 (14.7)	107 (29.7)	156 (43.3)	360 (99.9)
Improved pupil behaviour and discipline as a result of a whole school approach	44 (12.2)	70 (19.4)	127 (35.3)	119 (33.1)	360 (100)

* Because of rounding, percentages might not add up to 100.

29 per cent) or 'staff mobility' (43 per cent versus 32 per cent), but this may indicate reductions in an absence of such problems three years before in these schools.

Six out of ten key staff reported some or a lot of change when asked about the 'enhanced local reputation of the school'. Again, secondary staff were more likely to report a lot of change than their primary counterparts for school reputation. Between 50 per cent and 70 per cent of key staff reported some or a lot of change in terms of 'enhanced commitment and enthusiasm of staff', 'changes in the homework policies and practice', and 'improvements in terms of achieving an orderly and secured working environment' over the previous three years. There was a sector difference found here, with an even higher proportion of primary key staff reporting a lot of change compared to those in secondary schools.

For both the primary and the secondary sample, heads in the Low Start Group were most likely to indicate substantial improvement across their school over the previous three years in most areas related to school conditions, while no or little change was more likely to be reported by those in High Start Group (see Tables 5.5 and 5.6). This pattern of change is in line with school effectiveness and improvement research that points to the importance of the behavioural climate as a key characteristic of effectiveness (Sammons et al., 1997; Teddlie and Reynolds, 2000) and the results of previous case studies of improving and turnaround schools (Ofsted, 2000; Haydn, 2001; Henchey, 2001).

Over half of secondary heads (51 per cent) in the Low Start Group reported a substantial degree of improvement in terms of 'an enhanced local reputation' for their school during the previous three years, compared with less than one in three (30 per cent) in the High Start Group. A similar but less marked pattern was found for the primary sample.

A substantial degree of improvement in 'achieving an orderly and secure working environment' was reported by over half of primary heads in the Low Start Group (54 per cent), whereas only a third in the High Start Group (34 per cent) indicated this. The difference is more noticeable for the secondary sample. Almost half of secondary heads in the Low Start Group (45 per cent) reported a lot of improvement in this aspect, in contrast to only 18 per cent of those in the High Start Group.

In addition, 29 per cent (N = 45) of primary heads and 30 per cent (N = 49) of secondary heads in the Low Start Group indicated 'a lot' of improvement in terms of 'a reduction in staff mobility' in their schools, in contrast to only 12 per cent (N = 15) of primary heads and 11 per cent (N = 13) of secondary heads in the High Start Group.

Similar patterns were also found in the extent of change or improvements reported by head teachers in four other important areas: 'reduction in staff absence', 'improved homework policies and practice', 'enhanced commitment and enthusiasm of staff', and 'improved pupil behaviour and discipline as a result of a whole school approach'.

Significant associations were also found between key staff responses and the three improvement groups. Overall, those from schools in the Low Start Group were the most likely to report 'a lot' of change in the previous three years with regards to improvement across a range of school conditions. More differences were found within secondary schools than primary schools. In particular, there was an association between key staff responses and school improvement groups for the following items: 'enhanced local reputation', 'enhanced commitment and enthusiasm of staff', and 'promoted an orderly and secure working environment', including greater perceived change in the Low Start Group.

Taken together, the survey results for head teachers and key staff support the view that rapidly improving schools effect improvement across a range of areas to do with practice, climate and learning conditions that have a mutually reinforcing impact and help schools to break out of a low attainment state into an upward trajectory. It appears that such change is particularly associated with secondary schools that have a past history of low performance. The results thus point to the importance of studying school improvement processes according to the school's developmental trajectory related to its starting point at a given time in terms of pupil attainment levels and value added effectiveness. (See Chapters 7 and 8 for examples of this.)

Changes in curriculum, pedagogy and assessment

At the secondary level, the school improvement group was related to the extent of reported change in leadership practice in relation to almost all the aspects of school structures, culture, and curriculum, pedagogy and assessment. In contrast, far fewer associations were found for the primary sample, particularly in relation to change in school culture.

There were significant associations between school improvement group and the amount of change in leadership practice reported in relation to curriculum, pedagogy and assessment, but these were most evident in the analyses of survey responses by heads in the secondary sector.

For the primary sample, heads in the Low Start Group were somewhat more likely to report a moderate or a substantial amount of change in terms of 'using coaching and mentoring to improve the quality of teaching', 'encouraging staff to use data in their work' and 'encouraging staff to use data in planning for individual pupil needs'. For secondary heads, relatively more change was reported by those in the Low Start Group in relation to 'using coaching and mentoring to improve quality of teaching'. Half of the secondary heads in the Low Start Group (N = 85, 52 per cent) reported a lot of change in this aspect, compared with 40 per cent of those in the High Start school group.

In the secondary sector the school improvement group was also associated with the amount of reported change in relation to a number of other items on class observation and assessment. Heads in the Low Start Group were relatively more likely to report a substantial degree of change relating to 'regularly observing classroom activities' and 'working with teachers to improve their teaching after observing classroom activities'. Substantial change in 'regularly observing classroom activities' was indicated by 65 per cent of secondary heads of the Low Start Group, compared with 55 per cent of those in the High Start Group. Relatively more change in leadership practice was also reported by heads in this former improvement group for items related to 'incorporating research evidence into their decision making to inform practice' and 'using pupil achievement data to make most decisions about school improvement'. For example, a very large majority of 84 per cent of secondary heads in the Low Start Group reported a substantial amount of change in 'encouraging staff to use data in their work', compared with 70 per cent of those in the High Start Group. Nonetheless, it can be seen that this was an important emphasis in all of the sample of improving and effective schools.

All heads in secondary schools in our survey reported a considerable change in the extent of encouraging the use of data by teachers, but this was given a particular emphasis in Low Start secondary schools. It appears that heads in schools that make rapid improvement from a low base are likely to have focused more strongly upon the use of a range of specific strategies to change teachers' classroom practices, particularly in the secondary sector. Despite this difference in degree, it is clear that encouraging staff to use research and achievement data to inform their work was a key strategy for enhancing teachers' practice in the vast majority of successful schools in our sample and fits with the concept of promoting evidence-informed professional practice.

Strategies and actions: differences by developmental trajectory

Additional data collected from the surveys included details of the three strategies identified as most influential in improving pupil academic outcomes by the head teachers (see earlier discussion in Chapter 3 of overall findings). These were further analysed to establish which combinations of actions were perceived to have been most important in promoting improvement by head teachers in the three improvement groups. Tables 5.7 and 5.8 present details of the most important strategies and actions adopted by the schools over the previous three years, as reported by their head teacher, according to the three improvement groups. For ease of comparison the results are shown separately for the two sectors.

The results reveal considerable similarities in the three most important strategies head teachers reported they had adopted to promote improvement in pupil outcomes. Nevertheless, for primary schools, those in the Moderate Start Group seem to have placed more emphasis on initiating improvements

Table 5.7 Headteachers' responses to the most important actions/strategies used to effect improvements over three years by school improvement group (primary)

Strategy	Low Start Group (%)	Medium Start Group (%)	High Start Group (%)	Total* (%)
	N = 160 (42.4)	N = 94 (24.9)	N = 123 (32.6)	N = 377 (99.9)
A2 iv) Promoting leadership development and CPD	22 (13.8)	17 (18.1)	21 (17.1)	60 (15.9)
A3 iv) Strategic allocation of resources	32 (20.0)	22 (23.4)	23 (18.7)	77 (20.4)
A4 i) Providing and allocating resources	24 (15.0)	24 (25.5)	25 (20.3)	73 (19.4)
A4 v) Encouraging the use of data and research	42 (26.3)	26 (27.7)	37 (30.1)	105 (27.9)
E3 iii) Improved assessment procedures	40 (25.0)	32 (34.0)	34 (27.6)	106 (28.1)
E3 iv) Changes to pupil target setting	33 (20.6)	22 (23.4)	21 (17.1)	76 (20.2)
E5) Teaching policies practices	39 (24.4)	32 (34.0)	27 (22.0)	98 (26.0)

* Because of rounding, percentages might not add up to 100.

in assessment procedures and on teaching policies and practices than head teachers in the other improvement groups. Likewise for secondary schools, those in the Low Start and Moderate Start groups reported relatively more emphasis on addressing teaching policies and practices than those in the High Start Group. By contrast, head teachers in the secondary sector in all groups were more likely to have emphasized strategies to change their school culture than their primary counterparts, but this emphasis did not seem to vary much by school improvement group. The focus on improving the quality of teaching in schools that have low levels of pupil attainment has been stressed in studies of turnaround schools and schools that succeed against the odds (see Wendell, 2000; Henchey, 2001; Harris et al., 2006; James et al., 2006; Sammons, 2007). Nonetheless, the overall pattern of results suggests that, in terms of their three most important strategies, head teachers of highly effective and improved schools generally focused on similar kinds of approaches, irrespective of their improvement group. This suggests there are some common foci for school improvement and some essential features that can be seen as a common core of leadership practices. We return to this topic again in terms of evidence from our case study schools in Part 3 of this book.

Table 5.8 Headteachers' responses to the most important actions/strategies used to effect improvements over three years by school improvement group (secondary)

Strategy	Low Start Group (%)	Medium Start Group (%)	High Start Group (%)	Total* (%)
	N = 167 (46.6)	N = 76 (21.2)	N = 115 (32.1)	N = 358 (99.9)
A2 iv) Promoting leadership development and CPD	20 (12.0)	10 (13.2)	25 (21.7)	55 (15.4)
A4 i) Providing and allo-cating resources	30 (18.0)	12 (15.8)	27 (23.5)	69 (19.3)
A4 v) Encouraging the use of data and research	51 (30.5)	30 (39.5)	40 (34.8)	121 (33.8)
E3 ii) Monitoring of departments and teachers	27 (16.2)	10 (13.2)	21 (18.3)	58 (16.2)
E3 iii) Improved assessment procedures	35 (21.0)	8 (10.5)	23 (20.0)	66 (18.4)
E4) School culture	34 (20.4)	15 (19.7)	26 (22.6)	75 (20.9)
E5) Teaching policies practices	50 (29.9)	24 (31.6)	25 (21.7)	99 (27.7)

* Because of rounding, percentages might not add up to 100.

Conclusions

This chapter has outlined the way a sample of highly effective and improving schools was identified and has focused on the topic of schools' developmental trajectories, drawing attention to the differences between successful schools from three distinctive improvement groups, Low Start, Moderate Start and High Start, in terms of their initial attainment levels in 2003. It has provided examples of key findings from analyses of survey responses by head teachers and key staff and explored their relationship to the school improvement group. It has found, in summary, that:

1   *The categorization of schools into three distinctive improvement and effectiveness groups reveals statistically and educationally significant differences in certain features and practices.* In addition, these school improvement groups differ in terms of head teachers' years of experience in total and in time in their current schools, the number of head teachers in post in the previous ten years, school sector and socio-economic context.

2 *The challenges facing head teachers in schools in different improvement groups vary markedly.* Both primary and secondary head teachers from the Low Start Group were more likely than those from the other two school improvement groups to report that they had originally experienced major challenges of *poor pupil attainment, poor pupil behaviour* and *poor pupil motivation* in the first year of their headship in their current school. Also, for secondary schools in the Low Start Group *poor reputation within local community* and *falling pupil rolls* were more likely to be cited as major challenges in their early years of headship in their current school. Head teachers in the High Start Group were more likely to report challenges related to *coasting* or *complacent staff* rather than those related to pupils' learning behaviour or attainment levels.

3 *There are important relationships between school context and the school improvement group, and between school context and head teachers' time in post.* The less stable leadership histories of schools, particularly secondary schools in high-disadvantage, challenging contexts are evident and are a feature that points to the likely importance of supportive initiatives by the National College for Leadership of Schools and Children's Services and others in relation to leadership, training, development and succession planning.

4 *Respondents in the Low Start Group of improved schools were significantly more likely to report substantial improvement in pupil behaviour, attendance, attitude and motivation.* These findings are in accord with those of reviews of school effectiveness and improvement research (Teddlie and Reynolds, 2000; Wendell, 2000; Muijs et al., 2004; Harris et al., 2006; Sammons, 2007). These aspects are likely to be important precursors and facilitators for improvement in students' academic achievements, especially in high-disadvantage contexts. It must be remembered that many more of the Low Start improvement group served highly disadvantaged pupil intakes.

5 *Head teachers in the Low Start Group of schools were more likely to focus their attention on improving teaching and learning, school review and evaluation procedures and encourage teachers in the use of data and research to inform their teaching than those in the High Start Group.* Although a strong emphasis on these areas was found for all of the successful schools in this study, this focus was especially strongly evident for those in the secondary sector and in the Low Start Group. To achieve rapid, significant and sustained (over three years or more) improvement in academic outcomes from a low base, it appears that a strong focus on school structures, culture, curriculum and pedagogy and assessment practices is necessary,

especially in the larger and more complex organizational context of secondary schools.

The following chapters add further detailed evidence, rich descriptions and more nuanced, contextualized explanations of how heads' values, strategies and actions support successful school improvement and raised pupil achievement. Such schools' achievements do not happen by chance, but by highly reflective, carefully planned and implemented strategies which serve these schools well in meeting the many challenges along the path to success (Ofsted, 2009).

Taken together, the survey results suggest that nearly all head teachers in our survey had placed emphasis on the achievement of a common vision, or 'mindset' (James et al., 2006) and that such an emphasis is likely to play a particular role in motivating and focusing the collective efforts of staff to promote improvement in pupil outcomes as a high priority. Our evidence suggests that this is particularly important in schools that improved from a low start, many of which were in highly disadvantaged contexts. In addition to addressing mindset, however, there was a strong focus on a range of strategies and actions that supported the improvement of teaching and learning, enhanced pupil and staff motivation and well-being, improved pupil behaviour, and enabled a stronger focus on enhancing a wide range of pupil outcomes, including academic achievement.

PART 3
Who heads are and what they do to build and sustain success

6 Core values and practices
Leadership, learning and improvement

So far in this book we have discussed what the extant literature and national survey results have revealed about the relationship between headship in a range of effective and improving schools and pupil outcomes. This chapter will describe and discuss the ways in which school leaders in the 20 case study schools in the IMPACT study established the conditions in which staff could maximize pupil outcomes.

The data reinforce the findings presented in this book so far, that the leadership of the head is the key driver in the growth and sustained improvement of the school. The chapter focuses upon four core components which provide further reinforcement and elaboration of key elements of the four categories of leadership practices identified in Chapter 2:

1 'Setting directions'
   - defining the vision, purposes and directions

2 'Developing people'
   - enhancing teacher quality

3 'Refining and aligning the organization'
   - redesigning organizational structures, redefining roles and responsibilities
   - involving pupils
   - building relationships within the school community
   - building relationships outside the school community
   - involving parents and supporting families
   - working with other schools

4 'Improving the teaching and learning programme'
   - improving physical conditions for teaching and learning
   - developing high expectations

- consistent school-wide policies on pupil behaviour
- enhancing teaching and learning: refining and extending peda-gogical approaches
- using attainment data and observation
- redesigning and enriching the curriculum
- a focus on student attainment outcomes through the use of performance data and observation.

Setting directions

Defining the vision, purposes and directions

One of the first focuses of heads in leadership is to create and share their vision for the school with staff. Our data showed that one of the most powerful dimensions of effective school leadership was the establishment of a clear sense of direction and purpose for the school. Defining, discussing and commu-nicating a set of values to all in their school community in order to establish purposes and direction for school improvement which were clear, agreed and enacted by all was a consistent priority and revisited regularly. These were articulated through new organizational structures, and redesign of roles, responsibilities and relationships.

All the heads had a very strong and clear vision for their school that heavily influenced their actions and the actions of others. Heads were instrumental in driving it forward. The vision was shared with the senior management team and was a central driver of all leadership activity, shared widely and clearly understood and also supported by all staff. It was a touchstone against which all new developments, policies or initiatives were tested.

> The whole vision of the school probably comes from the head and the senior management team. But I think if anyone goes on to courses and gets inspired, and you say that was really good, he will say 'We'll try it; if you want to do it, well, go and do it.'
>
> (Primary Teacher)

Once created, heads and leadership teams effectively propagated the vision at all levels in the school and established appropriate optimal condi-tions for it to be realized. A long-term plan was formulated with different but interrelated strategies identified and the required resources acquired and allo-cated over time. The selection and recruitment of staff were especially important, since, through these, heads ensured that new personnel would share the vision for the school and embody it in their working practices.

All the teachers and support staff in the schools were clear about the vision and were able to articulate it and support it.

> I always had a vision of where I knew the school had to be. That was always there, but I did not sit down and think: this year we are going to . . . We do have a strategic long-term plan but it wasn't enough. I suppose I always knew that we needed a more creative curriculum but until you get some of the key things right, they just could not have coped with it. You know, we did some creative themes but it needed to be managed in such a way that people were not overwhelmed and felt quite secure and confident to trial things.
>
> (Primary Head)

Heads engaged staff in the decision making and evaluation of the school's development in order to determine the areas which needed further work.

> The head will steer the school in lots of different ways. He's very sure of where he wants it to go, so he's quite clear in his objectives, but he's also very collegiate in that he'll say 'What do you think?' and 'How could your department or your Key Stage add to this?', 'What do you want to do?', 'What do you need training in?', or 'How do you want to develop?'
>
> (Primary Key Stage Co-ordinator)

The school culture was heavily influenced, shaped and a consequence of the values and vision stated and reinforced by the head. Indeed, for many staff the head epitomized the vision for the school and on a daily basis demonstrated how that vision could be realized and fulfilled.

> He's got very good direction and he comes across as being hugely committed, almost a zealot, more strongly than I've seen in some of my other heads.
>
> (Secondary Deputy Head)

Core values, such as trust and high expectations, and a 'can-do' culture provided a strong basis for establishing and developing environments in which teacher morale and motivation, and student achievement and learning could be nurtured and improved. Thus, heads' values, as played out in the daily interactions and organizational structures and roles and responsibilities of staff and students, influenced pupil behaviour, attendance and achievement levels.

Now it's a culture of 'we can do' and 'the children can do', and there's no such word as can't. Everyone's involved in evaluation and perceptions.

(Primary Deputy Head)

The head teacher provides a can-do culture and one of the things that I learned from him was that there are not problems, there are only solutions.

(Secondary Assistant Head)

However, while the heads' actions and relationships were consistent with the schools' core vision and values, heads and SLTs found it necessary to adapt structures periodically, in order to reflect changes in the school's circumstances. The processes of adaptation were, however, based on situational analyses, horizon scanning and timely judgement.

Developing people

Enhancing teacher quality

All schools in the research were committed to improving and enhancing teacher quality as part of their drive to raise standards.

He very much develops people, he does see the potential in people and bosses them on to the next step. 'Here's this "leading from the middle" course and you may want to do this course.' In a sort of quiet but encouraging way. I mentioned that I wanted to do a course which prepared you to be a deputy head and it was like 'Right, that starts in November so we'll sign you up for that.' And then he started putting things about NPQH in my pigeonhole which I staunchly ignored. He definitely brings on individuals. If someone comes on as a dinner lady, he's encouraging them to become a teaching assistant. Especially if he sees potential.

(Primary Deputy Head)

Continuing professional development was seen as an entitlement. This was motivational for teachers and impacted positively upon their teaching practices. Schools provided a rich variety of professional learning and development opportunities for staff and placed a high premium on internal professional development and learning.

Professional learning and development were not limited to teachers; all heads emphasized the importance of training for support staff also. While all but two (secondary) schools provided a broad range of external training available to staff, all also emphasized the importance of internally led training and development, which focused upon meeting organizational and individually identified priorities, needs and concerns. In the case of training schools, opportunities to have trainee teachers in their classrooms were made available to all. There was a commonly expressed view, particularly among heads in secondary schools, that internally led training and development both provided an efficient means of training all staff and helped to strengthen whole-school policies and initiatives.

> Some people still go out on courses, but these courses tend to be rather expensive, both in terms of the cost and in terms of going out of the classroom too. So we are trying to do more and more in-house CPD, so we have quite an extensive programme. This is done after school, not the best time to do it because people have had a full day of teaching and are tired, but nonetheless we still think that it is effective.
>
> (Secondary Head)

While internal training and development were prioritized by most of the schools, staff were encouraged to take part in a wide range of INSET, and were also given the opportunity to access training leading to external qualifications. A combination of external and internal CPD was most often used to maximize potential and to develop staff in diverse areas.

Peer observation was commonly used as a way of improving teaching and learning processes. In particular, teachers valued informal observations; also, many schools implemented an 'open-door' policy, which was seen as a powerful tool for improving teaching and learning. In addition, schools used modelling, shadowing and informal discussions in order to develop teaching practices. Coaching and mentoring were also used across schools as a means of providing challenge and support for all staff.

> What you do need is a model: someone to work with you, to make you feel good about yourselves, to give you a few ideas, and then to validate and affirm what you have done, and make suggestions. And that is what I do.
>
> (Secondary Head)

> The other thing that has had a huge impact is the school's professional attitude to the appointment of a professional tutor in school and then creating widespread mentorship. She's trained mentors so that almost everybody's mentoring somebody. What I want to do is go that one step further and have everybody doing paired observation. We haven't quite got that far yet.
>
> (Secondary Head)

These and opportunities for collaboration among teachers were found to be a powerful means of securing higher quality. Greater opportunities for teachers and support staff to work together had a positive impact on teaching and were perceived to create greater understanding and empathy.

Staff collaboration also allowed for co-planning and the joint targeting of individual pupils. Heads ensured that time was scheduled for such planning meetings to take place and that the school timetable allowed for teachers to observe each other and work together. Teachers reported that they experienced a greater sense of collective responsibility from working more closely together more regularly and were more able to improve their practices through joint working.

> The relationship between the team is another indicator. I'm very big on relationships, working relationships and relationships working well. Having that time as a team to play together in the staff room is a big indicator to me about how things are going. If they are in there working together as a team, I am fairly confident that things are going along fine. When I see staff who are not in that situation, then for me that becomes a worry.
>
> (Primary Deputy Head)

Last, but not least, a feature of all the schools was a strong focus on succession planning and, in training schools, targeted recruitment.

> I am a great believer in internal promotion. Interviews don't really give you a true picture of what people are like, and how people will fit into the school. I would rather be secure in the knowledge that I knew how they fitted into the school and I knew what they can do, and to give them the opportunity to do it. So all of my senior appointments are internal appointments. They have all been appointed by me.
>
> (Primary Head)

Many schools also provided opportunities for 'acting up' or shadowing as a route to succession planning. Staff gained experience through taking on a new role for a fixed period of time.

> What being acting head gives the deputies is a week where they do have to think slightly differently, and one of the key differences between deputy headship and headship is that in deputy headship you tend to be quite task driven, you've got your very specific elements that you're responsible for. In headship you've got less to do and an awful lot more to think about.
>
> (Secondary Head)

In addition, teachers engaged in action research in order to test out ideas and to trial new ways of teaching. Heads encouraged staff to share their expertise across the school and to learn from each other wherever possible. By these means, heads built professional capacity and increased staffing stability within their schools.

Refining and aligning the organization

Redesigning organizational structures, redefining roles and responsibilities

Another strategy employed by the heads in our research to improve their schools was that they purposively and progressively redesigned organizational structures, and redefined and distributed more widely leadership and management responsibilities in order to promote greater staff engagement and ownership, and, through this, greater opportunities for student learning. While the exact nature of the restructuring, change in roles and responsibilities, and timing varied from school to school, there was a consistent pattern across schools of changing the existing hierarchy, using teaching and learning responsibility (TLR), payments to staff, advanced skills teachers (ASTs), and the wider use of support staff. Lines of communication and responsibility were improved, and new leadership and management responsibilities were clearly outlined. These were clear to all staff and allocated on the basis of ability along with recognition of people's strengths and organizational needs.

In the early phase of headship, especially, a new senior leadership was formed and/or team members' roles and responsibilities were reconfigured. In most cases, however, the primary focus was upon the SLT. Members of the SLT were deployed more strategically then previously and, in particular, attention was placed on identifying staff members who could work together and create an effective team. Communication channels were improved between the management layers and better use was made of staff time in meetings with the SLT. There was evidence that such restructuring and redefining of roles and responsibilities had been welcomed by staff and that the new patterns were perceived to be more effective. Staff found the clarity around new roles to be helpful, and generally appreciated the new leadership and management structures.

> The reduction in the administrative load of teachers meant that teachers were more able to focus on providing high-quality teaching. This has proved to have had a major impact on raising pupil achievement. Increasingly I'm trying to move more and more people who are not teachers either into the leadership group or into positions of responsibility, for example, as year leaders. The reason I'm doing this

is that I don't believe that it's now feasible to have somebody who is involved in some way in teaching and learning at the same time doing a fairly complicated job like being a year leader or looking after the buildings of schools.

(Secondary Head of Department)

Systems of pastoral care were strongly in evidence across all the schools, and while different schools developed these at different times, they were a feature of heads' strategies in each phase. A common feature in several case study secondary schools was the introduction of vertical tutoring. This was discussed by the participants as an important way that pupils were given more peer support as well as more opportunity to talk to their tutor if they had problems.

The change from a horizontal structure to a vertical structure, based on the idea of community and with permanent pastoral posts rather than year heads, I think, over time will have an immense impact. It's in its infancy at the moment. Two or three years down the line, I think that people will see the groupings are really strong, and the relationships between the kids of different ages are really strong and I think it will have a very beneficial impact on the future of the school and what we're trying to do in terms of both the idea of community, the extended school and the personalized curriculum. I think it will be very positive.

(Secondary Assistant Head)

A second feature was the introduction of non-teaching pastoral staff to immediately provide pupils with emotional and behavioural issues with a greater range of opportunities for support and care. In primary schools this involved giving more responsibility to support staff. In secondary schools there were non-teaching support staff at every level to deal with pastoral issues. These measures also had the effect of freeing up teachers' time to concentrate on academic issues. These schools also provided a coherent and consistent support system for pupils' social and emotional development. In primary schools this meant more teaching assistants and learning mentors, nurture groups or a learning support unit where a member of support staff was constantly available for children's needs.

So one of the biggest changes that has been implemented is putting a teaching assistant in every class . . . The teaching assistants are an absolutely crucial element in every classroom not only for raising standards but also for PHSE. I would say that emotional confrontation is an issue, not just in the school but on the Estate.

(Primary Head)

New teams that included support staff were perceived to make a difference to the teaching capacity within the school. In addition, several of the schools created new pastoral teams to support teaching and learning. The combination of teaching and support staff in these played an important role in the success of efforts to raise achievement.

In both primary and secondary schools, career paths were also created for support staff, resulting in membership of the SLT, with many new roles created for heads of year or pastoral support leaders in secondary schools, and many additional leadership responsibilities developed for class teachers in primary schools. In secondary schools the titles for these staff varied across schools from learning mentors to learning managers or inclusion officers, but the principle was the same.

> We were mindful that learning mentors did not have a career struc-ture, so now we have a career path. So you could come in as a teaching assistant, you could become a higher learning teaching assistant. If you fancy that, you could then become a learning mentor or an assistant learning manager; if you are good enough and highly skilled, you could then become a learning manager and then a senior learning manager, and then there is a place for support staff to actually come on the leadership team.
>
> (Secondary Deputy Head)

Restructuring across the schools also extended leadership configurations and practices. The distribution of leadership roles and responsibilities was a developing feature in all the schools. This was a pattern of leadership that was initiated and nurtured by the heads over time.

> Leadership is distributed fairly well now. When the head first came, that wasn't the case, but we have clear strata so people know where people sit in a linear way.
>
> (Primary Key Stage Co-ordinator)

> In short, everybody does have a leadership role in school, absolutely everybody.
>
> (Primary Head)

Distributed leadership was a feature of all schools to varying degrees. Those who were in leadership roles were held accountable for the tasks they undertook. They were also supported with targeted staff development oppor-tunities and internal support from the SLT.

All the schools had strong internal accountability systems where they set their own professional standards and judgements. Schools evaluated their practices systematically and gathered a wide range of data that was used to improve performance.

> I think getting teaching staff to feel accountable in a supported manner, if that's not a contradiction. Everyone is accountable for their outcomes but we will support you in getting there. I think that goes along with the drive for improvement. As a school, how can we get more efficient? As a teacher, how can you get more efficient? What is it that we can change? What sort of support do you need from your head of department?
>
> (Secondary Head)

In secondary schools, departments evaluated their practice regularly, and changes were made to further improve their practice. Individuals were held accountable for their performance and were responsible for refining their own teaching practices. The constant focus on improving teaching and learning was a common denominator of success across all primary and secondary case studies.

Involving pupils

Distributed leadership also included pupils. Through school councils and other forms of participation, schools provided opportunities for pupils to participate in the decision-making process. These opportunities included involving pupils in job interviews for school staff. In addition, pupils were given responsibility to lead projects and, in some cases, training so they could undertake their new leadership responsibilities effectively. This involvement in leading and leadership of the schools was highly motivating for young people and had a positive impact on motivation and subsequent learning.

> The leadership has got to come from, and it is not just the staff, it is from the children as well. The leadership qualities from the children, we try to encourage peer tutoring, buddying, we have a very active school council, and they all play a part in the leadership.
>
> (Secondary Head)

Building relationships within the school community

Building positive relationships in school was an important feature of the heads' leadership. The impact this had on pupil outcomes was not only noted by staff but also by Ofsted.

> Excellent relationships exist between everyone in the school. Pupils have a very positive attitude towards their learning and their

behaviour is excellent. They clearly love coming to school. A strength is the way in which pupils' efforts and achievements are recognised.

(Primary Ofsted report)

The unequivocal and overwhelming evidence from staff in all schools was that heads were supportive of the staff and made them feel valued.

If I need support, then I will go and get it. He's there if you need anything. You can always knock at his door and go in and have a discussion with him and we have regular assessment-type meetings and management meetings so on those occasions we get the support we need, and we've had several of those already this academic year and we're due to have another one after the holiday.

(Secondary Head of Department)

Heads listened to and respected staff, valuing their opinions.

He does listen to you and although he has a set steer for the school, he makes that very open and we know what the school improvement plan is, what our priorities are, but he's not the sort of head who says I'm going to do it this way and this is what you're doing, he does listen to people. You just feel part of it.

(Primary Senior Leader)

I think the staff feel valued, cared for in their needs and aspirations are very much in the forefront of the [head teacher's] mind and the leadership team are very good at keeping in touch with what's going on, what's happening with people and people's feelings about things.

(Secondary Head of Department)

Heads were seen as approachable and communicative. They involved staff in discussions about future planning and strategic thinking.

The fact that he shares all the new things that he hears about, all the things that he knows are coming up. He will talk to us about them and have them included in teacher training days so that we always try to be one step ahead of what is going to be implemented in school. And that strategy of looking to the future and planning ahead is vitally important.

(Secondary Teacher)

So, as I say, we are open, and, as I say, we are an honest staff and if people see something and they're not happy with that, then let's say

> so. You do need to have good relationships, open systems of communication to move things along.
>
> (Primary Deputy Head)

Promoting participation through distributing leadership, acts of care, encouragement, inclusivity and involvement in development activities all contributed to staff motivation, high expectations and positive relationships within the case study schools.

> I think he tries to encourage us. If it's a whole staff, then he tells us in the briefing. When we go to our individual meetings, he tries to motivate us. If you've got strengths, he always tries to identify those strengths. He doesn't play on the weaknesses, he tries to pick on the positives so people are encouraged in their area, and they know that they can go and talk to him as well if they have issues.
>
> (Secondary Head of Department)

The relationship between the heads and their senior leadership team, in particular, was one of mutual respect. They engendered loyalty from parents, staff and pupils.

> He walks round the school all the time, he'll go into lessons, he'll cover, he leads assembly, he goes in both staff rooms and he knows the children, he knows the parents, he's got an open-door policy in terms of staff and parents, he's got a good relationship with the governors.
>
> (Primary Deputy Head)

> All staff know that they are communicated to, they know what is happening, they know that there is a change of staff, or if there is a change of events. Small, day-to-day things actually mean a lot because it shows that staff are important. We hold weekly team meetings so that is an opportunity to make sure that everyone can get together. That is what I feel is central, communicating, because it changes the whole atmosphere in the school. If people are happy and they feel that they are informed, then they are happy in their job.
>
> (Primary Key Stage Co-ordinator)

They called children by name, knew about their concerns so that they felt cared for and respected. When asked in the pupil survey what the best things about their school were, pupils commented on this.

Understanding teachers, you can always talk to your teachers, if you don't understand your work, the teachers explain.

(Pupil Survey: Primary)

The remodelling of the workforce in English schools, which was given impetus by the signing of the 'Raising Standards and Tackling Workload – a National Agreement' in 2003, was used as another means of building relationships within the school communities. The greater use of support staff, in particular of classroom assistants, and the different ways in which they were deployed led to the creation of more effective teams. This in turn led to a decrease in teacher workload and increased staff motivation.

The largest changes are the learning managers and the support staff taking on more of the admin roles that were originally done by teachers because teachers are there to teach and anything that can be done by other staff ought to be done by other staff.

(Secondary Business Manager)

All heads worked on building trust with staff and pupils. They regarded this as essential for developing the capacity of the school as a learning community, able to be collectively responsive to change, and resilient in the face of anticipated and unanticipated challenges:

We've always had good relationships but I think that relationship develops over time and it's not something that's going to happen overnight because there's got to be trust on both sides. They've got to trust me and I've got to trust them but it is something you can foster, it's dependent on time, commitment, a degree of frankness and openness, but also a sense of being prepared to be challenged and that's not always easy especially if you're feeling a bit tentative or vulnerable.

(Primary Head teacher)

The nature of trust and processes of trust building will be explored further in Chapter 9.

Building relationships outside the school community

Last but not least, building relationships outside the school community should also be seen as a crucial component of leadership development.

All schools sought to improve the level of engagement of parents and the community by employing home–school liaison personnel, offering adult education classes, or developing stronger links with other schools, either through the Specialist Schools and Academies Trust (SSAT) in the case of secondary schools or, in both primary and secondary, with local feeder schools. For example, using the specialism to run a 'fun day' for primary school pupils.

> We did a lot of work with building up with parents. We accessed the money and got a home–school liaison person who did a lot of work with parents.
>
> (Primary Head teacher)

In some cases this was linked with a new policy of Extended Schools in disadvantaged areas that involved multi-agency working.

> We get on well because we are an early adopter extended school, so we do . . . It's not an easy community to link with, because we are in a deprivation factor 9 or whatever it is, but we do have strong links. It's just that I suppose really that the community [is involved] . . . This school's not really in a middle-class area where, you know, there's a mega involvement by parents in school life, as there are in some areas. . . . That's one of our school development priorities, you know, engaging with the community.
>
> (Secondary Head of Department)

The reputation of the schools in the community was important to the heads, and so they paid particular attention to improving the school profile. Many had secured a better reputation for the school though improved community links, more positive media attention and, for some schools, achieving 'Specialist School' status. Specialist status was not only an accolade for the schools but also an important means of securing more resources to improve the physical learning spaces.

> Once we became a specialist school, especially in the arts – because lots of our students here are into the arts, visual arts and performing arts – we were starting to get into the newspapers much more and then we got this new building we are sitting in now. So suddenly it was, yes, there is something about this school which is special.
>
> (Secondary Assistant Head)

Heads in our research pointed out the importance of community engagement as an important component of their vision and essential to their success. They and their SLTs had developed positive relationships with community leaders, and had built a web of links across the school to other organizations and individuals, and strong links with key stakeholders in the local community, which benefited the school.

Our reputation is very important in the community. We don't have a nursery [as] most schools in the area do so we have to fight very hard for our children. If there is an accident or a dispute . . . I had a dispute recently and I wonder whether the gossip coming from the dispute will cause people to look at us differently. I think at the moment we are all right.

(Primary Head)

Involving parents and supporting families

Heads also made a great deal of effort to communicate with parents. Parents were informed about all aspects of their child's education and constant attempts were made to make contact with the 'hard to reach' parents. They were actively engaged in setting targets for their child and ensuring these targets were met. They were encouraged to participate in school activities and to support classroom teaching. Heads had an open-door policy with parents, and parents were constant visitors to the school. Emphasis was placed on supporting parents to support learning in the home.

Working with other schools

Links were forged with other schools, allowing staff and learners to develop new skills and for the pooling of resources. Links were also made with external agencies and local services.

We have got a particularly close relationship with another school in the area. Managing from the middle is a course that one of their staff and one of our staff did together. We have been doing a lot of optimum learning, and we have done a lot of INSET days with them. We have talked a lot about different issues. That is our particularly close school. We have links with other schools through sport; also getting together for festivals in that kind of thing, that all the preparation for going on to secondary schools that they get to know other people in a year group. In years 4, 5 and 6 we do a lot of that.

(Primary Deputy Head)

These schools also maintained links with external agencies, such as social services. This multi-agency work led to more complete provision for the pupils. Links with universities for research purposes or as training schools also provided an extra dimension to their work.

The pastoral assistant head works with the support agencies and social services and whatever unit there is out there for the attendance and the education, the School's SENCO (Special Educational Needs

Co-ordinates) works with the educational psychologists and those who come to assess children for their needs. So on both fronts we approach that, so we do have a multi-agency.

(Secondary Head)

Some students' behaviour is very challenging. Progress in assisting their learning can be very challenging, because of external circumstances, their external circumstances, but in a sense it isn't too much of a challenge, because there is an excellent network of connection within external agencies. We do have, for example, our own school intervention officer, police officer, we have a youth justice worker who is on site. We have excellent connections with various external agencies like CAMHS and Social Services so, in that sense, it isn't a challenge because we do have that excellent network of connections.

(Secondary Head of Department)

We have external links with five universities, have 25–30 trainee teachers each year and try to recruit to staff because they already know and understand the ethos of the school, can develop their skills and increase their responsibility.

(Secondary Head)

Heads were also skilled in using external agencies as a resource to further improve provision.

I developed a strategy in conjunction with HMI. They thought they were coming here to inspect me but I used the opportunity to interview them and tried to pull out all the bits of good practice that they had observed over the country. I used them as a resource. I have got an awful lot of time for HMI. I worry about the structure that they work with . . . but I have never yet met a bad HMI inspector.

(Secondary Head)

All of the heads were 'ahead of the game' and responsive to change. They were adept at identifying shifts in the external environment and ensuring that their school was best placed to capitalize on that change.

Improving the teaching and learning programme

Improving physical conditions for teaching and learning

Although all the heads in our research recognized the need to improve the conditions in which the quality of teaching and learning could be maximized and pupils' performance enhanced, they achieved this in different ways. For example, in many cases, at the start of the heads' tenure, the physical condition of the school was not conducive to effective teaching and learning. Therefore, there was a deliberate and continuing strategy by the head to improve the school buildings and its facilities. By changing the physical environment of the schools and improving the classrooms, heads provided a very clear signal of the level of importance they attached to associations between high-quality conditions for teaching and learning, and staff and pupil well-being and achievement.

> We had a very big change in terms of the building work so a very physical change in the building, in that Key Stage 1 and Key Stage 2 swapped over. So that was quite a tricky six months. But the rooms that the Year 6s and the Year 5s now have, and Reception are now in the main building, it has really improved the educational environment.
>
> (Primary Teacher)

Emphasis was placed on display and brightening up the learning environment.

> The children respect the classrooms more; there's no vandalism here. There used to be writing on displays years ago, pen marks on the walls, but for years there's been nothing. Even outside, even the community, because we visualized the apparatus in the nursery playground and the new junior playground getting vandalized, but it hasn't.
>
> (Primary Teacher)

Positive changes in the physical environment prompted positive changes in pupil behaviour. Pupils had more respect for an improved environment and this created a greater sense of calm and order across the school.

Developing high expectations

The development and embedding of high expectations, what others have termed 'academic optimism' (Hoy, Hoy and Kurtz, 2008), for behaviour, teaching, learning and achievement were a second key feature in the work of all heads at the beginning of their headship, and remained a focus throughout all phases.

> High expectations are essential here and not allowing that to slip, and that belief that every child can achieve is really important in this context. And I think just being very organized and efficient and

keeping on top of things, dealing with things very quickly so nothing gets out of hand.

(Primary Deputy Head)

Staff recognized the effect this had, both on staff and pupils. Indeed, it was particularly important in schools in more disadvantaged contexts, as it raised both staff's and pupils' self-esteem, and there was a reinforcement of the belief that improved outcomes were possible.

I do firmly believe that everybody has got the potential to do well in life; no one from my family had gone to university but I was encouraged to do very well. I really do want to get that over in my teaching. If they have got enthusiasm and ability and they want to get on, they can do. That is constantly what I am trying to get over to them.

(Primary Deputy Head)

The most important aspiration has been to raise students' expectations. If it's something I try to communicate to staff, it would have to be raising expectations. Moving the standards up had engendered faith in colleagues, and had done a lot to raise self-esteem and self-confidence. We're try to make the school as successful as it can be by raising public accountability and the reputation in the community, which is what was holding the school back.

(Secondary Head)

That these high expectations extended through every aspect of school life was seen as essential to the effective communication of this whole-school vision of achievement.

I think it permeates through everything from classroom expectations and expectations of how the school expects people to behave, in terms of uniform being correctly worn, the way they behave in the classroom, expectations of behaviour, and also expectations of work because there are high expectations of students here: the school's very into target setting.

(Secondary Head of Department)

Consistent school-wide policies on pupil behaviour

One area where high expectations were particularly important was pupil behaviour. This was seen as essential in improving outcomes across the school, and staff recognized the importance of this coming from the leadership and being consistent across the school.

Standards of behaviour, expectations throughout the school are really high. I think that's important because when you are in a classroom that time is for working and I don't feel like any time is wasted on discipline or that kind of thing.

(Primary Senior Leader)

Improvements in learning were also secured though the development of school-wide policies that were deliberately focused on improving pupil behaviour and attendance, both seen as necessary conditions for this. There were consistent, whole-school approaches to behaviour based on clear procedures and high expectations. Emphasis was placed upon attendance and punctuality. Both were monitored and any absenteeism was addressed without delay. The establishment of clear, consistent rules and norms of behaviour was further supported by strong pastoral systems that reinforced respect between staff and pupils and a collective view of what constituted positive behaviour.

The school has a positive climate – displays, good behaviour, no gang culture. We use assertive discipline which is very helpful. It's firm and gives the pupils' boundaries. All staff have a consistent approach to behaviour.

(Secondary Head of Department)

Staff spoke of the importance of a positive attitude toward behaviour that focused on learning, and misbehaviour as a barrier to learning. Teachers said that they responded to misbehaviour calmly and led by example. In some cases this was expressed through school-wide policies which explicitly related behaviour to learning, which were perceived by staff to have a big impact on student outcomes.

The most significant change has been the introduction of this 'behaviour for learning' strategy. I think we were aware . . . that the behaviour of the school was getting in the way of their learning. So the introduction of this has helped that. I think the classrooms in corridors are much more quiet as a result of that. But I think there is, also, a by-product of that, . . . that the success culture has been growing.

(Secondary Head of Department)

The heads and other staff interviewed reported that improved pupil behaviour contributed directly to improvements in homework, less conflict between pupils, a feeling of safety within the school and improved attendance. These factors, along with setting high expectations and high standards for academic achievement, were found to impact positively upon pupil learning.

> I want kids to feel confident . . . I want the children here to see beyond [this neighbourhood], not in a derogatory way because I think they should be proud of where they come from, but I want them to see that there is life beyond [this neighbourhood], and they can do anything they want if they've got the experiences and the choices to choose from.
>
> (Primary Key Stage Co-ordinator)

Thus, by creating a culture where poor behaviour was not tolerated and high expectations were the norm, heads improved both staff and pupil motivation and created an environment where it was acceptable to learn and to succeed.

Enhancing teaching and learning: refining and extending pedagogical approaches

A key strategy in all schools was to create consistency in the organization of teaching and learning without prescribing particular classroom pedagogies.

> I understand it more now we have a standard lesson plan template, which has always worked using a three-part lesson: a starter, a middle and plenary. So everybody follows that format. But what we are developing at the moment is that bit at the beginning and that middle bit. At the start of every lesson sharing that success criteria and every lesson given that opportunity to reflect on their work.
>
> (Secondary Teacher)

Schools were all persistent in the pursuit of improved teaching, learning and achievement. Teachers were encouraged to go beyond their usual teaching models and to try new or alternative approaches. Heads encouraged staff to be leaders in their own classrooms and to take informed decisions to extend their teaching approaches. They provided an infrastructure where it was safe to try things out. Staff responded to this opportunity positively. It affected the way they saw themselves as professionals and improved their sense of self-efficacy. This, in turn, had a positive impact on the way they interacted with pupils and other staff members in the school.

> He allows you to take risks, he allows you the freedom to make mistakes, and he backs you up if you need backing up.
>
> (Secondary Head of Department)

> We have an influx of younger teachers who will take risks: for example, one teacher has taken up an initiative called computer clubs for girls.

> And she has run with it and they have won an amazing award. And that was someone who has only been teaching for a year. And she felt powerful enough to do that.
>
> (Secondary Assistant Head)

> I've let people run with things; I have given people free range initiatives for as long as it's reasonable. I've encouraged people to take risks and I have worked at the kids; I have an open-door policy.
>
> (Secondary Head)

The schools' contexts, phase of improvement, heads' leadership strategies and other factors contributed to schools' different levels of innovation in teaching and learning.

> We have a very clear policy on how lessons are delivered, so we teach at Key Stage 3 with a starter, a main activity, a plenary and so there's constant reviewing [of] lesson objectives. And the pupils are so familiar with that format that they now expect all lessons to be taught like that and have time to review.
>
> (Secondary Teacher)

> However, I have some reservations of it [the school's lesson] being too prescriptive. I tend to teach in some unusual ways, and I had excellent Ofsted always from when I started at the school, and for me it feels 'let me do it my own way because I know what I do'. But, it is more about learning rather than teaching and how you do it and maybe we need to go through that phase.
>
> (Secondary Teacher)

The use of information and communciation technology (ICT) as a tool to enhance teaching and learning had made a difference to classroom processes in the majority of schools. There was widespread use of interactive whiteboards and evidence of schools investing in technology such as educational computer games to enable independent and more interactive learning. This proved to be motivational for pupils.

Using attainment data and observation

Data were used extensively to inform changes in teaching and learning. Pupil data were used in both formative and summative ways to scrutinize performance and to plan appropriate teaching strategies. The use of data to identify and support the progress of students who were not reaching their potential and/or who were disaffected was also high on the agenda.

> Each half term [the deputy head] and I sit and go through everybody's assessments and we look then at those children who are not reaching their full potential. It might be a high achiever or it may be a child with special needs but we know they haven't made adequate progress, so we go through and jot down, say, if there's been attendance issues, etc., and we need to keep a tally on this.
>
> (Primary Head)

Classroom observation was used in a developmental way to provide support, guidance and advice about further improvements. This was welcomed by teachers as a way of sharing practice and refining teaching approaches. It was viewed as a form of professional support, rather than surveillance, and an opportunity for a dialogue around teaching.

> Well, one of the things that she does is she has a programme of observing everybody. It doesn't matter if you're the newest person in. I was observed, just before half term. So she actually knows what's going on in the classroom, and she does know individual teachers' strengths and weaknesses, and does what she can to support that. And I think that that's a really good practice. It certainly paid dividends when we had an Ofsted.
>
> (Secondary Head of Department)

Schools had also incorporated into their classrooms Assessment for Learning processes. Teachers planned for Assessment for Learning (AFL) and used these data to set individual targets.

> Sharing targets for parents on parent evenings are something we do, we all have targets displayed in the classroom so that children know what the targets are, and it's a matter of keeping a close eye on them, and you're looking carefully at the assessment material they gather to make sure children are achieving as expected. It's in the vocabulary that the children use as well, they talk about their own targets.
>
> (Primary Key Stage Co-ordinator)

Across all the schools targets and levels were clearly understood by pupils, and this enabled them to play active roles in progressing their own learning. This emphasis on independent and interdependent learning had a positive effect on pupil motivation and engagement.

Redesigning and enriching the curriculum

Heads had made changes within the curriculum in a deliberate attempt to broaden learning opportunities and provide access points for each child, making the redesigning and enriching of the curriculum another crucial aspect that contributed to their schools' success. Interestingly, most, though not all, of these changes were very much in line with government initiatives. The emphasis was upon 'stage not age' learning, with the curriculum being adaptable to the needs of all pupils rather than some. At primary level there was a particular emphasis upon greater flexibility and continuity between Key Stage 1 and Key Stage 2. At secondary level there was a focus on the provision of different pathways toward vocational qualifications and an emphasis upon personalized learning.

> Each student is doing a personal curriculum, something we have tailored for them to help them get the best out of the school while they are pursuing their various curriculum options.
>
> (Secondary Head of Department)

> Regarding personalized learning, we've got a whole strategy working in collaboration with five schools and the college. One of the schools had got the opportunity to open a sixth form, which has been approved.
>
> (Secondary Head)

Teachers were encouraged to teach for a wide range of different pupil learning strategies, and extra specialist classes (booster classes, gifted and talented) were offered to encourage all pupils to reach their potential. Pupils were encouraged to work toward individual goals and to focus on their own specific needs. In addition, they were able to choose subjects suited to their skills and consequently were able to achieve better results.

A number of the schools had introduced more emotional support into the curriculum through PHSE (personal health and social education) or SEAL (social, emotional and affective learning) programmes. Creativity and self-esteem featured heavily in curriculum provision, as did a focus on the development of key skills. There was a major emphasis on enjoyment of learning, and the recognition that when pupils enjoy learning, they are more effective learners.

> I think that the big thing about the school is the PHSE curriculum: it is very caring, and throughout the school we are teaching the children right from nursery to be caring and respectful of each other and to share things, to respect each other's differences and to look out for each other. And when the visitors come to the school they notice how polite the children [are], even the very, very young children.
>
> (Primary Teacher)

There was also evidence of an emphasis on the provision of a broad range of extracurricular activities, and schools offered a wide range of options including lunchtime and school clubs as well as holiday activities.

Conclusions

These cross-case study results confirm and extend the results identified from the quantitative survey phase of the research. The analyses reveal a high degree of consistency in leadership values and range of practices across the case study schools. Heads deployed the same strategic leadership approaches although, as we will show in later chapters, the combinations, sequence, timing and intensity of these approaches varied. They were highly context-specific and related to the particular phase of the school's improvement journey.

The strategies, also, provide key areas of focus for designing programmes which enable support for school leaders' own professional development:

- Becoming lead learners and recognizing that raising teachers' expectations of themselves and providing targeted support for their learning and development needs are keys to increasing their sense of well-being, morale, motivation, commitment and retention, and, through these, achieving better learning outcomes for pupils.
- Maximizing all the influence at their disposal, securing the trust of others, and making a difference to learning outcomes through enhancing conditions at the school, teacher and pupil level. To achieve this improved performance, they need to employ not only the appropriate strategies, but also the core values and personal qualities demonstrated daily with colleagues and pupils.
- Placing pupil care, learning and achievement at the heart of all their decisions by having as a central focus the creation of appropriate conditions for teaching and learning; the development of personal qualities such as a strong sense of moral responsibility and a belief in equity and social justice; a belief that every child deserves the same opportunities to succeed; respect and value for people and a real passion and commitment to education; and encouragement in risk taking and innovations.

For these to be successful, however, it is crucial to learn how the sequencing, timing, ordering and combinations of these strategies many be applied in different contexts. Most importantly, heads need to be supported in how to be most acutely attuned to context and recognize, acknowledge, understand and attend to a range of human development motivations and needs, to allow them to choose the most appropriate and effective strategies for their school at a particular time. The next chapter provides further unique insights into the ways heads contribute to the improvement of their schools within and across different phases of their development.

7   Phases of school improvement

Introduction

This chapter will discuss the ways the core practices identified in Chapter 6 were enacted within and between a number of school improvement phases.

Toward the end of the field research, we used focused interviews to discuss the school's improvement trajectories and the school's leadership since the head's appointment. Heads and their key staff identified the strategies and practices which had contributed to school improvement during their tenure. By plotting these on a time graph, then identifying significant turning points, each head created a detailed 'line of improvement' which extended through a number of development phases during their time at the school.

While there were differences in the number and variations in the length of these, on close analysis three broad development phases were identified: early (foundational), middle (developmental) and later (enrichment).

Heads' personal diagnoses of internal contexts (e.g. staffing, physical conditions for teaching and learning, success history of the school, SES) and external policy initiatives were identified by them as being important influences on the decisions they had taken about the nature, timing and implementation of their strategies and actions. It should be noted, also, that while government strategies and policies influenced some of the decisions made by these heads, they did not dictate their actions.

> So long before the government introduced it, if you read my Ofsted report, I was passionate about my every child matters and suddenly I see that the government have a programme called Every Child Matters.
>
> (Secondary Head)

School improvement phases

While these leadership values, qualities and strategies were common factors in the improvement of all schools, there were others which, although present in all phases, were emphasized more in some than in others, according to the heads' diagnoses of policy, organizational, community and individual contexts of need and judgement about the timings, length and intensity of their application. For example, primary heads tended to place an intensive focus on creating, establishing conditions and communicating an agreed set of values and direction for the school, and were able to establish these in the early phase. Secondary school heads' responses, however, suggested that establishing appropriate structures and relationships which were consistent with a collective vision took longer.

> To build an ethos, as you know, in any institution you have to let staff know in simple language exactly what your vision is. I told them it was very simple, I want a happy school where the ethos is one that can best be defined as a relaxed yet disciplined ethos.
>
> (Secondary Head)

> He has the vision. He had the vision when he came of what he wanted a learning environment to look like and what he wanted pupils to look like. I don't think really we had ever spent enough time looking at that sort of . . . what do we want to get to? And I think that was the big thing for him; he came with that vision, we shared bits of it, we developed further bits, and more and more we see where we're going and what we're doing.
>
> (Secondary Deputy Head)

> I think it is providing the vision to the school; he is quite keen to push the school forward and I think he is keen to push everything along. And kind of keeping it asked as up-to-date as possible to keep us right at the front of new ideas. I think he is quite open to change. He's prepared to take a risk and to push the school forward.
>
> (Secondary Head of Department)

> I think she has a very strong vision of exactly how she wants things to be. She will have an idea and she will be very driven and enthusiastic about a change. So she is very positive and encouraging like that.
>
> (Primary Teacher)

Early (foundational) phase of heads' leadership

Key strategies which were prioritized in this phase related to improving the physical, social, psychological and emotional conditions for teaching and learning. They were used to ensure that certain 'basics' were in place. Three particular strategies were prioritized in this foundational phase:

a)   improving the physical environment of the school for staff and pupils in order to create positive environments conducive for high-quality teaching and learning;

b)   setting standards for pupil behaviour and improving attendance; and

c)   restructuring the senior leadership team and redefining the roles, responsibilities and accountabilities of its members.

Improving conditions for teaching and learning: the physical environment

Heads recognized the importance of creating a physical environment in which all staff and students felt inspired to work and learn. Changes to the school buildings varied in scope, from increasing visual display in classrooms, corridors and reception areas, to the creation of internal courtyards and entirely new buildings.

> When [the head] first came here the biggest impact that she made her number one priority was the environment. And everything went into the environment. That was the focus, nothing else, which I think is great because if you try to do too many things too soon, I don't think we'd have got where we are today. So that was the one big thing.
>
> (Primary Teacher)

Improving conditions for teaching and learning: pupil behaviour

Strategies for improving pupil behaviour initiated in the early phase often included changes to uniform, systems for monitoring attendance patterns, and follow-up of unauthorized absences:

> We were very strict. We went in immensely hard as you have to and the children couldn't breathe without permission, which was really hard because it wasn't us, it's not the way we are, but we had to do it.
>
> (Primary Deputy Head)

> We set out very good school systems and I think that is what you have to stick to. . . . We established the rules with the children and in fact we did them all together and kept going over them and the children agreed to these rules so, it was an agreement in assemblies and things

like that and if they broke the rules, there were consequences. And we stuck to it as a staff and we were consistent.

(Primary Head)

Behaviour was seen as a whole-school collegiate approach. We refined classroom rules and had the same classroom rules and expectations displayed in each classroom, so we were having, I think, more emphasis on a unified approach to behavioural issues so students knew the ground rules and what to expect.

(Secondary Head of Department)

Redesigning organizational roles and responsibilities: the senior leadership team

Both primary and secondary schools distributed more leadership and responsibility first to the SLT and later to middle leaders and other staff. Heads saw the early creation of a team around them that shared and championed their values, purposes and direction for the school as essential in order to enable the development of other important improvement strategies.

So then [in the first phase] there was the reshaping of the senior management team and we started to look at accountabilities a lot more. The job descriptions were revised to reflect the national standards far more closely . . . After that the senior management team was extended to incorporate all the core subjects. Prior to that, it had been extended by having a guest member of middle leadership on there, so we had an AST (Advanced Skills Teacher) for two years to drive assessment for learning.

(Secondary Deputy Head)

In the first year [of the] new SLT structure, that was partly good luck because the existing senior deputy left and that gave me the chance to restructure. . . . Basically bringing more people onto the team. The previous structure had been a head, two deputies and two senior teachers, and I made it a head, a deputy, and five assistant principals. The number of assistant principals has increased with time. The idea was to have more people involved, that has been a key plank all the way through to try and be less hierarchical than it had been before.

(Secondary Head)

Primary school heads also moved toward more clearly defined (though not inflexible), flatter structures.

I found on entry to the school that some people were doing jobs that they shouldn't be and some people weren't doing the jobs that they should be in terms of just sticking their oar in, and as a new head I'd not worked that way before and quite quickly thought I don't want to work that way either. So this restructuring has helped to put people not in boxes but focusing on what their role is.

(Primary Head)

This restructuring, which often involved new roles being created on the SLT and having a member of the support staff on the SLT, was a common feature of team building in both primary and secondary schools.

Also on the SLT we have got an HLTA [higher learning teaching assistant], and so she represents the teaching assistants. That's really good because she had such brilliant ideas and can see things from a very different perspective.

(Primary Teacher)

And that's where our strength is. It's in that team approach. I have all these ideas but I leave it all in chaos and they pick it all up, matching it in, and they're making it work. They deliver the support timetable. I think we have a strength in the symbiotic relationship the management team have. We will switch roles and I have no problem with that. There's no defined roles as such. I go out into my school and walk the walk, I talk the talk. I don't talk the talk very well, but I can walk the walk and make it work.

(Primary Head)

We have a senior management team, which consists of two senior teachers, Key Stage 1 co-ordinator and Key Stage 2 co-ordinator, and myself. But I would also say that all staff at the school has a managerial responsibility and a curriculum areas, so they all have budgets, and they all have responsibilities for overseeing their particular curriculum area. So they all have curriculum co-ordinator files, so they have that as part of their brief. We also have a very good strong governing body, who make decisions.

(Primary Head)

Middle (developmental) phase of heads' leadership

Two key strategies were prioritized in this second phase. These were

a)   the 'wider distribution of leadership' – for most schools this had begun with the SLT in the earlier phase, extending then to middle leaders in the middle phase and finally other staff in the later phases; and

b) enhancing the use of data-informed decision making to improve the quality of teaching and learning.

Redesigning organizational roles and responsibilities: extending leadership

Increased participation in leadership processes and decision making in the foundational phase was largely the provenance of a smaller group of staff who made up the SLT.

> Under the head teacher's leadership she's made us quite autonomous, she has her finger on everything. She knows everything that's going on but there's a balance of letting us get on with it. Some heads would be in every meeting, but she'll be in enough just to keep herself informed.
>
> (Primary Deputy Head)

> In the early days it was very much in our hands because there wasn't anybody else. Since then, the team of assistant heads has grown. They are developing in capability and confidence. They remain a mixed-ability team, but they have come on hugely. They are taking on more responsibility and more is being left in their hands.
>
> (Secondary Head)

By the middle phase all but two of the twenty case study heads were distributing significant decision making both to this leadership team and to a larger group of middle leaders; and by the later phase all schools were distributing leadership throughout the school.

> We all [provide leadership] in a sort of way because every teacher has an area of curriculum responsibility or a role that they have to take the lead in.
>
> (Primary Teacher)

> Everyone in the middle leadership is included in the decision making.
>
> (Secondary Teacher)

> Every member of staff has a subject area of responsibility and the classroom assistants have responsibilities as well and they get feedback from the learning co-ordinator.
>
> (Primary Deputy Head)

The middle leadership team was appalling. . . . Now they have come along huge leaps and bounds. . . . People have come on to the school and gained confidence . . . Part of what we have at the moment is that we have a head of department who has paired with an assistant head who has the appropriate experience.

(Secondary Head)

In our fields, we all have a leadership role. So the teachers have a leadership role because they're a class teacher, the senior management team, the deputy head, fantastic deputy head, they rub off each other. They're different characters and they bounce off each other. They really are a good team.

(Primary Secretary)

Leadership is well spread out at all levels and everyone knows what they have to do.

(Secondary Head of Department)

This additional responsibility was very much a function of growing trust and trustworthiness. (See Chapter 9 for a full discussion of the relationship between trust and the progressive distribution of leadership.)

Enhancing teaching and learning: use of data-informed decision making

Using data to inform them of pupils' progress and achievement was a key feature of practice in all schools. Data were used to identify those who needed extra support, facilitating increases in opportunities for personalized learning. Of the 20 heads, 11 showed clear progression to a more sophisticated generation and application of these in the later phases, in order to target pupils who were working close to examination grade boundaries.

[These] data are what then help us to track progress within the school on [a] whole-school level and for a department because clearly each pupil is set targets when they join us in Year 7.

(Secondary Head of Department)

In stage 3 we took that a stage further, and one of the big decisions we took between stages 2 and 3 was to employ a systems manager who would look at making our data work for us, and what we really wanted was traffic-lighted reports.

(Secondary Deputy Head)

Once schools began to use data as part of their practice, systems became embedded, in practice, continuing but with less intense focus. The priority placed upon the use of data by heads within each phase differed. This is illustrated in Figure 7.1, which shows how many heads in primary and secondary schools prioritized this strategy in each phase of their school's improvement journey. The prioritization of one strategy did not mean the abandonment of others. Rather, it denoted the areas which heads highlighted as key priorities within a number of action in each improvement phase.

Figure 5.1 shows that, for primary schools, while all heads discussed the use of data, there was no particular phase regarding when this strategy was prioritized. However, the trajectories seem to show that there was a significant and steep increase in the use of data by secondary schools in the middle phase of these heads' leadership. There are two explanations for this:

1   Size and complexity meant that other priorities and preconditions were established in the early phase of their leadership (e.g. policies for pupil behaviour, restructuring and reculturing).
2   Understanding data was an important precursor to later strategies such as personalizing the curriculum, which tended to be a priority in the later phase.

It should also be noted that both using data and curriculum personalization were linked to changes in government policy, and this may have impacted on the timing of the heads' actions. Nevertheless, due to the differences in the length of headship, the middle phase did not occur at the same time for all the heads, so policy alone cannot explain this trend.

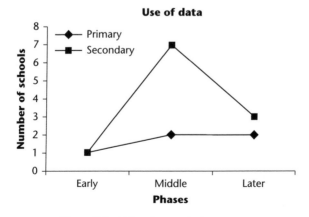

Figure 7.1   Using data – priority strategy

Later (enrichment) phase of heads' leadership

Redesigning the curriculum: personalization and enrichment

Building further upon the growth of achievement and its positive effects upon teachers' and pupils' sense of confidence and stability, the key strategies that heads prioritized in this phase focused upon the further personalization of learning and enriching of the curriculum.

Personalization

Personalization of the curriculum was reflected in an increasing emphasis upon teaching, which promoted interdependent, independent and flexible learning, which supported a range of pupil learning styles. In the case of secondary schools, this included increasing the curriculum options for pupils, particularly vocational options or pathways. The relationship between the increased use of data in the middle (development) phase and personalization of the curriculum in the later phase was identified by an overwhelming majority of the heads, and this was also highlighted by staff as a key enrichment strategy that impacted positively on pupil outcomes. This applied, particularly, to schools which had been placed by Ofsted in 'special measures' just before the appointment of the current head. In these schools, the quality of the teaching and learning, pupil behaviour and staff motivation and commitment had been a clear, early and urgent priority in the early (foundational) and middle (developmental) phases:

> The next difference that I made, alongside this, I feel, was to do with the curriculum. When we first started, when I arrived, the curriculum was very simple, in that it was mainly a GCSE programme for Key Stage 4. Key Stage 3 is much more governed and driven by the DfES sort of requirements, but with Key Stage 4 we began to be very creative with it, purely because we recognized the needs of the students.
>
> (Secondary Head)

The relationship between the extended use of data and personalizing the curriculum was also highlighted by staff as a key strategy that impacted on improved pupil outcomes:

> It would be the assessment and tracking systems. I think that has got to be, it has taken a long time to get there and I think at some stage that people thought that Mr T. was just filling in more forms for us, but I think that now people have realized that there is benefit, that from the systems we can narrow it down to individual pupils who might need differentiated approaches, personalized learning. It is not just one size fits all. The government is now saying that as well.

But I agree totally, you want to make sure that every child is getting what they need. So I think [that means] the assessment and tracking systems are essential.

(Primary Deputy Head)

Primary school heads' personalization of the curriculum focused on assessment for learning and individual pupil target setting. Primary teachers spoke of planning for different learning styles as a key ingredient of a personalized curriculum:

As far as personalizing the learning, I think we've done a lot in terms of teaching styles. The teachers know which styles . . . the children are more au fait with. All the kinaesthetic and all of that. So in terms of that we've got quite a lot of knowledge to do with that. So I think we're quite well on the journey to personalizing. Homework's personalized quite a lot in school with parents. That's over and above the special needs children.

(Primary Deputy Head)

For all secondary heads, the focus on providing appropriate options was the key to personalization. The provision of a broad curriculum and 'use of data' to help target individual pupils' needs were also identified as key strategies by the secondary teachers. These schools tended to have a range of vocational options available and different pathways for pupils to follow, based on their skills. Although this tended to be a higher priority for schools in areas of higher socio-economic disadvantage, all of the schools were either broadening or deepening their work in this area in the later, enrichment phase. Nonetheless, this was done without neglecting the academic areas in which these schools were highly successful.

Our work-related curriculum began in this third phase . . . It isn't now just for the disaffected, it's for any pupil who would be better suited to learning in a college; one branch is for those are not academic full stop . . . and the other group of students are those who want to follow a vocational route from early on, . . . it's very strong, we get very able students going on this alternative provision depending on the courses they want to study . . . they're on a very flexible timetable.

(Secondary Teacher)

Each student is doing a personal curriculum, something that we have tailored for them to help them get the best out of the school while they are pursuing their various curriculum options.

(Secondary Head of Department)

Many teachers commented on the positive impact this work had had on pupil outcomes, and saw a direct link between personalizing the curriculum and higher academic results.

> So two years later when the school moved from 26 per cent to 42 per cent, that major curriculum innovation was shown to have quite a phenomenal impact and that exceeded the target that was set for the school so that was very good . . . Phase 2 was really the implementation of the vision of the new head and that was based very much on personalizing learning, and I suppose the key strands of that were curriculum reform, a broadening of the curriculum quite considerably, taking a wider range of qualifications.
>
> (Secondary Deputy Head)

> There have been a lot of things that I think together have moved. A more tailored curriculum; we have been moving toward a more personalized curriculum as well. Whole-school efforts getting coursework finished, various things like that.
>
> (Secondary Head of Department)

> I think [the improved results] reflect the great choice that children have, especially GNVQs that they have been doing which offer a better GSCE, if you like: two for the price of one or something. . . . I have applied to do five at history because eventually we have heard that the model will have different awards. When it started it was a lot of the less able kids, but now the kids are seeing the possibilities of it and the fact that you move onto the A level with this, and a lot of the brighter ones choose it now.
>
> (Secondary Head of Department)

Enrichment of the curriculum

Curriculum enrichment refers to broad pupil outcomes and development of the whole child; it focuses on social and emotional learning and provision of creative, cross-curricular or skills-based learning, such as off-timetable focus days on learning to learn, thinking skills or topic-based learning. The pattern was similar for the introduction of enriching extracurricular activities.

> We've done a lot of in the past two or three years, it's what's broadly called enrichment, but what I would call pupil personal development. We had to focus very strongly on the academic, to start with, and now we're confident that we're maintaining [and] improving that. We've put in a lot of effort, and the actual quality of the pupil experience in school is much richer now than it was three or four

years ago, so I hope it's a better school now to come to. It's more enjoyable.

(Secondary Head)

I think there are other areas, and other aspects of schooling beyond mere exam results, and I'd like to think I work in an education system where you look at the person that leaves the school, rather than just the certificate that leaves the school, and how you've moulded them socially, or emotionally, or whatever, or you've given them opportunities that they might not have otherwise had, if they'd not come here.

(Secondary Head of Department)

It is about the whole of the person, and we work fundamentally with students on their social skills, emotional literacy, their ability to relate to other people, other adults, other students, to work in groups, to be able to express their feelings, their ideas and so on in the right way and to have aspirations of where they want to go, to be aware of themselves as people.

(Secondary Assistant Head)

For primary schools the emphasis tended to be on making the curriculum more creative, flexible and enjoyable for the pupils, aiming to inspire and interest them, with the aim of producing a more rounded individual.

Now, it's more of a focus on the creative and the enjoyment of speaking and listening. We've got a school teacher that comes in, we've got drama and just linking the creative partnerships to get them involved in school. We've still got the focus of impacting it on writing, a very clear focus, but it's how can we inspire children. I feel that's the phase the school's [in] at the moment.

(Primary Deputy Head)

It is also giving them a wider curriculum than just what is normally there. We try to get them out and about around the area and we try to get people in and we try to widen out what they experience. So we have realized that targets are important but they are not the be all and end all of education of children at school. We are looking for more of a rounded child rather than the concept of education today, which has targets.

(Primary Acting Head)

For secondary schools, flexibility and enjoyment were also central. This would sometimes involve whole days off timetable working on cross-curricular projects or skills-based learning. Specialist school status often helped to focus these days and use the specialism as a guide, such as science fun days or adding extra dimensions to sports days.

> [The focus days are] looking very much at skills-based learning, so making the connections across subject areas is still . . . I know it's been going on since the national strategy started in cross-curricular approaches. It's quite a hard nut to crack in secondary and I think we are starting to get there and our focus days help us with that, but it's still about making it clear to the students, the connections they can make across the curriculum and also staff to see how they can enhance their own classroom by having that enhanced in other areas as well.
>
> (Secondary Deputy Head)

> We've used our Sports College status more since 2006, and as well as incorporating the outward bound activities and the activity weeks, we've also done things like, for example, as head of English I've got some boys doing dance and learning some of the poems through dance, and I send some of my gifted and talented pupils out to inter- view pupils on sports day, and we're doing a newspaper magazine. So trying to incorporate sport into and across the curriculum has helped, I think, especially with boys' underachievement and we have tried to use that more as we've become more secure in our Sports College status.
>
> (Secondary Head of Department)

Tables 7.1 and 7.2 provide examples of the focus and relative intensity of the strategies in the later (enrichment) phase. For example, for 'Pupil behaviour' the heads may have employed three actions: instigating a whole-school 'behav- iour for learning' policy, consistency of application by staff and students, and changing the school uniform. Three actions such as these are represented by deeper shading. A single strategy was considered to be more intense if it built on and extended work that had gone before. The tables show how the emphasis on curriculum redesign increased in the later phases.

Heads of schools which had no urgent standards issues to resolve (School 11 and 14 in Table 7.2) were able, it seemed, to focus upon enriching the curriculum earlier than others. For schools in 'special measures' when the current head began (School 3, 7 and 10 in Table 7.1), however, enrichment had to wait until the middle phase once more urgent quality issues had been addressed.

> There were still children within the school that had not had a proper curriculum because when the school was put in special measures the teaching was completely unsatisfactory and so was the learning. So we

Table 7.1 Curriculum personalization and enrichment across phases (primary schools)

School																							
School	2			3			4			5			6			7			8			10	
FSM level	2			3			3			4			3			4			2			3	
Length of headship	11 years			11 years			17 years			12 years			24 years			9 years			19 years			7 years	
Phase	E	M	L	E	M	L	E	M	L	E	M	L	E	M	L	E	M	L	E	M	L	E	M	L
Curriculum personalization																								
Curriculum enrichment																								

E = Early
M = Middle
L = Later

Table 7.2 Curriculum personalization and enrichment across phases (secondary schools)

School	11	12	13	14	15	16	17	18	19
FSM	1	4	3	4	4	2	3	2	2
Length of headship	6 years	9 years	8 years	12 years	18 years	15 years	7 years	12 years	9 years
Phase	E M L	E M L	E M L	E M L	E M L	E M L	E M L	E M L	E M L
Curriculum personalization									
Curriculum enrichment									

E = Early
M = Middle
L = Later

were kind of looking at enriching the curriculum then, but it was really that the teaching had to be right. The children had to be seen to be learning and making progress. So here [in the later phase], we decided to enrich that even more; it had to [be] more of a creative curriculum. So it was not just maths systems and English systems. It had to be more creative.

(Primary Head)

No school employed personalization strategies without first prioritizing learning how to collect and use data. School 13 is a very clear example of this. This school has a high number of pupils receiving free school meals (FSM 3), is in an area where a low value is placed on education, and was in special measures when the head began. Since then academic results have improved and there are higher expectations for all. Although the head began to focus on data-informed teaching in the early phase, once this became embedded in the school, the middle and later phases witnessed a focus upon the development of personalization strategies.

Each student is doing a personal curriculum, something that we have tailored for them to help them get the best out of the school while they are pursuing their various curriculum options.

(Secondary Head of Department)

Figures 7.2 and 7.3 show that more secondary school heads' prioritized personalization and enrichment in the later phase, while in the middle phase more heads prioritized enrichment than personalization. Indeed, enrichment in both primary and secondary schools was a priority for more heads in the later phase, when half of the primary heads and three-quarters of the

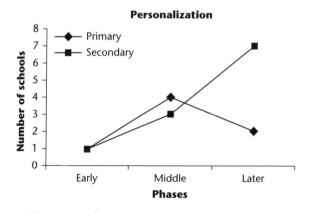

Figure 7.2 Curriculum personalization – priority strategy

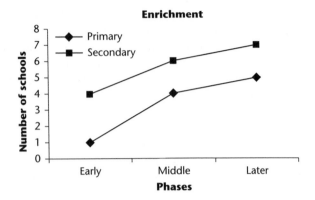

Figure 7.3 Curriculum enrichment – priority strategy

secondary heads claimed this was a key strategy. Similarly, the majority of secondary heads prioritized personalization in the later phase, a significant increase on the number who focused on this in the middle or early phase. However, fewer primary heads than in the middle phase prioritized personalization in the later phase, when they focused on curriculum enrichment.

Table 7.3 provides an illustration of the introduction of these key improvement strategies in difference phases of the schools' improvement journeys.

Table 7.3 Phased combinations and accumulations of improvement strategies

Strategies	Phase 1 (Foundational)	Phase 2 (Developmental)	Phase 3 (Enrichment)
Improving the physical environment	Primary and secondary		
Setting standards for pupil behaviour	Primary and secondary		
Restructuring the SLT	Primary and secondary		
Distributing leadership		Primary and secondary	
Using data		Primary and secondary	
Enriching the curriculum and opportunities for pupil voice			Primary and secondary
Personalizing the curriculum			Primary and secondary

Conclusions

The evidence from our research shows clearly that while these successful heads shared similar sets of educational values and leadership qualities and employed a range of core strategies, it was the different ways in which they deployed these in different phases of school improvement, together with the clarity and consistency of the values and qualities which they displayed, which enabled them to establish, build and sustain success. The selection, timing and timeliness of combinations of strategies and the accumulation, intensity and sustained application of these were a result of the heads' contextually sensitive diagnoses of changing individual, organizational, community and national policy concerns and needs. The next chapter will explore this in greater depth through detailed case studies of one primary and one secondary school. We call this phenomenon 'layered leadership'.

8   Layered leadership strategies
How leaders achieve and sustain successful school improvement

Chapter 7 showed how, within and across the three broad foundational, developmental and enrichment phases, successful heads combine, apply and accumulate combinations of strategies for school improvement of school improvement. This chapter builds upon this by providing a more nuanced, contextualized picture of the complex ways in which heads build their success. It examines these in more depth and shows how they were closely aligned to the heads' contextually sensitive diagnosis of externally defined needs and internally identified concerns and capacity, and founded upon consistent, clear and repeated communication of their values, purposes and visions for the school. Heads tended to prioritize some strategies during each phase of development, while simultaneously 'seeding' others, which themselves later were prioritized. It is important to note, therefore, that for these successful heads school improvement was not viewed as a linear process, but multi-layered. Our research provides rich illustrations of the qualities of diagnosis, differentiation, decision making, emotional understanding and practical wisdom which successful heads display though the contribution of who they are and what they do.

How successful heads use combinations and accumulation of strategies to influence school improvement directly

The following two cases (one primary and one secondary school) provide examples of the heads' attributes and how they selected, combined and accumulated strategic actions, placing relatively more or relatively less emphasis upon one or more at any given time and over time, in order to ensure school improvement. In doing so they were demonstrating not only the possession and use of key qualities and skills (an ability to diagnose and problem solve, and an ability to exercise judgements about selection, timing and combination of strategies which were sensitive to individual, organizational and individual contexts), but also their highly attuned cognitive and emotional under-standings of the needs of individual staff and students and of the concerns of both national government and local community. The first case, Greenpark Primary School, illustrates how the head laid foundations for growth in the early, foundational, phases of her leadership, developed capacity within the school in the middle, developmental, phases and extended this in the later, enrichment, phases.

Greenpark Primary and Nursery School

The school had been established for 3 to 11-year-old pupils in 1992 and had a current population of 250. The pupils, the majority of whom entered the school with levels of attainment well below the national average and many of whom had special educational needs, were housed in a mixture of buildings dating from 1912 to which various extensions had been added over the years. The school was in the FSM3 band, with 25.5 per cent of pupils being eligible for free school meals. It had extensive grounds, including a large playground, field and environmental area. The school hall was used as a gallery for professional, amateur and children's work. There were many extracurricular clubs and strong community links with youth clubs and a local church. Pupils received regular visits from working artists and dance companies and visited the theatre.

There was a high number of transient families in the catchment area, which meant that there was significant pupil turnover. In addition around a tenth of children were from ethnic minority backgrounds and, of these, very few spoke English as their first language. These circumstances presented a number of challenges to staff in the school. The head, Joan, was from a deprived background herself and was very driven by strong values about equal opportunities and equity. She had taught for a number of years and, immediately prior to taking the post at this school in 1992, she had worked as a school Early Years adviser. When she began as head, she inherited a new staff of eight teachers and one support staff, all with different backgrounds, all from different schools. One of the first jobs was to create a shared philosophy and set the vision for the school. In 2007, Ofsted reported that Greenpark was an outstanding school, with outstanding leadership and management, which provided excellent value for money.

Head's attributes

Consultative and approachable

Joan had a consultative approach, was open to ideas and suggestions and was seen as approachable by the staff.

She's very personable, very easy to have a chat, just come and knock on the door. She's always wandering around the school seeing what you are doing and she is always very supportive. If there's anything that you need to develop or there's anything that she thinks could have been done slightly differently, she'll come and speak to you in a very professional way and also in a very friendly and supportive manner. In terms of whether there are ever any issues in terms of parents or children, she is very supportive in that way as well and will always meet with you with parents if needs be. She is very supportive and very friendly to approach, which is important. I don't want somebody I'm scared to talk to. She is very good and I enjoy working for her.

(Teacher)

Supporting, caring and listening

She was supportive and gave the staff confidence, she was described as kind and caring and a good role model. She was strong also in developing people's skills, recognizing their strengths, and enabling them to play on these.

Very supportive, . . . She is very good at supporting and making you feel confident, if there are things that I have come to her and said 'I need to do this' and 'how might this person react', she is very approachable, she doesn't make you feel that if you go and ask, it's because you can't do it. You are going to ask because you need support. There is no hesitation in going to see her. Again she will come in and work with the children as well as being that leadership, she will get down and be there as well, which is good. I think the children see that is good because she is there.

(Senior Leader)

Fantastic, a good role model. Very accommodating, and willing to embrace the idea that anybody has, and will actively support, if possible, and finances allow; she is quite willing to have a go at something. If it works, that's great we will carry it on, if not we will put it down to experience and take that from that. But very, keeping up with the times, I think. She realizes that the kids are changing and it is different to what school was ten years ago. So we need to keep up with the times, and not get stuck in our ways really.

(Learning Manager)

Staff trust or, they know, that she is a caring person, that she is a kind person, that she is a listening person. And you know there are different types of listeners: you have your active empathetic listener, and you have the person who is hearing you but actually in their own minds they are doing something else. You have to do that as a leader anyway, because sometimes people will come in and want to offload. But at other times, you have to make that judgement, 'No, it's crucial to hear what this person is saying'. So, for example, if she wants to introduce something, she is still quite open to someone coming back to her and saying again in a professional way 'Have you thought [it] out properly?'. And because you know she is open to that, you will listen to her every time

(Senior Leader)

I am a touchy-feely type of person, so I will often buy flowers and things like that. Little gifts to show my appreciation.

(Head)

I think [the head's biggest contribution is] supporting the staff, supporting the students, and opening the doors so that if people want to do something, there is the support to do that. If they want to do something really exciting, then it is not pooh-poohed. Barriers are not put in the way if it is an exciting idea, and 99 per cent of the time it is supported. Being here for the children, they will come down when the head is not busy with the meeting. They will go in and sit down and have a drink and talk about what they have done. If they have a problem, if they don't like something, they come down and they tell her. They really do. If they have got something to say, then they know they she will listen.

(Senior Manager)

Coaching and counselling skills

Joan felt that she had developed her coaching and counselling skills and that her skills with relationships had developed over time.

I'm a better counsellor now. I've had counselling training in the past and I've continued to regularly go on child protection training and domestic violence training because I'm more and more coming across those experiences here. So my skills have developed in order to build better relationships because I've got a better understanding both in the real world, as my family has experienced that, and through the training that I've had over time. Also, I watch people and you learn from other people, so my skills have developed over time. My nature and personality are probably the same and my own upbringing has given me my sound philosophy and belief for every child: that's never changed.

(Head)

I am an outgoing, gregarious type person but my skills with relationships certainly have developed over time because clearly I was a very young head when I came here and I think all life experiences make you better.

(Head)

Understands the needs of staff and pupils

Joan had a very detailed understanding of pupils' families and community and how the school needed to develop around these. She was adept at looking carefully at the development needs of staff and those of children, so that both were met.

I think she is very authoritative, she understands the children's needs, and she makes sure that everybody else understands, I presume; like I say, her finger is on the pulse all the time. She portrays this in the daily things that she does. In staff meetings, she will make sure that staff are aware of what she expects and the results.

(Administrator)

If the children are quite happy and doing well, then that's what she wants: she wants a happy school and a successful school, and the staff in here are all very happy. She was very open about where we are going and anything we are going to try, and we are in the way at the moment of developing a children's centre. She's very good at keeping us up to date with exactly what's happening and what might not be happening and all the changes.

(Teacher)

Again, it is about my belief in them and valuing the pupils' lives and home backgrounds. I know there are other institutions that don't bring the child's homelife into the school and it doesn't make for the best success because I know some colleagues will say that whatever happens there, happens there, when you come here it's separate, and I don't believe in that. So I think having a belief in them as individuals and valuing whatever it is their background is. I'm not judgemental about the families; I do have my judgements, that's normal, but it doesn't affect my care and attention to that child as it [wouldn't] to any other child. And so that's very important and the other thing is because I'm consistently fair to staff and children, the children know that I respect them.

(Head)

The head is the driving force. Her warmth, friendliness and extensive knowledge of every pupil are key strengths and mean that their individual needs are well known and individual potential is recognised. Those who are not doing as well as expected are quickly identified and supported.

(Ofsted, report for Greenpark primary and nursery school, 2007)

Strong vision and strong values

Joan had a strong clear vision, clear values and a strong drive for success. This included a strong focus on ensuring that every child had the best opportunities to succeed.

> I think my aspiration is to give every child the best opportunities possible and that has not changed. What has changed is because of a lot of factors in increased resourcing and funding, CPD, and we have more opportunities to do that now. When I started off as a head teacher I had only one additional adult but now I have more support staff and teachers, and because of that you are better able to fulfil that aspiration. So that is the difference, it has not changed my core value: that has remained constant.
>
> (Head)

> She leads the school forward. She can deal with people who come in who want to see the success of the school, she can show them the success.
>
> (Senior Leader)

> I think she has a very strong vision of exactly how she wants things to be. She will have an idea and she will be very driven and enthusiastic about a change. So she is very positive and encouraging like that. She is obviously in the office sometimes but she also spends a lot of time wandering around school and dropping into classrooms. So I think that children see her as very approachable. She always wants children to come and see her and she will sometimes teach little groups within your class so that children see her within different situations.
>
> (Teacher)

Firm, fair and flexible

The head was described as fair and firm and also flexible. She would change things if feedback indicated a change was necessary.

> Firm but fair, we have two meetings every week. We have meetings at various times, informal times. If you want something doing she will tell you. But she will be fair about it . . . Flexible is a word I also apply to her: firm and fair and flexible.
>
> (Senior Leader)

Phases

Defining the vision was an important priority in the early, foundational phase, along with the high expectations, which were often a feature of creating academic optimism and renewing hope for the future. The focus on teaching and learning was evident throughout, as was the focus on pupil behaviour. This head identified five phases of her leadership success during her 16 years of headship of the school. As mentioned in the previous chapter, it was not uncommon for heads to identify up to five development phases, and these were grouped in the cross-case analysis to highlight the strategies typical of the early, middle and later phases of school improvement.

Alongside the distribution of leadership to a small team, the focus on pedagogical approaches was first apparent in the early phase of headship, although it continued to feature in the middle phase. 'Enhancing teacher and teaching quality' also featured in both the early, middle and later phases through observations and discussions with staff. This illustrates a difference in approach between the early foundational and later enrichment phase, in which the head also demonstrated a higher level of trust and consultation with staff through a higher level of leadership distribution. Leadership responsibilities were not, however, distributed to the pupils until the later phase when pupil voice was given a higher priority. The use of internally led professional learning and development was cited as being important, and typically external courses were not given the same priority. This internal training included support staff, with particular attention being given to the lunchtime staff. It was not until the later phase that there was a focus on broad-based systems of integrated care when the provision of a new children's centre caused a new post of responsibility for inclusive education to be established. This also provided a greater opportunity to engage with the community and parents, which was also prioritized in the later improvement phase in this school. Similarly, networking and linking with other schools were prioritized in this later phase. Finally, a further restructuring of the SLT and a broadening of its membership came in the later phase. This was a common feature in all the case study primary schools.

Table 8.1 shows the strategies employed and prioritized during each of the four phases of development which the head initially identified.

Joan's interpretation of her school's own trajectory of improvement was represented graphically. She identified which strategies were prioritized in

Table 8.1 Greenpark Primary: leadership strategies

Strategy list	Phases				
	Early		Middle		Late
	1	2	3	4	5

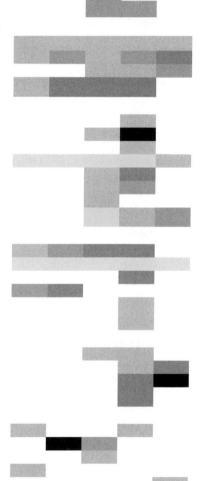

Defining the vision
Creating a vision
Establishing conditions
Communicating the vision

Improving conditions for teaching and learning
School building
Pupil behaviour
Restructuring systems
Developing high expectations

Redesigning the organization
Rethinking structures
Restructuring SLT
Workforce development
Pastoral care
DL – SLT
DL – others
Accountability and evaluation
DL – pupils

Enhancing teaching and learning
Pedagogical approaches
ICT as a tool
Using data
PM and observation
Assessment for learning
Pupil motivation

Redesigning the curriculum
Changing
Personalizing
Enriching
Extracurricular activities

Enhancing teacher quality
Internal collaboration
Internal CPD
External CPD
Modelling, coaching observation
Succession planning
Collaborative action inquiry

(Continued)

Table 8.1 (*Continued*)

Strategy list	Phases				
	Early		*Middle*		*Late*
	1	*2*	*3*	*4*	*5*
Internal relationships					
Building relationships					
Staff–pupil relationships					
External relationships					
Community					
Parents					
Schools					
Agencies					
Agendas					

Notes:
DL = distributed leadership
PM = performance management
The darker shades represent a greater emphasis in terms of either more strategies that focused on those issues, or building on what had gone before through a greater intensification.

each phase together in the significant turning points in the improvement journey of the school. Other staff expressed similar perceptions of the most important features of success within each phase, thus providing triangulation and support for this interpretation. Joan's line of school improvement trajectory is illustrated in Figure. 8.1.

Phase 1: setting expectations (1992–94)

This first phase was described by the head as 'setting out the stall'. It was a period of diagnosis and reflection, with careful analysis of what needed to be prioritized while at the same time making her expectations clear to all. Joan identified five key strategies which were employed during this initial phase. The first of these, which continued throughout all phases, was relationship and team building. Staff were encouraged to work together, and the strength and depth of her own relationship with staff were developed over time. Expectations were set with regard to pupil behaviour, with a whole-school policy established. The final three strategies focused on teaching and learning: first, the head observed all staff teaching to evaluate their

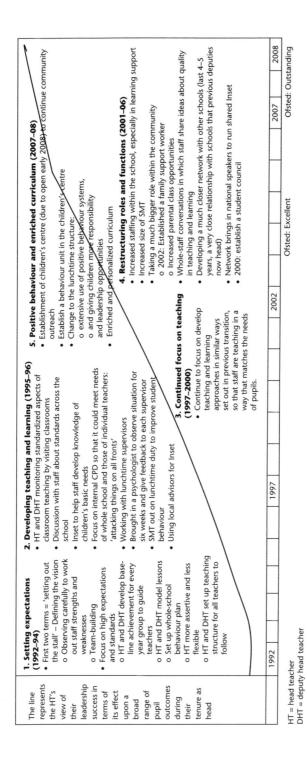

The line represents the HT's view of their leadership success in terms of its effect upon a broad range of pupil outcomes during their tenure as head

1. Setting expectations (1992–94)
- First two terms = 'setting out the stall' – Defining the vision
  - o Observing carefully to work out staff strengths and weaknesses
  - o Team-building
- Focus on high expectations and standards
  - o HT and DHT develop base-line achievement for every year group to guide teachers
  - o HT and DHT model lessons
  - o Set up whole-school behaviour plan
  - o HT more assertive and less flexible
  - o HT and DHT set up teaching structure for all teachers to follow

2. Developing teaching and learning (1995–96)
- HT and DHT monitoring standardized aspects of classroom teaching by visiting classrooms
- Discussion with staff about standards across the school
- Inset to help staff develop knowledge of children's basic needs
- Focus on internal CPD so that it could meet needs of whole school and those of individual teachers: 'attacking things on all fronts'
- Working with lunchtime supervisors
- Brought in a psychologist to observe situation for six weeks and give feedback to each supervisor
- SMT out on lunchtime duty to improve student behaviour
- Using local advisors for Inset

3. Continued focus on teaching (1997–2000)
- Continue to focus on develop teaching and learning approaches in similar ways set out in previous transition, so that staff are teaching in a way that matches the needs of pupils.

5. Positive behaviour and enriched curriculum (2007–08)
- Establishment of children's centre (due to open early 2008) to continue community outreach
- Establish a behaviour unit in the children's centre
- Change to the lunchtime structure:
  - o extensive use of positive behaviour systems,
  - o and giving children more responsibility and leadership opportunities
- Enriched and personalized curriculum

4. Restructuring roles and functions (2001–06)
- Increased staffing within the school, especially in learning support
- Increased size of SMT
- Taking a much bigger role within the community
  - o 2002: Established a family support worker
  - o Increased parental class opportunities
- Whole-staff conversations in which staff share ideas about quality in teaching and learning
- Developing a much closer network with other schools (last 4–5 years, a very close relationship with schools that previous deputies now head)
- Network brings in national speakers to run shared Inset
  - o 2000: establish a student council

1992	1997	2002	2007	2008
		Ofsted: Excellent		Ofsted: Outstanding

HT = head teacher
DHT = deputy head teacher

Figure 8.1 Head teacher's line of success – Greenpark Primary School

strengths and weaknesses;, then she laid out a clear and consistent teaching structure for all teachers to follow and this was modelled by her and the deputy head; she then developed a base-line achievement for every year group to guide teachers and make expectations clear. In this school, then, the head may be said to have had a direct effect on teaching and learning in the classrooms.

Relationship and team building

In setting out the vision in this early phase, Joan identified whole-school and team approaches as key elements. She worked to establish a collective vision in a meeting with staff, parent and governors at the beginning of each year. In building effective relationships, Joan always ensured that she shared her vision with the SLT and the staff. She had a strong vision but was always supportive of ideas from her team.

All staff were included in activities and events in school. Everyone had the opportunity to contribute as much as they wished to these and were given training to ensure they could do this well. This added to the feeling of team-work within the school.

> And if we go out for a meal, every single person is invited, kitchen staff and everyone. When we went out last week there was representation from teaching, cleaning, the kitchens, everyone. We are a team, we are not in little pockets.
>
> (Teacher)

Pupil behaviour policy

At the beginning there was a period of 'very poor behaviour' (Head). Therefore, one of the first key strategies implemented in the early phase was the formation of a cohesive, whole-school behaviour plan which worked alongside a strong pastoral care system and a focus on establishing a calm atmosphere throughout the school.

> Behaviour, establishing a calm atmosphere around school and focusing on the ethos, really beginning to pull together with the whole school ethos, it was really beginning to embed itself in that time.
>
> (Deputy Head)

This behaviour policy was implemented alongside a strong PHSE programme and an emphasis on emotional well-being.

Classroom observations of all staff

Joan systematically and carefully observed all the staff to evaluate each individual's strengths and weaknesses. This allowed her to gauge what was needed in terms of professional development and identify potential for career advancement internally.

> We then would monitor that by regular visits to each other's classrooms with this in our hands, what does a quality classroom look like? So I began then to make sure that there was continuity of progression of provision for children.
>
> (Head)

Consistent teaching structure and modelling

A clear lesson structure for all teachers was established. This was modelled by Joan and her deputy.

> In that early period, in the first five years, my deputy at that time shared exactly the same philosophy as me. We were able, between us, to role model teaching. We introduced consistency of practice, consistency of classroom management, consistency of classroom layout.
>
> (Head)

> We introduced structures for the whole school . . . I introduced structures and we looked at the quality of the learning environment.
>
> (Head)

Base-line of achievement

Since all teachers came together from different backgrounds and experiences in other schools, at the beginning, there was a need to make standards consistent. In this early phase, setting standards and expectations was, therefore, a key priority. Joan set up base-line achievements for each year group and worked hard to ensure staff understood each individual child's needs, always pushing for higher achievements.

> We wrote, because this was pre-National Curriculum, base-line achievements for every year group. We modelled lessons, we set up a teaching structure that all staff had to follow and we introduced this in Key Stage 2.
>
> (Head)

Phase 2: developing teaching and learning (1995–96)

The second phase saw a continuing focus on high expectations for teaching and learning, the associated professional learning and development of staff, and a continued focus on standards of pupil behaviour.

High expectations in teaching and learning

Joan developed effective monitoring procedures to ensure high standards of teaching. These included a rolling CPD programme which included walk-abouts, work scrutiny and formal and informal lesson observations.

> We do try to ensure that we have high expectations and we make sure the children to do their best. It is one of the principles of our school is that every child will do their best, that we want them to do their best.
>
> (Head)

Professional learning and development

As new changes and initiatives were being introduced to raise achievement, professional learning and development of staff were paramount.

Joan introduced a wide-ranging CPD programme, drawing upon school staff and external consultants, which catered for all teaching and support staff.

> We are all involved in different things in different training. Everybody comes into contact with the children so we are all . . . any CPD that we do in the school, everyone is invited and the majority of them do.
>
> (Administrator)

She recognized the need for internal opportunities for professional learning and development at a time when there were few opportunities to attend external courses. This led her to develop a school-based programme that was focused both on organizationally defined priorities to help staff develop further knowledge of children's basic needs and on development needs identified by individual staff.

> In those days CPD was not valued very much and not many staff got to go on these courses, so having our own internal planned INSET matched to the teachers' needs and the school's priorities meant that we were attacking on all fronts.
>
> (Head)

Improving pupil behaviour

In the second phase there was a continuing focus on pupil behaviour. Lunchtime was identified as a problem area, with the supervisors unable to control the children during their break, leading to further disruption in the afternoon. The school had 'inherited' lunchtime staff from the middle school, who were initially unaware of the positive behaviour policy which Joan had put in place. Joan took a number of steps to improve this, including bringing in a psychologist to work with the lunchtime supervisors and provide training, encouraging them to become more involved in school life. This was complemented by having members of the SLT share duty at lunch times.

Phase 3: continued focus on teaching (1997–2000)

The third phase was essentially a broadening and deepening of the strategies already in place, with careful reflection on how these were developing. The main areas for further, detailed attention were teaching and learning approaches and relationship building.

Broadening teaching and learning approaches

Approaches to teaching and learning were constantly being developed and improved. Through the increased monitoring of quality, collective understandings of teaching and learning approaches and their effects grew.

> We utilized any courses that were available to us which were led by the authority. So over time as each member of staff was more skilled we then had a common theme about how we would monitor and look at the quality. As time moved on we then began to share an understanding of what quality means in terms of learning and teaching and again along this path was introduced the appraisal system. It was round about this period I think that the appraisal system came into place so we then improved our understanding of the quality of teaching.
>
> (Head)

Communication and participation

Communication and relationships were also a constant leadership focus. Joan worked hard to ensure that staff felt included in decision making, while still pursuing her vision for the school.

When it is necessary there are some things that she will have to bring into school, or want to happen in school, where, as the head, she makes it clear what is going to happen. But when she delivers it, she does not deliver it as a fait accompli, she presents it as this has got to happen, now let's take a step back and look at why. I want this to happen, this is why, this is what I think the impact will be, and equally, let's run with people. Let's see how it goes, if it works well, let's come back and review it. If not, we'll come back and review it and we won't do it again. So people know most of the time that if we are having a drive of something, there is a secure reason behind it. It is part of the vision, and we keep coming back to that all the time.

(Deputy Head)

Staff relationships and teamwork were also further encouraged through regular staff meetings and opportunities for collaboration. Joan's constant focus on positive relationships was a priority throughout. Pupils were given lots of praise, and achievement was rewarded.

My great belief is that children should also be aware, not only of their successes but also of their teachers' successes. And in the school it is a praise-based ethos. Success is through praise, not by fear and negativity.

(Head)

Phase 4: restructuring roles and functions (2001–06)

In Phase 4, the head sustained existing strategies and also extended her focus to other areas. Firstly, professional development was given further consideration. In addition to the full school-based CPD programme, staff were given opportunities to attend external courses, and support staff were able to attain new qualifications. Within school, staff were given a variety of different experiences to aid their development and development potential. With staff now confident in their ability to make a difference to pupils' well-being and achievement, they were able to work together more closely. This phase also saw some redesigning of the staff roles and restructuring of leadership teams. This commonly occurred in the later phases in primary schools, when leadership teams were expanded and new roles created. This restructuring went hand in hand with a wider distribution of leadership responsibilities and accountabilities. Typically, this was more limited in the earlier phases. The enrichment of the curriculum also received more attention in this phase, with teachers offering more variety, creativity and an ability to cater to different learning styles. This was accompanied by a greater use of data and target setting. Finally, it was in this phase that Joan began to apply more strategies to extend relationships outside the school, both with the local community and with other schools.

Deeper professional development strategies

While CPD that was specific to the school was still very important, Joan also ensured that staff were able to take advantage of courses offered by the local authority. Funding was provided for external training where this was required. A number of people commented on the excellent opportunities provided for support staff to attend courses and gain qualifications to help them in their work.

Ensuring a variety of teaching experience for staff in school was key to their development in this phase: for example, teaching a range of year groups.

> Your best teachers are those that have experience in many year groups and different phases and that have taken on different responsibilities, as opposed to staying in the same year group. I am working in a school where the same teacher has worked in the year group for ten years and surely that is not inspiring for that teacher. In order to keep teachers engaged and inspirational, variety is the spice of life, I believe.
>
> (Head)

A strong culture of learning from each other developed in these later phases. Staff with special skills, such as ICT, could be approached by other staff who needed support in that area. There were also mentors for all staff and opportunities to observe model lessons and be observed themselves, both by the leadership and by their peers.

Restructuring

The staff sense of team spirit grew stronger as the years progressed. A number of new roles were also created. An ICT 'lead practitioner' was seconded to the school to help develop the school's ICT capacities.

Joan was careful to appoint new staff who shared her vision for the school. This improved the quality of the teaching team.

> One of the key things is that I have made successful appointments. Standards will only improve with good teachers and I've had opportunities to make those appointments.
>
> (Head)

Distributing leadership

In this phase, also, Joan began to distribute leadership further, firstly to the SLT and then to all staff. She created a 'flat' management structure which encouraged staff to make decisions. By this phase, then, she had begun to view leadership as something to which all staff should contribute, not just the SLT.

> I have a flat management approach, if you like. As head sometimes I have to make decisions but I believe firmly in staff members recognizing the need for them to make decisions, developing their individual management styles, so that I don't need to be there all the time.
>
> (Head)

> We've always been involved in leading but I think it is distributed more between the whole staff now rather than just the senior leadership.
>
> (Deputy Head)

Staff were fully supported in developing their leadership skills. Leadership was now distributed and everyone worked as a team, with all roles equally valued.

Enriching the curriculum

An important feature of this fourth phase was the further development and enrichment of the curriculum, with an increased emphasis on cross-curricular work, creativity and variety in lessons now that standards and teaching quality had been assured. Training was provided to enable all staff to meet these challenges.

Using data

Also in this later phase there was an increased use of data to inform decision making, and higher priority placed on target setting and tracking. Rigorous data analysis was undertaken and used to set specific targets. There was an increasing responsibility placed upon teachers to work together to collect and analyse classroom data, moderate work and set targets. This, along with the close tracking and monitoring of pupils, allowed the school to better address external accountabilities.

> Well, we are very much data-led: we do rigorous data analysis year on year, tracking through the year, particularly in a year where the baseline for the children is very low. We have to justify what we are doing and how it impacts so we can see that there is value added right from

the word go, even though a significant group of children might not meet the national average. You are so accountable these days you have to have that information in place.

(Deputy Head)

Establishing relationships outside the school community

Finally, it was in this phase that Joan began to prioritize extending and deepening relations with the community, particularly parents, and also to build stronger relationships with other schools. A newsletter was established and sent out to parents and they were invited in to assemblies once a term. There was an open-door policy for parents who were also encouraged to come into the school on an informal basis to 'help out'.

Involving the parents in their children's work and helping them to understand the expectations and targets were also given a higher priority in this phase.

Although in many ways Greenpark had been what might later be termed an 'extended' school since the head arrived, relationships with the wider community were also given a greater emphasis in this phase. Parenting classes, day-care, breakfast and after-school clubs were further developed. The school opened to the community at the weekends and ran activities during the summer holidays. There was a 'mums and tots' group. All these initiatives aimed to involve the community in using the school and for young children to feel comfortable there. There was also a community charity group that worked within the school and organized a range of events throughout the school year.

Relationships with other schools were also given greater emphasis in this later phase, and the school benefited from opportunities to learn from exchange of good practice.

Joan was instrumental in setting the foundation of a strategic network in order to develop expertise across six schools. This provided development opportunities for staff and mutual support from the leadership teams.

Phase 5: positive behaviour and enriched curriculum (2007–08)

In this latest phase Joan worked to embed, develop and deepen strategies in key areas. The main foci were further development of the curriculum, including both more enrichment and the development of a more personalized curriculum, and embracing new national initiatives, particularly in ICT and literacy. Alongside this was a deeper focus on the learning needs of pupils with particular learning and behavioural needs.

Developing the curriculum

The school made a number of changes in teaching strategies which Joan believed had a large impact on the school's success. These included new approaches in ICT and initiatives such as 'boxing clever' and Ros Wilson's 'big writing'.[1] The curriculum was more finely tailored to meet the pupils' needs through identifying barriers that impeded student learning and employing more curriculum integration. There was also development in the transition process between Key Stage 1 and Key Stage 2.

There was an ever wider range of extracurricular provision at the school, including summer camps, breakfast clubs, lunchtime games and a range of after-school activities relating to the school's aim of promoting social and emotional well-being. There remained a strong focus on PHSE and on the 'Excellence and Enjoyment' agenda.[2] There was a strong focus on a play-based curriculum at the Foundation stage and also at Key Stage 1. Independent and personalized learning were important features of the head's vision and cross-curricular work was constantly being developed.

Continued focus on pupil behaviour

With the recent opening of a children's centre[3] in 2008 the school was now able to offer even better provision for teaching and learning for both pupils and their parents. Behaviour strategies were enhanced by the opening of the behaviour unit within the Children's Centre.

Another key feature of the deepening of the behaviour strategies was the development of pupil voice and distribution of leadership to pupils. Pupil park helpers, lunchtime supervisors and planners for sports tournaments after the national tests were introduced. Pupil voice was heard and listened to in the school through an active student council.

The layering of leadership

When this example of a line of improvement is examined, it is clear that Joan was able to introduce new strategies within each phase, while continuing to build on strategies that were already in place. Team building and focusing on

---

[1] New methodologies and initiatives for teaching punctuation in primary school.

[2] One of the five elements of the Every Child Matters agenda.

[3] Children's centres provide not only an early years curriculum for nursery children, but also holistic support for parents, families and the community. They were introduced in 2003 under the Labour Government 1997–2010 with a particular focus on deprived areas as a means of promoting interagency working and supporting children and families to give children a better start to life.

pupil behaviour were not established in Phase 1 only to be abandoned in subsequent phases. On the contrary, these were important features throughout and, although they were given more emphasis in some phases than others, they were constant characteristics of the leadership approach. However, as the positive effects of these strategies grew, and became more established within the school, Joan was able to introduce or place more emphasis upon others, which were built on the foundations laid in Phase 1. In establishing new priorities, without losing sight of her original objectives, Joan demonstrates what we identified as 'layered leadership', typical of the successful heads in this project.

Figure 8.2 represents graphically the way that Joan built on her strategic actions in each phase, so that by the fifth phase she was confidently able to develop new strategies which relied upon the continuing successful effects of previous priorities. A clear example of this was the way that leadership was distributed only when the foundations of good relationships, opportunities for professional development and an understanding of high expectations were all safely in place. Similarly, the introduction of an enriched and creative curriculum could only be successful because it was underpinned by a consistent teaching structure and well-established teaching and learning approaches. It was this layered approach to leadership that enabled Joan to have a positive influence on pupil outcomes.

Eyhampton High School

Eyhampton is a 13 to 19 mixed comprehensive school, designated as having a specialism in sport.[4] It was situated in an area of high industrial deprivation, where few parents had a history of accessing further education. Aspirations and academic expectations in the community were typically low, although students came from a range of backgrounds. At the time of our visits the school was below average size with 793 pupils on the roll. It provided a range of opportunities for trips and visits, opportunities for achievement through sport, opportunities for performance through theatre and music arts, and opportunities for citizenship through involvement in a range of community activities.

The school was struggling and had low attainment, poor behaviour, a poor reputation locally and a poor inspection report when Graham arrived, and he felt that strong authoritarian leadership was what was needed at that time in order to raise aspirations and change the under-achieving school culture. He had worked as a modern foreign languages teacher and senior leader in a number of schools in a different region of England before joining this school

---

[4] Specialist schools had been promoted as a means of raising standards under successive governments since the mid-1990s in England. Schools received extra resources and support when designated.

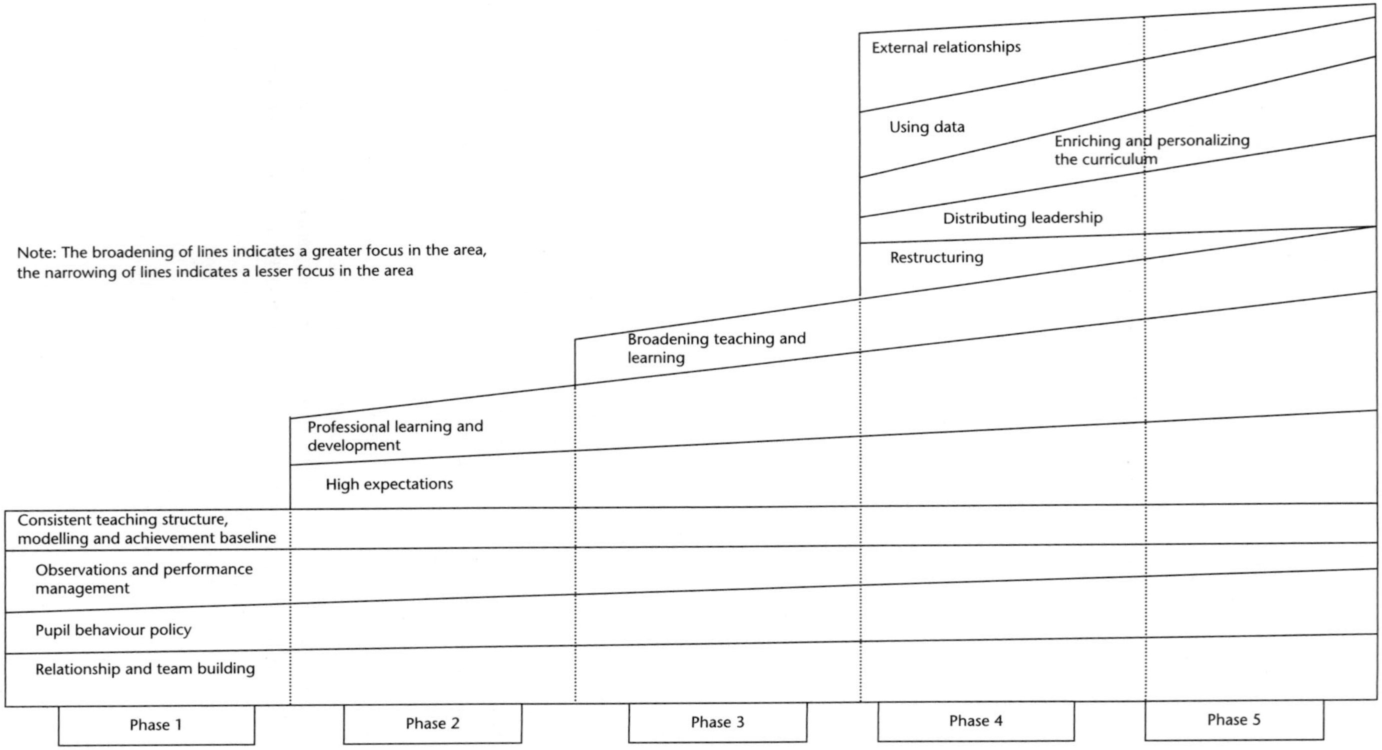

Note: The broadening of lines indicates a greater focus in the area, the narrowing of lines indicates a lesser focus in the area

External relationships

Using data

Enriching and personalizing the curriculum

Distributing leadership

Restructuring

Broadening teaching and learning

Professional learning and development

High expectations

Consistent teaching structure, modelling and achievement baseline

Observations and performance management

Pupil behaviour policy

Relationship and team building

Phase 1	Phase 2	Phase 3	Phase 4	Phase 5

Figure 8.2 Layering leadership strategies: Greenpark Primary School

ten years previously. Over the years, he had worked hard and successfully to change the initially poor physical environment of the school to make it more conducive for teaching and learning. He had established an open-door policy with staff and pupils and high expectations of all, supported by school-wide academic and behaviour systems, and a senior leadership team with shared educational values. He was visible around the school, had a strong presence, and continued to work hard to sustain a friendly but purposeful ethos. In 2006 the leadership of the head and senior staff was described as outstanding by Ofsted, and by 2010 the school itself achieved an overall grade of outstanding.

Head's attributes

Open and visible

Interviews revealed that the staff experienced the head's leadership style as very open, with a strong SLT and an open-door policy.

The head was also described by key staff as 'very visible'. Although he no longer taught, he was seen as being closely involved in the day-to-day activities in the school and as approachable by staff and students. He also paid great attention to the quality of teaching and appointment of teachers.

> The head is very visible in school and at the gates. He's approachable through the school council and assemblies. Pupils see him as someone who could be trusted and know he's pushing the school forward.
>
> (Key Staff)

> The head leads from the front and has strong opinions on the direction he wants the school to go in. He's interested in all aspects of the school and knows what's going on. You see him around the school, although he doesn't teach any more. He talks to pupils and stands at the school gate at the beginning and end of the day.
>
> (Key Staff)

> We see him sometimes. He sits and eats his dinner with the kids, which I think is really nice, and he goes out on the gate, so you do see him around the school, but he's very much sitting in his office figuring out what he can do next. So the things about and the things he employs, the kids get the benefit from. So you do see him, it's not in a visual way, more in actions, things that happen.
>
> (Teacher)

Striving for improvement

Graham was always striving for improvement. If he achieved success in one area, he would look for another area in need of attention.

> There are bound to be limits on what we can achieve, but we can always do better than we're doing now, so it's a matter of pushing those boundaries all the time, and there's always going to be an area in the school which is weaker than it should be.
>
> (Head)

> But that preparedness is finding alternative solutions to what appears unsolvable. Finding a way round things. So that's a characteristic.
>
> (Assistant Head)

High expectations

Graham was described by his staff as very competent, with high expectations of himself and others.

> The leadership of the head teacher is excellent. He's on the ball and knows where he wants the school to go and wants people to get involved.
>
> (Head of Department)

> He's very reflective, he's got a very clear vision . . . he has developed and is developing more what I would call a human approach. . . . He's very straight, if he likes what you're doing, he will say; if he doesn't like what you're doing, he will say, but he doesn't put you down.
>
> (Teacher)

Clear vision

Graham had a very clear vision of what he wanted for the school and he was effective in communicating this to the staff.

> I think the head's got a very clear vision, and I think that's a major influence. I think from the top things are filtered down in a very clear way; we have no doubt about what expectations are and how we deal with them as a school, and because we see ourselves as being successful with the pupils that we have through our door, then I think that spurs you on, so you do appreciate that that is working . . . There are clear expectations of high standards and I think from that everything kind of gels together from there.
>
> (Head of Department)

Team-building skills

The head himself saw his team-building skills as an important part of his leadership which had a direct effect on raising pupil outcomes. The staff also recognized his 'ability to build teams'.

The ability to be a figurehead, very much so in the early years but now deliberately less so and putting other people into the limelight, but when it's needed to be there. The ability to work with governors . . . Strategic thinking, the ability to extract the important from this morass of detail with information overload that we have. And looking ahead, trying to look two or three years ahead so the things that are going to impact on the school negatively are tackled and raised first with SLT and then with the staff.

(Head)

I felt supported by the head when I came back after being ill. I had a phased return. I wanted to come back straight away, but he said no and he was right. If I have a problem, I go to see him and it's sorted out.

(Head of Department)

Honesty and commanding respect
In general, Graham commanded great respect at the school. He was trusted by the staff, and seen as a good motivator.

I feel trusted by the staff – I put all information I have in the public domain and tell the staff of any innovations that might be on their way so that we can start thinking about them as a team. I don't go behind their backs and I give them the bad news as well as the good news.

(Head)

This secondary school also illustrated a number of the features reported in Greenpark Primary School. For example, here the distribution of leadership to all but a small group of colleagues was also developed over time, with a relatively autocratic approach adopted in the first phase, when the school faced many challenges and pupil behaviour and attainment outcomes were poor. The leadership became progressively more distributed as the relationships and competences of staff increased. High expectations and a focus on pupil behaviour were common throughout and gradually broadened and deepened over time. Graham identified four improvement phases, each of which will be explored in this section.

Phases

Graham demonstrated many features typical of the successful secondary schools in our sample, including increasing distribution of leadership and a focus on high expectations throughout. The use of internal training and development was also cited as a priority in each phase, with different strategies being employed to enhance teacher and teaching quality, such as coaching and observations. As was typical in most of the secondary schools in our study, the restructuring of the SLT was a focus in the early phase, and networking with other schools was given greater attention in the later phase. Use of data to inform decision making in the school and classrooms and monitor student outcomes was viewed as a key strategy in raising standards. It began in the middle phases and was developed throughout, enabling a more personalized and enriched curriculum in the later phases. Finally, there was extensive restructuring of the pastoral care system, with non-teaching pastoral staff responsible for social, emotional and behavioural issues. Marked improvements in pupil behaviour and motivation were experienced by teachers as a result.

Table 8.2 illustrates the strategies prioritized and employed in each of the phases identified by Graham. The deeper the shade, the more emphasis there was on the strategy. In some cases a deepening of strategies can be seen where previous strategies were built upon. For example, the pastoral care system was addressed in the early, foundational, phase, and then adjusted and more holistic strategies employed in the middle, developmental and, later, enrichment, phases.

Graham's graphical interpretation of his trajectory of school improvement can be seen in Figure 8.3 and Table 8.2. As in Table 8.1, the darker shades represent a greater emphasis.

Table 8.2 Eyhampton School: strategies for improvement

Strategy list	Phases		
	Early	Middle	Late
	1	2	3	4

Defining the vision
Creating a vision
Establishing conditions
Communicating the vision

Improving conditions for teaching and learning
School building
Pupil behaviour
Restructuring systems
Developing high expectations

Redesigning the organization
Rethinking structures
Restructuring SLT
Workforce development
Pastoral care

Table 8.2 (*Continued*)

Strategy list	Phases				
	Early		Middle		Late
	1	2	3	4	5

DL – SLT
DL – others
Accountability and evaluation
DL – pupils

Enhancing teaching and learning
Pedagogical approaches
ICT as a tool
Using data
PM and observation
Assessment for learning
Pupil motivation and responsibility

Redesigning the curriculum
Changing
Personalizing
Enriching
Extracurricular activities

Enhancing teacher quality
Internal collaboration
Internal CPD
External CPD
Modelling, coaching observation
Succession planning
Collaborative action inquiry

Internal relationships
Building relationships
Staff–pupil relationships

External relationships
Community
Parents
Schools
Agencies
Agendas

Notes:
DL = distributed leadership
The darker shades represent a greater emphasis in terms of either more strategies that focused on those issues, or building on what had gone before through a greater intensification.

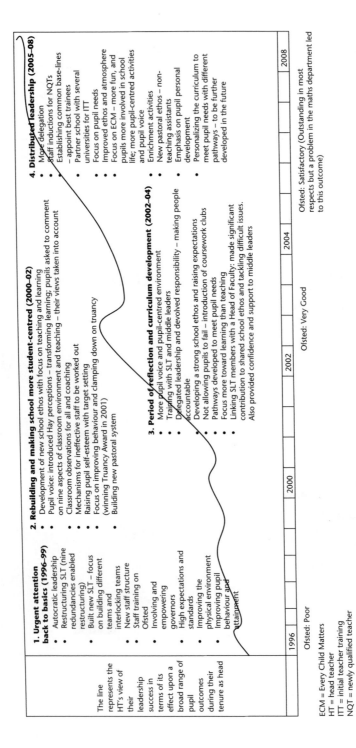

1. Urgent attention back to basics (1996–99)
- Autocratic leadership
- Restructuring SLT (nine redundancies enabled restructuring)
- Built new SLT – focus on building different teams and interlocking teams
- New staff structure
- Staff training on Ofsted
- Involving and empowering governors
- High expectations and standards
- Improving the physical environment
- Improving pupil behaviour and attainment

The line represents the HT's view of their leadership success in terms of its effect upon a broad range of pupil outcomes during their tenure as head

2. Rebuilding and making school more student-centred (2000–02)
- Development of new school ethos with focus on teaching and learning
- Pupil voice: introduced Hay perceptions – transforming learning; pupils asked to comment on nine aspects of classroom environment and teaching – their views taken into account
- Classroom observations for all and coaching
- Mechanisms for ineffective staff to be worked out
- Raising pupil self-esteem with target setting
- Focus on improving behaviour and clamping down on truancy (winning Truancy Award in 2001)
- Building new pastoral system

3. Period of reflection and curriculum development (2002–04)
- More pupil voice and pupil-centred environment
- Training with SLT and middle leaders
- Delegated leadership and devolved responsibility – making people accountable
- Developing a strong school ethos and raising expectations
- Not allowing pupils to fail – introduction of coursework clubs
- Pathways developed to meet pupil needs
- Focus more toward learning than teaching
- Linking SLT members with a Head of Faculty: made significant contribution to shared school ethos and tackling difficult issues. Also provided confidence and support to middle leaders

4. Distributed leadership (2005–08)
- More delegation
- Staff inductions for NQTs
- Establishing common base-lines – appoint best trainees
- Partner school with several universities for ITT
- Focus on pupil needs
- Improved ethos and atmosphere
- Focus on ECM – more fun, and pupils more involved in school life; more pupil-centred activities and pupil voice
- Enrichment activities
- New pastoral ethos – non-teaching assistants
- Emphasis on pupil personal development
- Personalizing the curriculum to meet pupil needs with different pathways – to be further developed in the future

1996 — 2000 — 2002 — 2004 — 2008

Ofsted: Poor

Ofsted: Very Good

Ofsted: Satisfactory (Outstanding in most respects but a problem in the maths department led to this outcome)

ECM = Every Child Matters
HT = head teacher
ITT = initial teacher training
NQT = newly qualified teacher

Figure 8.3 Head teacher's line of success: Eyhampton Secondary School

Phase 1: urgent attention: back to basics (1996–99)

Typical of the secondary schools in the sample, this head began his tenure with a wide-ranging redesigning of organizational roles and responsibilities, particularly within the leadership team. The head had a strong moral purpose and desire to raise standards and unique opportunities for pupils in this disadvantaged and declining ex-mining area. There was a clear emphasis on high expectations and raising aspirations, which continued throughout. This led to a major focus on pupil behaviour and teacher and teaching quality as well as an improvement in the physical environment.

Redesigning the leadership and staff teams

Initially, Graham built a new SLT and focused on building and interlocking teams. He made a number of key appointments in the early stages and then later reduced the number of middle managers and the size of the SLT, to widen participation and make the leadership structure stronger and flatter.

The organization of the leadership team changed significantly and many saw this as a fundamental move in bringing about change. There had previously been a large group of middle leaders, which had become a bit of a 'moaning shop' (Assistant Head). This number was reduced, and heads of faculty were appointed instead. A member of the SLT was linked to each faculty, providing confidence and support to middle leaders. This made a significant contribution to the shared school ethos and tackling difficult issues.

> I have an excellent SLT and middle leader team and now have a positive 'can do' ethos. Teams have to inter-relate. There's a senior management member linked to all Head of Departments so that there's trust, and potential mistrust of management teams is avoided.
> (Head)

Training and development for all

After a poor Ofsted result before his arrival, Graham's first job was to prepare teachers for external inspections and observations in the future.

Typically, he focused on school-based and school-led professional learning and development, which he saw as better value for money than external training. He provided a comprehensive range of training and monitoring for all staff, and in this first phase the emphasis was on raising standards, using Ofsted judgement criteria.

School ethos and high expectations

One of the first of Graham's strategies was to change the negative relationships culture within the school and raise expectations for pupils and staff. Changing the culture and ethos of the school was one of the first key features of his leadership success. This was not easy. However, the head was 'fortunate' as many of the staff who were initially resistant to change chose to retire or move, thus leaving the way clear to develop the new ethos and 'get the floating voters on board'.

The previous ethos of the school was described as 'not positive'. The school had a poor reputation in the local community in the early 1990s. There was a gang culture, misuse of uniform, and poor behaviour and attendance. This culture had become ingrained in the school and 'it was a struggle to change it' (Head Teacher).

Pupil behaviour

The early change to a school uniform and the development of a focus on discipline and high behavioural expectations were key elements in instilling the new culture into the school. These measures were accompanied by the development of a new pastoral system, headed by a member of the SLT to ensure that the higher expectations were accompanied by pupil support and guidance.

> The school has a positive climate – displays, good behaviour, no gang culture. We use 'assertive discipline', which is very helpful. It's firm and gives the pupils boundaries. All staff have a consistent approach to behaviour.
>
> (Head of Department)

In addition, Graham worked hard on improving pupil attendance, which was problematic when he started. This resulted in a Truancy Award for the school.

> Attendance was very poor and we moved it from 87 per cent to 94 per cent in three years, which put us in the top 50 schools in the country. That was part of the first phase, getting the standards up.
>
> (Head)

Improving the physical environment

The fabric of the building was in poor condition before the head came to the school. With a pre-existing budget deficit, the required improvements placed a strain on finances. Nonetheless, the physical environment and resources were made a priority in this early phase.

Some of the buildings were completely remodelled and this was ongoing. One of the first changes made by the head was to create environments in each classroom that were conducive to learning. For example, matching chairs and tables were bought for every room, and displays were put up in classrooms and around the school. A new entrance to the school was a source of pride and enhanced its image.

Phase 2: rebuilding and making school more student-centred (2000–02)

Phase 2 saw a continued focus on performance management, high expectations and improving teacher and teaching quality. Pupil behaviour was also a continuing priority and addressed through the pastoral care system. Pupil voice was given greater importance.

Performance management; observation and coaching

All staff were regularly observed, and strengths and weaknesses were identified. Coaching and support were available for all to enable them to meet the high expectations. Peer observation also began to play a role in development. It was in this phase that the school increased the number of students in teacher training it hosted.

High expectations and use of data

To continue to raise aspirations, Graham introduced the use of data and target setting. This was seen as crucial to promoting higher academic standards and change in staff and student attitudes, and in the school culture. In addition, he established an exclusion centre and a flexible learning centre, which were also used to manage teaching and learning for pupils with a range of special learning and behavioural needs.

> We track the [special needs] children really closely, which is not some-thing that all of the departments do within the school, or are trying to do. And we are then able to send letters home, for example, termly, to tell the parents where they're at, . . . and what percentage, so on and so forth. We're also quite motivational.
>
> (Head)

Pupil behaviour and pastoral care

The focus on pupil behaviour continued into Phase 2 and, to ensure pupils had the support they needed to achieve, the pastoral care was strengthened.

A holistic approach to behaviour was adopted by all staff, and classroom rules were refined early in Graham's headship.

> Behaviour was seen as a whole-school collegiate approach. We refined classroom rules and had the same classroom rules and expectations displayed in each classroom, so we were having, I think, more emphasis of a unified approach to behavioural issues so students knew the ground rules and what to expect.
>
> (Head of Department)

Pupil voice

In this phase Graham increased the profile of pupil voice. He introduced a questionnaire through which pupils could comment on lessons, teachers and other aspects of school life.

A student council was also introduced early on and this grew in its influence over time. The school council was consulted at every level, including staff recruitment. Their opinions were taken into account and had a significant influence on new appointments. The school council grew in many ways and provided the pupils with leadership opportunities.

Becoming a training school

The school also enjoyed strong links with universities, and in this phase became a training school, enabling it to develop and then recruit newly qualified teachers who understood the ethos of the school.

> We have external links with five universities, have 25–30 trainee teachers each year and try to recruit to staff because they already know and understand the ethos of the school, can develop their skills and increase their responsibility. We've had problems when teachers have joined the staff from other schools; it's not been successful because they won't go the extra mile. Teachers here have to be determined.
>
> (Head)

Phase 3: period of reflection and curriculum development (2002–04)

In this phase Graham began to distribute leadership more widely. He also expanded the curriculum significantly, enriching the experience of the pupils and making their options more personalized and pupil-centred. It was also in this phase that the school achieved specialist status as a Sports College.

Distribution of leadership

The distribution of leadership is something that changed throughout the headship. Initially there was a more autocratic style that served to build vision and 'get the staff on board'. In the early phase Graham was described as authoritarian by some staff, but he gradually began to distribute leadership to others.

Graham and his assistant head took most of the strategic decisions originally, but over time this process became more distributed. In the third phase, decisions were taken with the whole of the SLT, although the ultimate decision always lay with the head.

Curriculum enrichment, personalization and pupil-centred learning

As with Greenpark, this phase saw the development of an enriched curriculum. Personalized and pupil-centred learning was paramount. The curriculum became more geared to meet pupils' needs, and pupils took more responsibility for their own learning, having a greater awareness of and responsibility for identifying and achieving their learning objectives.

The most significant effects on teaching and learning, however, involved the design of a new curriculum.

> It's a very complex curriculum but it's one that allows the flexibility to meet the enormous range of needs that we have in the school right from children who can't cope in the classroom full stop to pupils who will go to Cambridge. We've got five different pathways so we've got the traditional academic curriculum, which 50 per cent of the population do, then we have a group who follow vocational, then we have a group who are college-based. Then we have a group with a very restricted curriculum because of very low academic abilities, and they're given just confidence-boosting courses.
>
> (Assistant Head)

Graham identified the alternative pathways and the expansion of provision in the sixth form as changes that had had the most impact on pupil outcomes. Broadening the curriculum in this way to meet the needs of the pupils was, he believed, key to the school's success. There was variety and choice that enabled pupils to choose the route that was best for them, and one in which they could succeed. The sixth form now offered a range of different types of courses beyond traditional A-levels, and there was a flexibility that encouraged pupils of all levels of ability to excel.

This expansion of the curriculum took place not only in the sixth form, but throughout the school. While this created logistical difficulties, it had a powerful effect on pupil outcomes.

Developing the school ethos and raising aspirations

There was a renewed focus on developing the school ethos in this phase.

> The school culture is one of understanding, at the forefront, respect, warm and friendly. It's fast and demanding as well.
>
> (Secondary Key Stage 4 Co-ordinator)

This was accompanied by a continued emphasis on raising expectations. This supportive culture of hard work and respect led to the promotion of success within the school and this was supported by the target-driven culture of the school.

Graham also aimed to create in staff and students a sense of individual and collective achievement and reward for hard work.

Specialist status improvements to building environment

It was in this phase that the school achieved specialist status, which released funds for further improvements to the physical environment.

> We got lots of new sports facilities: the Astro-turf pitch, the sports hall, two dance studios, new changing rooms and lots of new gym equipment and machines. So that's been a massive improvement.
>
> (Secondary Assistant Head)

Phase 4: distributed leadership (2005–08)

In Phase 4, Graham took further steps toward developing and distributing leadership more widely, ensuring all staff were able to take on leadership responsibility. Perhaps the most important change in this phase was the introduction of non-teaching staff as 'inclusion managers' responsible for pupil behaviour and emotional issues. Finally, the deeper strategic work on the curriculum also had a big impact in this phase, with a more highly personalized and enriched curriculum.

Further distribution of leadership

By the third phase Graham had already begun to distribute leadership to the SLT. More responsibility was given to the faculty leaders to run their own departments. In this phase, also, leadership responsibilities were further devolved to middle leaders and other staff. Where the head used to lead all the staff meetings, in this phase he encouraged staff to take the lead in meetings.

They were supported in their decision making, and encouraged to find their own solutions, knowing that they could approach the head whenever they needed guidance.

> [The head] wants staff to think of solutions, not to bring him problems. He gives responsibility to people.
>
> (Assistant Head)

Further pastoral restructuring: focus on learning and inclusion

There were further, significant changes also in this phase to the pastoral structure. The introduction of non-teaching pastoral staff was a common feature in many of our case study schools, and all reported how much this benefited behaviour. With the increased support, the pupils cooperated more with staff.

> [The inclusion managers] are actually round and about the school all the time because they don't teach, picking up behaviour issues, dealing with children who are in trouble, phoning parents, sitting with children in classrooms. We have got three, one for Year 9, 10 and 11. And we put in admin support so there's an admin person in each year group as well. So whereas before, your head of year was spending time filing, etc., now it's the quality issues, managing the learning.
>
> (Head)

The new pastoral system helped provide an environment that was strict and yet supportive, regarded as 'essential in this context'. New 'learning' and 'inclusion' managers focused on behavioural issues and worked regularly with those pupils who required it. This focus on pupil needs was a crucial element of the development of the culture in the later phases.

This monitoring and learning support allowed the school to meet the needs of individuals and work, essential in an area where the pupils have diverse needs and capacities.

Further curriculum enrichment and personalization

Further development of the curriculum in this phase meant, also, that pupils had an extensive range of options available to them, and this provided opportunities for all pupils to succeed.

> We've also got students that are educated at the Eyhampton Resource and Information Centre, and that's for students who are struggling in particular lessons, or need some one–to–one mentoring support. We've also got the new pathways structure in place as well, so all

pupils should have an option where they feel they are best catered for. So you've got Pathway 1, which is for the more academic students, and we call those your ones and twos, because we have an effort grading system. People who are working hard, and perhaps look towards FE and higher education. Then you've got students who perhaps need extra support with maths and English, and that's Pathway 2 and they do an extra three lessons a week of those core subjects. But they're also offered half a BTEC in PE or perhaps an option that's available. So perhaps art could be available . . . Then you've got Pathway 3, which is health and social care, or PE BTEC . . . Then there's Pathway 4, which is for your alternative curriculum. So, students who can go to college. There's different types of strains because you've got those that perhaps go to college one day a week, you've got students that might be doing an apprenticeship. . . . Then you've got students that, we don't want to exclude them; we want to make sure they've got access to education, so there's something that's called the Bridging Project . . . and they're there full-time. They do a college course that would best suit them. We've got quite a few success stories.

(Senior Leader)

In addition to the increased personalization of the curriculum, in this phase there was also more work on enrichment and making the pupils' experience of school far broader and more enjoyable, giving opportunities for different types of learning.

Key elements of this new focus were 'enrichment' days and community involvement.

Just for example, for Year 10 we had a crime and punishment day. So we had the justice system in, we had judges in, we set up a mock trial, we had the police in talking about forensic science, we had a youth offending team, we had convicted people in talking about what happened to them. So it's citizenship and I think it's true, it's for them really.

(Head)

Many teachers commented that the pupils felt 'happy' in school and that it was a 'safe' and 'pleasant' place to be. The emphasis on extracurricular activities and school trips means that there was diversity for the students.

We took all our Year 9 to an outdoor pursuits centre, we paid for them as a school, where they all did rock climbing, abseiling, canoeing, potholing, archery, orienteering, you know, to develop their teamwork and their personal independence when they came into the school.

(Head)

The layering of leadership

This school provides another example of the way that leadership was layered and developed over the course of the school's improvement journey. Figure 8.4 shows how Graham built upon strategies over time. While some strategies, such as restructuring, which was a particular feature of the early phase, did not continue through each phase, others grew in importance, and others formed foundations upon which other strategies could build. For example, the growing confidence in using data, which began in Phase 2, was a necessary step on the way to developing a complex personalized curriculum in Phases 3 and 4. The two strategies then continued to develop in tandem. By the latest phase a range of strategic actions were being simultaneously implemented, though not all with the same degree of intensity. While some had a higher priority than others, it was the context-sensitive combination and accumulation of actions, along with timely broadening and deepening of strategies, that allowed the later strategies to succeed, and made it possible for Graham's leadership to have such a powerful impact on pupil outcomes.

Conclusions

These two case studies are illustrations of the abilities of the successful heads in this study to acknowledge and diagnose internal needs, organizational history, culture and external demands, and to respond to these holistically rather than in segmented ways. In doing so they exercised timely and informed judgements and applied context-sensitive strategies which aligned with their core values.

From the evidence in the larger study, as illustrated by these two exemplars, it is clear that certain combinations of key school improvement strategies are prioritized within and across all the phases of leadership, while others are given particular emphasis in particular phases, and that decisions about this relate to the heads' abilities to diagnose complex sets of external, organizational, staff and pupil needs and concerns. However, ensuring quality of teaching and learning and consistency of teaching practices and performance management of teachers were initiated during the early foundational phase and remained a feature in all phases. Curriculum enrichment was rarely evident until the later phases, when standard-raising issues had been resolved, trust established and confidence of staff and pupils in their ability to succeed had grown. Strategies in some phases built on those developed in others. For

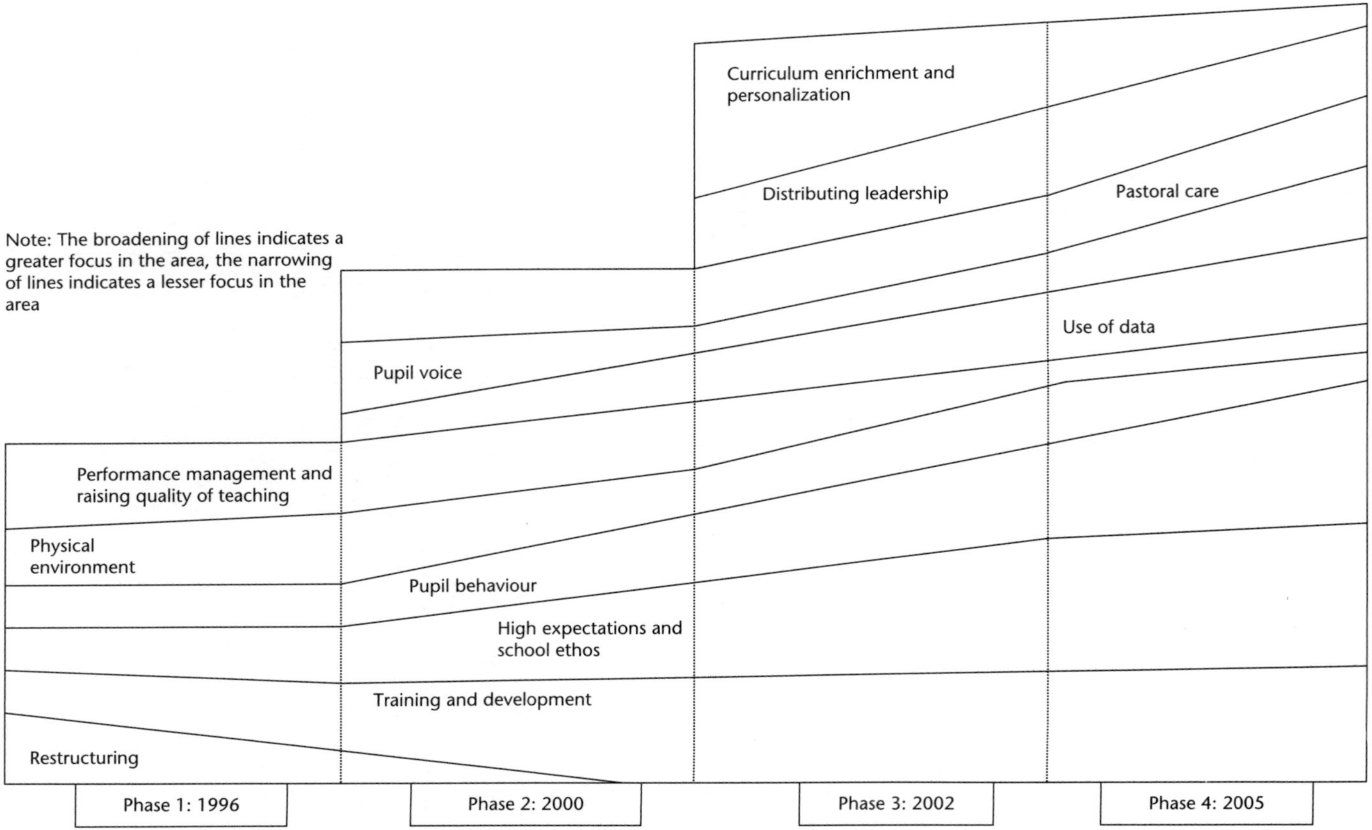

Note: The broadening of lines indicates a greater focus in the area, the narrowing of lines indicates a lesser focus in the area

Curriculum enrichment and personalization

Pastoral care

Distributing leadership

Use of data

Pupil voice

Performance management and raising quality of teaching

Physical environment

Pupil behaviour

High expectations and school ethos

Training and development

Restructuring

| Phase 1: 1996 | Phase 2: 2000 | Phase 3: 2002 | Phase 4: 2005 |

Figure 8.4 Layering leadership strategies: Eyhampton Secondary School

example, schools learned to use and analyse data effectively to inform teaching decisions before they introduced a personalized curriculum.

We may conclude, then, that it is heads' selection and application of appropriate combinations and accumulations of strategies, at appropriate times and in particular contexts, that enable them to impact positively on raising standards of teaching and learning; and that these increase the motivation, participation, engagement and commitment of staff, pupils and external communities, and lead to enhanced pupil outcomes. However, it is important to note that these strategies are not discrete, or stand-alone. Nor do they necessarily end once a task has been completed; rather they develop, broaden and deepen over time, forming a foundation upon which further actions can be built. It is the ability to construct and layer leadership in this way – together with the possession, articulation and communication of certain personal and professional values, qualities and dispositions – that makes the heads in our study so successful.

PART 4
Future progress and prospects

9 Organizational democracy, trust and the progressive distribution of leadership

There has been much writing internationally about the ways in which successive government interventions in many countries since the late 1980s have increasingly constrained teachers' abilities to exercise discretionary judgement in what have increasingly become 'low-trust' environments dominated by external results-driven target setting, external inspections and other forms of what many commentators deem to be punitive public accountability (Ball, 1993; Goodson and Hargreaves, 1996; Day and Gu, 2010). In other words, power in the form of responsibility of individual teachers and schools for decisions and actions appears to have been eroded at system level. In the schools in our research, however, this was not necessarily the case. Nevertheless, they were responsive to the external context. A number had been judged to be poor by inspections or in terms of pupil attainment in the past, and incoming heads in such schools saw raising achievement as a high priority. Crucially, they valued it in its own right, not just because of external pressure. As we have shown elsewhere in this book, successful heads have a strong sense of agency, moral and ethical responsibility for the education and achievement of all students, and recognize that this is best achieved by exercising power and influence through and with rather than over staff (Day et al., 2000). They demonstrated this through fostering staff's authority in ways which were perceived as being both meaningful and beneficial. In their schools, leadership distribution was common, and distributed sources of leadership co-existed alongside or in parallel with more focused or individually enacted sources of leadership. However, we also found that the distribution of leadership responsibility and power between individual and distributed sources varied in relation to the heads' responses to and assessments of individual, relational, organizational and external social and policy conditions or challenges which they identified in their schools.

This chapter will focus upon the nature and different purposes of forms of distributed leadership in schools. It will show how, in successful schools, distributing leadership takes time and is associated with the growth of organizational democracy and a strong belief by heads in the professionalism of their staff. Those in our research demonstrated this by providing, nurturing and developing opportunities for consultation, participation, engagement and the exercise of agency in individual and collective decision making which led to increases in job satisfaction, efficiency, effectiveness, and a sense of the work of teaching and learning as a collective endeavour which encompassed shared instrumental and moral purposes. The chapter will show, also, however, that the success and extent of the distribution of leadership power and authority depend upon the development of trust and trustworthiness and what has been called an 'economy of regard' (Halpern, 2009). Thus, in our research, we found that in the early phase of headship (see Chapter 7), while all heads entrusted leadership roles and functions to a small group of colleagues, the senior leadership team, it was not until the middle and later phases of their tenure, when trust had grown among a greater number of staff, that leadership authority and responsibility and accountability were more widely distributed, reflecting their confidence in the capabilities and capacities of staff and following their strong emphasis on developing people as well as restructuring the organization.

Organizational democracy

Much has been written over the years about organizational democracy in schools and, within this, the nature and effect of relations between heads and staff and staff and principals. Rizvi (1989), for example, suggested that participation by staff in decision making is 'a necessary condition for bringing about greater efficiency', and supported others in claiming that 'participation induces . . . enterprise, initiative, imagination and the confidence to experiment' (cited in Grace, 1995: 59). Thus:

> For schooling, this argument implies that the realization of a school's mission statement is more likely to be achieved where a head teacher uses high levels of participation rather than hierarchical enactment.
>
> (Grace, 1995: 59)

Leithwood and his colleagues wrote in much the same way about the effective uses of power by heads as being for the purposes of achieving ends rather than controlling people, and empowering others. They associated this latter as being directly related to transformational leadership, the central purpose of which is the enhancement of the individual and collective problem-solving capacities of organizational members (Leithwood et al., 1992: 7) Such leadership, Bennis and Nanus (1985) claimed:

is collective, there is a symbiotic relationship between leaders and followers and what makes it collective is the subtle interplay between the followers' needs and wants and the leader's capacity to understand these collective aspirations.

(Bennis and Nanus, cited in Leithwood et al., 1992: 8)

Such subtle interplay was observed in the kinds of collaborative cultures which had been nurtured and developed in the schools of the successful heads in our research and which had contributed to raising individual and collective levels of self-efficacy among staff and students for, as Leithwood and his colleagues point out:

> Central to the concept of a collaborative culture is the more equitable distribution of power for decision-making among members of the school. Especially when the focus on the decision making centers on cross-classroom and school-wide matters, this will involve school administrators [heads] in at least delegating, if not giving away, sources of power traditionally vested in their positions . . . With power, of course, comes the responsibility for decisions and actions
>
> (Leithwood et al., 1992: 142)

The recent literature on conceptualizing differences in the forms of distributed leadership in schools reflects this. For example, seven of the ten central chapters in the text edited by Leithwood, Mascall and Strauss (2008) offer unique conceptions: additive and holistic patterns (Gronn, 2008); autocratic and ad hoc patterns (Harris, 2008); leader-plus and parallel performance patterns (Spillane, Camburn and Pajero, 2008); planned alignment and spontaneous alignment patterns (Leithwood et al., 2008), as well as pragmatic and opportunistic patterns (MacBeath, 2008). Researchers such as those cited here have often chosen to focus on different dimensions along which patterns of distribution might vary. To date, these dimensions attempt to capture

a) differences in the range of organizational members to whom leadership is distributed;
b) the degree to which distributed forms of leadership are co-ordinated;
c) the extent of interdependence among those to whom leadership is distributed;
d) the extent to which power and authority accompany the distribution of leadership responsibilities; and
e) the stimulus for leadership distribution.

A handful of factors influence the extent to which leadership is distributed. These include, for example:

- the extent of both leader's and staff members' expertise;
- the prevalence of policies and regulations that influence the direction of work in the school (what Kerr and Jermier (1978) called 'substitutes for leadership');
- the leadership functions(s) to be performed; and
- the scope of the goals to be accomplished.

More significant leadership distribution seems likely, for example, when staff have significant amounts of relevant expertise, and when there are relatively few substitutes for leadership in the organization.

This new evidence suggests that:

- It is often some form of external pressure that prompts efforts to distribute leadership more broadly: for example, pressure to improve disappointing school performance, often linked with external accountability mechanisms, introduction of new policies, and programmes requiring new teaching and learning capacities. Greater distribution of leadership outside of those in formally established roles usually depends on quite intentional intervention on the part of those in formal leadership roles.
- School heads can easily, if unintentionally, sidetrack efforts to distribute leadership. Among the important conditions influencing leadership distribution that depend, in part or whole, on what heads do, are: providing time to exercise leadership, acknowledging the importance of such leadership, creating opportunities to develop leadership skills, targeting or encouraging people to take on leadership tasks, ensuring the leadership task is clear.
- Such factors as heads' experience, self-confidence, dispositions toward collaborative organizational cultures, compatible personal relationships, and adequate resources also have important influences on the development of distributed leadership.

The best documented effects of distributed leadership in the literature concern its contribution to school improvement processes (e.g., Harris and Muijs, 2004) and the amelioration of the often negative effects on schools of leadership succession (Fink and Brayman, 2006). Mascall, Moore and Jantzi (2008) have reported new evidence confirming both the negative effects of many leadership successions and the promise of distributed leadership as an antidote. Moreover, Mascall, Leithwood, Strauss and Sacks (2008) found a significant relationship between a co-ordinated form of leadership distribution which they label 'planned alignment' and a teacher variable labelled 'academic optimism' (Hoy, Hoy and Kurz, 2008). Planned alignment entails members of a leadership group planning their actions together, periodically reviewing their impact and revising accordingly. Academic optimism was measured as a composite of teacher trust, teacher efficacy and organizational citizenship behaviour, each of which has been significantly associated with student achievement.

Trust leadership

In many countries schools as organizations operate within external environments in which, it is claimed, the pace of life, the resources which people, neighbourhoods and families once had to organize and support themselves to deal with problems have 'gone into steady decline' (Putnam, in Hardin, 2006: 4) as 'activities which isolate us from one another have steadily increased' (Seldon, 2004: 34). One consequence of the increase in the pace, intensity and complexity of life in the twenty-first century is that the kinds of face-to-face interactions which are demanded for individuals to be able to manage this have declined. This, in turn, has led to a decrease in trust. One example of this is to be found in the increase in bureaucratic accountability measures which have been put in place in public services and which, since the late 1980s, have led to what O'Neill (2002) terms a 'culture of suspicion', although this is not true of all countries. In Scandinavian countries, for example, social disengagement and the corrosion of trust associated with society in the USA and the UK are contrasted with so-called 'solidaristic individualism', in which social interactions and social trust have increased (Halpern, 2009: 10). However, even in Sweden the free school movement – where parents run schools – and the challenges faced by the state to fund parents' choices to educate their children in private schools indicate that trust in public education has declined. It is in this context that most leaders in English schools and those in many other developed countries including the USA, Canada, Australia and New Zealand find themselves. This chapter now discusses:

- how successful heads build and sustain trust (aka social capital) progressively, according to their judgements of individual, relational and organizational readiness; and
- the reciprocal relationship between trust and trustworthiness.

Finally, it places trust and the economy of regard in the context not only of the school as an organization in its own right but also of the school as an important microcosm of society in which heads potentially exercise immense power and influence.

As role models, leaders across society must meet two key criteria of trustworthiness: behave ethically and be technically proficient. The

> power of leaders to build or destroy trust is vast. Without honesty and
> competence, suspicion will grow . . .
>
> (Seldon, 2009: 26)

In these words Seldon captures the power of school leaders to determine the moral purposes and culture (the norms of behaviour, the way we relate to each other) of the school.

We have written elsewhere in this book of the key dimensions of successful leadership (see Chapters 3, 4 and 6) and, within these, the importance of leadership values, but it is important to note that trust as a value and as a practice cannot be forced upon staff and students. To nurture, grow and sustain trust in others requires that leaders show themselves to be trustworthy.

The *Oxford English Dictionary* defines trust as 'confidence in or reliance on some quality or attribute of a person or thing'. Trust is also associated with 'The quality of being trustworthy; fidelity, reliability, loyalty' (www.oecd.com). In other words, trust and trustworthiness are in a reciprocal relationship. It is claimed that 'a presumption of trust rather than a presumption of mistrust helps individuals and organisations to flourish' (Seldon, 2009, Preface), and that:

> Trust builds better communities . . . It facilitates people working together for common purposes, rests upon bonds rooted down at local level – in schools, clubs and professional organisations – and can only be built up over time.
>
> (Seldon, 2009: 10)

Trust and trustworthiness are reciprocal, then, in terms of:

a)   people – trust is the result of a two-way process and it changes as a result of people's needs; and
b)   the relationship of trust with actions and strategies – trust both sets the environment which can determine the success of strategies (such as distributing leadership or communicating the vision) and is also a consequence of these strategies.

Thus, in order to create a culture of trust, it is not only the actions of leaders that are important but the values and virtues which they possess, articulate and communicate. In our research, we found that these included those said to be fundamental to teaching: honesty, courage, care, fairness and practical wisdom (Sockett, 1993: 62).

> Teaching necessarily demands these virtues – although many other virtues may be contingently significant. First, since teachers deal in knowledge and trade in truth, questions of honesty and deceit are part

of the logic of their situation. Second, both learning and teaching involve facing difficulty and taking intellectual and psychological risks; that demands courage. Third, teachers are responsible for the development of persons, a process demanding infinite care for the individual. Fourth, fairness is necessary to the operation of rules in democratic institutions or, indeed, in one-to-one relationships. Finally, practical wisdom is essential to the complex process teaching is and, of course, may well demand the expertise of those virtues (such as patience) that are contingent to the teaching situation.

(Sockett, 1993: 62–3)

Since trust relies on the values and attributes of another person, people or group, their predispositions and reactions, it cannot be viewed as simply a characteristic. There are qualities that contribute toward the creation of trust, but these interact constantly with other variables to create an environment for improvement, making trust 'a necessary ingredient for cooperative action' (Seashore Louis, 2007: 3). Trust is an individual, relational and organizational concept, and its presence and repeated enactment are as vital to successful school improvement as any expression of values, attributes and the decisions which heads may make. Indeed, it cannot be fully separated from any of these elements of leadership. Indeed, research has suggested that 'trust in leaders both determines organizational performance and is a product of organizational performance' (Seashore Louis, 2007: 4).

Seashore Louis notes a number of behaviours that leaders and followers identify as central to a trusting relationship. Not only are these qualities that a leader must have, but they must also manifest themselves in the chosen behaviours and actions. We can compare these to a similar set of 'trust-generating qualities' suggested by Fullan (see Table 9.1). These may be demonstrated through almost all strategic actions taken; they must be central to everything heads do from the outset if their actions are to be successful.

There is a clear interplay, then, between heads' qualities or attributes and the development of trust. Seashore Louis suggests that 'teachers' trust in administrators is based on behaviour and . . . teachers do not clearly discriminate between interpersonal behaviours (caring, concern, respectfulness) and

Table 9.1 Trust-generating qualities – creating a trusting relationship

• Integrity (honesty and openness)	• Integrity
• Concern (regard for others)	• Personal regard for others
• Competence	• Competence
• Reliability (consistency)	• Respect
(Seashore Louis, 2007: 4)	(Fullan 2003: 59)

administrative competence and reliability in initiating and orchestrating a complex change' (Seashore Louis, 2007: 17–18).

Whitaker (1993) uses MacGregor's (1960) two theories about human behaviour to distinguish between different assumptions that leaders hold about their staff. Theory X states that 'people dislike work and try to avoid it. They have to be bribed, coerced and controlled, and even threatened with punishment to perform adequately' (Whitaker, 1993: 30). Conversely, Theory Y claims that 'people do like work and don't have to be forced or threatened. If allowed to pursue objectives to which they are committed most people will work hard and not only accept responsibility, but actively seek it' (Whitaker, 1993: 30–1).

> The heart of both the practice and strategy of building trust is first building self-confidence and self-trust: trust in one's own abilities, skills, knowledge, preparation and know how, as well as trust in one's own body and body language, impulses, emotions, self-control, moods, thinking, intelligence and sensitivity to others.
>
> (Solomon and Flores, 2001: 121)

A leader holding the assumptions of Theory X is likely to be predisposed to establishing hierarchical leadership structures, will delegate some tasks, but in a 'functional' way and accompanied by tough performance management, short lines of upward accountability and a clear intolerance of incompetence. In other words, where leadership is distributed, it will be in the context of low-trust environments. Theory-X heads 'will tend to build management structures and systems designed to: direct the efforts of staff; control their actions; modify their behaviour to fit organizational needs'; they will often use language of 'persuasion; reward or punishment; instruction and command' (Whitaker, 1993: 31). Leaders who take a Theory-Y approach, however, tend to 'build management structures and systems designed to: make it possible for people to develop; seek responsibility; take risks; set ambitious targets and challenges' (Whitaker, 1993: 31). This latter was clearly demonstrated in our case study schools:

> I allow people to make decisions, the area that they are responsible for. If they make mistakes, they make mistakes. I'm prepared to accept that as part of the risk element of leadership. I think people respond to that well, once they have started to understand that they can make decisions in their own area of responsibility they become more confident, they, I think, believe in distributed leadership themselves. That impacts further down the school.
>
> (Secondary Head)

An assistant head commented on his head of 12 years and how he encouraged risk-taking in a supportive way, designed to build trust:

There's no blame basically. If the Head does encourage risk-taking, then he does and if it doesn't work, then it's not taken in a negative way. He's done it in a supportive way.

(Secondary Assistant Head)

Whitaker notes, however, that 'No single style of management can be regarded as relevant to all situations. What is needed is behaviour appropriate to the needs and circumstances of varying situations' (Whitaker, 1993: 31). Indeed, it may be difficult for an incoming head who is predisposed to Theory-Y values to follow a head with Theory-X values, and people may initially treat the new head with mistrust. Whitaker suggests that 'To gain support it is necessary to overcome this powerful inheritance factor first by explaining your beliefs, concerns, assumptions and expectations and then making your interpersonal style as consistent as possible with these' (Whitaker, 1993: 33). This primary school head from our research articulates well the importance of setting out her values and beliefs at the outset and how this contributed toward a trusting environment.

And things kind of developed and sparked something else off, so the environment was definitely that key thing and then when it was the first Inset day, and I talked to the staff, I talked a lot about my beliefs and my expectations and I suppose I felt that trust was a huge part of a successful school and that I acknowledged that I'd just come out of the classroom as well, and what it was like in the classroom.

(Primary Head)

Progressive distribution

A new trust environment usually requires an initial conscious act of will, but then becomes a habit; only when challenged or violated does trust become a visible issue again.

(Seldon, 2009: 2)

Successful heads recognize that building successful leadership takes time and depends upon the establishment and maintenance of individual and collective vision, hope and optimism, high expectations and repeated acts of leadership integrity in order to nurture, broaden and deepen individual, relational and organizational trust. The extent and depth of initial or provisional trust will depend upon a number of past as well as present factors, including the organization's current culture and past history of improvement. As we have seen, if the head inherits a school whose members have a history of experiencing distrustful relationships, then it may take longer than if the reverse were to be the case.

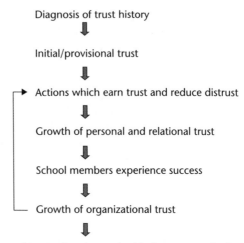

Figure 9.1   The progressive distribution of trust

Figure 9.1 illustrates the ways in which trust may be progressively distributed and embedded.

This is not a linear process, since the growth of trust in human relationships exercised in policy, social and personal contexts of change will be subject to many challenges, not all of which may be anticipated. Thus, Figure 9.1 illustrates the need for each growth point of trust to be followed by further actions which earn trust and reduce distrust. It is the interplay of trust and trustworthiness that creates reciprocal trust and the development of a culture of trust within the school. This is a constant process, and the head must continually assess his or her 'trustworthy reputation' (Seashore Louis, 2007: 18). Heads must scrutinize 'how their own behaviour and context are interpreted by others . . . [and develop] strategies for getting honest assessments' (Seashore Louis, 2007: 19). This may include being reflective, self-critical and communicative with staff.

Our data suggest that while successful heads hold Theory Y values, they enact these in different ways and over different time periods according to their diagnosis of past and present practices of trust in the school and based upon their judgements of the willingness, abilities and capacities of staff and students to engage in distributed leadership as one of a number of expressions of a culture of trust. It is notable that heads in schools that were deemed to have severe problems adopted different approaches and strategies to build staff relationships and capacities before distributing leadership more widely.

The main significant change, I think, is the transformation of the school ethos. When I came here 12 years ago I had inherited a very stressed-out staff and I told them that my main aim was to de-stress them. They didn't believe me at the time because the previous head teacher had a totally different leadership style from mine. So it took them months and months, and after six months I told them, 'Surely I can't be such a good actor, what you see is what you're getting'. So when Ofsted came three years ago they said, 'You have a very happy school'. . . . I think it's a happy school, because I believe for you to learn properly you have to be comfortable, safe and happy. I think that's the biggest contribution I've been able to make, and that's due not to anything written but that happens to be part of my psyche and I can't work in an unhappy place so I try to make everybody happy as well.

(Secondary Head)

Nor does the exercise of trust always meet with unbridled success.

Because now I've learned I can trust them to do it, whereas before I didn't know whether I could or I couldn't so I started off not trusting them. Although it has backfired on me once this year when I thought something was being done and it wasn't. So it's getting that balance of when to trust and when to check, but I would say I delegate more now than I used to.

(Secondary Head of Department)

Elements that were commonly discussed as preliminary actions to generate trust included: 'setting out the stall', 'explaining values', 'communicating the vision' and 'building relationships gradually'. Another secondary head spoke of the ways in which his autocratic approach to leadership at the beginning of his tenure, when Theory-X assumptions led him to keep control and delegate only in a functional way, changed over time.

For the first five years of headship here I was more autocratic because I needed things to be done. I kept people in the loop but didn't involve colleagues. The next five years, I started to delegate leadership across SLT and middle managers. I'm the king pin – I have high expectations of myself and of others. Devolving sometimes means you get high standards back, but I have to watch people make mistakes – people have to try new things. I've put systems in place throughout the school.

(Secondary Head)

Twelve years on he had established a high-trust environment:

If a member of staff needs a day off, it's not a problem. The head trusts the staff and he likes to stand back and let the SLT do the role he used to do and he adjudicates, giving neutral feedback. Any staff can have training, they just have to sign up and go and the head trusts that it will be good for the school.

(Secondary Assistant Head)

Some behaviours will act as significant enhancers of trust:

1 perceived influence over how decisions are made
2 a sense that decision makers take stakeholder interests into account
3 an agreed upon and objective measure of the effects or outcomes of implemented decisions

(Seashore Louis, 2007: 20)

These actions echo those of the heads in our research in the ways they redesigned organizational roles and responsibilities in the first phase of their headship.

The implication for administrators is that trust cannot be easily separated from expanded teacher empowerment and influence. Teachers are not passive actors in the school, but co-constructors of trust. As active professionals, teachers who feel left out of important decisions will react by withdrawing trust, which then undermines change.

(Seashore Louis, 2007: 18)

Staff often recognize the difference between notional involvement in decisions, especially when the end is interpreted as a functional outcome rather than a personal one. Here we refer to the work of Fielding, who distinguishes between one type of organization where '[t]he functional is for the sake of/expressive of the personal', creating a person-centred learning community, and another where '[t]he functional marginalises the personal', creating an impersonal organization (Fielding, cited in Day and Leithwood, 2007: 183). In the democratic 'distributed leadership' organization, people are not merely seen as the means to an end. In employing strategies that aim to build trust in the organization, the leader will have to place trust in others. There will thus be a difference between those heads whose trust in staff is ethically driven, aiming to develop individuals' motivation and commitment to their work and to the organization, and those whose trust is pragmatically or functionally driven, aiming to get tasks completed on a specific timescale regardless of the cost or benefit to the individual. A person-centred approach to leadership is able to be identified by

[the] creation of an inclusive community; emphasis on relationships and ethic of care; creation of shared meanings and identities through the professional culture of the school; staff development programmes

and arrangements for teaching; learning and assessment which encourage dialogue; a discourse of the personal; reciprocity of learning; encouraging new approaches to learning; remaining restless about contemporary understandings of leadership and management.

(Day and Leithwood, 2007: 184)

It follows that the progressive distribution of trust is an active process which must be led and managed. To do so successfully, however, requires more than actions. It requires that the leader possesses qualities of wisdom, discernment and strategic acumen. Moreover, trust in organizations is not unconditional:

> Discerning the proper level of trust requires wisdom and discernment on the part of the educational leader. Optimal trust is prudent, measured and conditional.

(Tschannen-Moran, 2004: 57)

Seldon (2009) has suggested that such active trust is exercised 'where our critical faculties are engaged when deciding who to trust or not to trust [that] we must make reasoned calculations on the trustworthiness of other individuals and organizations' (p. 6) and that it is 'the opposite of blind trust . . . Trust has to be earned' (p. 26). The data in our research show clearly that the heads exercised active trust in this way but also that such trust was informed, nurtured, broadened, deepened and embedded over time. For the heads in our research, the process of trusting others was not only calculated but also an expression of their values and dispositions:

1   *Values and attitudes*: beliefs that (most) people cared for their students and would work hard for their benefit if allowed to pursue objectives to which they were committed.
2   *Disposition to trust*: a history of received trust and observing in others benefits deriving from trusting relationships.

These values and dispositions caused them to engage with others over time in:

3   *Acts of individual, relational and organizational trust*: the increasing distribution of internal and external leadership influence and broadening of stakeholder participation.
4   *Building, broadening and deepening trustworthiness*: through repeated trustful interactions, structures and strategies which show consistency with agreed values and vision.

In charting how heads continued to build success, it is clear that key components were the structured opportunities that heads initiated in those settings which enabled individual and collective leadership capacities to be developed. They did this by:

- modelling care in their relationships with staff, pupils and parents;
- enhancing teachers' professionalism through CPD (internal and external) and enabling and encouraging collaboration between teachers so that responsibilities and professional ethics were shared; and
- demonstrating that, while care was not used as a means to improve pupil performance, its presence did, nevertheless, have an indirect effect through the associated increases in pupil attendance, engagement with learning, self-efficacy, sense of agency and commitment.

Schussler and Collins (2006), in research with students aged 10 to 12, identified five components of care:

1 opportunities for success;
2 flexibility (in teaching and learning);
3 respect by teachers for students;
4 a 'family' ethos; and
5 a sense of belonging.

These were all present in the schools of the successful heads in our research; and they were foundational rather than functional, part of the core values which they led, part of the conditions for improving teaching and learning.

Relational trust

> Trust is cumulative in relationships and grows with each encounter, so continuity of relationships is all-important.
>
> (Seldon, 2009: 91)

The leader's attitude to trust and to people also significantly affects the way that relational trust develops.

The development of relational trust is essential for improvement. Fullan suggests that trusting relationships must be established in advance of improvement efforts (Fullan, 2003: 32). Key elements include: contact, consistency, doing what you say, showing concern, acting on solutions and not tolerating incompetence. As relational trust develops, it has a significant impact on the effect of strategies employed by the head in the following ways:

i) Relational trust reduces the sense of vulnerability when staff take on new tasks.

ii) Relational trust facilitates joint problem solving.

iii) Relational trust undergirds systems of control in the school community.

iv) Relational trust creates a moral resource for school improvement [Teacher motivation, commitment and retention may be affected by this].

(Fullan, 2003: 42)

The fourth point here is particularly important in understanding the impact of relational trust on the success of the school. However, trust is also built through the layered and cumulative application of a variety of strategic actions. The growth of organizational trust is driven by actions at all levels, but all strategic actions rely on cooperation from other members of the organization. Communication, modelling actions, coaching staff, developing staff, sharing the vision, explaining values and beliefs, making visible and viable pedagogical and curriculum decisions, and appropriately restructuring organizational structures and cultures and redesigning roles and functions all contribute to fomenting the moral imperative needed to improve a school.

> Only when participants demonstrate their commitment to engage in such work and see others doing the same can a genuine professional community grounded in relational trust emerge. Principals must take the lead and extend themselves by reaching out to others. On occasion, the principal may be called on to demonstrate trust in colleagues who may not fully reciprocate, at least initially. But they must also be prepared to use coercive power to reform a dysfunctional school community around professional norms. Interestingly, such authority may rarely need to be invoked thereafter once these new norms are firmly established.
>
> (Fullan, 2003: 64)

Our heads built relational trust in a number of ways by, for example, 'involving subordinates in planning, implementing, and making adjustments in the change as it is carved out' (Seashore Louis, 2007: 4). Trust was built through progressive strategies, and involving staff in significant whole-school decision making. In this way trust became an active ingredient in change, working iteratively and gradually improving the conditions for strategies, allowing heads to move toward more complex versions of their initial actions in the later phases of leadership. Seashore Louis observed certain areas that were particularly related to the development of relational trust including vision, cooperation and teacher involvement (Seashore Louis, 2007: 8). With our heads, these factors were elaborated as cultures of trust through which their schools grew stronger.

It is not, then, the assurance of trust alone which will improve teaching, learning and achievement in schools (though if it is absent, there is less chance of improvement), but its manifestation through the quality and consistency of the leader's values, dispositions, and actions and interactions, as expressed, in particular, through organizational structures and individual and social relationships within. In addition, it needs to be developed in combination with appropriate actions and strategies, particularly setting directions, restructuring the organization and developing people. Bryk and Schneider identified three settings in which relational trust present in improving schools was exercised:

- Principal and teacher
- Teacher and teacher
- School professionals and parents

(Bryk and Schneider, 2002: 41)

Two others identified in our research are:

- Principal, teachers and support (non teaching) staff
- Principals and external agencies (including schools)

(Tschannen-Moran, 2004: 42)

Although Tschannen-Moran found that relationships became 'fairly stable' within 18 months in her study of three urban elementary schools, in our schools, individual, relational and organizational trust were not only broadened and deepened over a much longer period but were a continuing focus of heads' attention. They recognized that trust needed to be exercised and repeated in each of these settings if success for all was to be achieved.

Organizational trust

Trust requires a balance of individual and collective needs . . . a sensitive balance between the freedom of expression of the individual . . . and the claims of the collective.

(Seldon, 2009: 26–7)

Research in five high schools in the USA over a three-year period by Seashore Louis (2007) identified institutional trust as an important indicator of trust and predictor of student achievement: The research identified 'social cohesion' as an important indicator of institutional trust. Her findings are confirmed in the data from our research. In the schools of our successful heads, staff, students and parents spoke of the collective sense of purpose and participation, application of common behaviour protocols, cooperation and data-informed (rather than data-led) decision-making as the norms of their schools. One important finding from our research is that the growth of individual, relational and organizational trust which underscored change took time. While some norms were reported to have been established in the early years of the head's tenure, others were developed over a longer period. Choice and combinations of strategies, timing, sequencing and pace depended upon heads' judgements about the contexts which they inherited as well as their aspirations for the future.

> Trust is established through a commitment period during which each partner has the opportunity to signal to the other a willingness to accept personal risk and not to exploit the vulnerability of the other for personal gain . . . As participants begin to feel more comfortable with one another, there may be a tacit testing of the limits of trust and influence and attempts to arrive at a mutual set of expectations.
>
> (Tschannen-Moran, 2004: 42)

Progressive leadership distribution and the building of trust

As the first part of this chapter has shown, much has been written about the nature, forms and desirability of distributed leadership in schools, but there has been much less which addresses how, when and in what contexts it occurs over time.

The ways in which heads develop individual, relational and organizational trust relate closely to the decisions about distributed leadership. These may include building relationships based on respect, a feeling of being part of a team, a caring, supportive environment with low stress, and at the same time an environment of high expectations based on competence and professionalism.

> One of the governors said to me when I got the job that my job was, in five years, to make myself redundant. Your job is to empower everybody in the school to do your job. I think he's right. Any head who's doing this job today and trying to balance everything, can't do it. You've got to give it out, but do it in a way that you stand by them and take the flak.
>
> (Primary Head)

The evidence from our research is that trust is a value, a disposition and a strategy of heads, and that there is a qualitative relationship between the growth of trust and the distribution of leadership. Both are developed over time. This is so, particularly if levels of trust with a previous leader have been low.

> Administrators need to assess the current level of trust in a building prior to initiating a significant change. If trust is low, trust issues need to be addressed if other organizational improvements are to be introduced on solid ground.
>
> (Seashore Louis, 2007: 18)

For this reason, one of a new head's first tasks is to develop trust and raise staff morale as a necessary condition for introducing change, since 'trust is a mutual condition of a relationship' (Sockett, 1993: 117). However, the head may not distribute leadership immediately until staff capacities have been developed appropriately (see Chapters 3 and 7). How, when and to what extent power is distributed will, at least in part, depend upon trust. Sarason (1996) long ago noted, in writing about the culture of the school and the problem of change:

> The problem of change is the problem of power, and the problem of power is how to wield it in ways that allow others to identify with, to gain a sense of ownership of, the process and goals of change. That is no easy task; it is a frustrating, patience demanding, time-consuming process. Change cannot be carried out the calendar, a brute fact that those with power often cannot confront.
>
> (Sarason, 1996: 335)

Rizvi also recognized that, 'the introduction of more developed forms of organizational democracy in schools will be a slow and locally variant process depending upon existing historical and cultural experience' (cited in Grace, 1995: 59) and that, 'Changes can only come about when the individuals who belong to a particular organization can see the point of changing' (cited in Grace, 1995: 59). This contextually sensitive approach to distributing leadership of the kind which increases organizational democracy was a feature of the work of the successful heads in our research.

While the progressive distribution of leadership by the heads in our research occurred throughout each phase (see Chapter 7 for a discussion of phases of development), its spread and intensity varied. This is illustrated by Tables 9.2 and 9.3. The schools are represented by the columns and the school number is shown at the top of the table.[1] The phases are marked E, M and

---

[1] A full analysis of nine of the ten secondary schools and eight of the ten primary schools was undertaken for this phase data. The three schools were excluded from this analysis because of problems with the round 5 data due to the head leaving the school during the first year of the study.

Table 9.2   The nature of the distribution of leadership across phases (primary schools)

School	2	3	4	5	6	7	8	10
Length of headship	11 years	11 years	17 years	12 years	24 years	9 years	19 years	7 years
Phase	E M L	E M L	E M L	E M L	E M L	E M L	E M L	E M L
DL – SLT								
DL – Others								

Note: DL = distributed leadership

Table 9.3   The nature of the distribution of leadership across phases (secondary schools)

School	11	12	13	14	15	16	17	18	19
Length of headship	6 years	9 years	8 years	12 years	18 years	15 years	7 years	12 years	9 years
Phase	E M L	E M L	E M L	E M L	E M L	E M L	E M L	E M L	E M L
DL – SLT									
DL – Others									

L for early, middle and later phases. The different shadings signify when distributed leadership strategies were employed, in the upper row to the SLT, and in the lower row to middle leaders and other staff. The darker shadings represent more intense strategies, or more instances of distributed leadership than the lighter shadings.

The structural equation modelling (Chapter 3) showed that heads who responded to the national survey in our research distributed leadership to their senior leadership teams, and all 20 of the case study schools confirmed that they did so in limited ways in the early phases of their tenure. Tables 9.2 and 9.3, however, show increases in the wider distribution of leadership during the middle and later phases. For example, in primary schools 6, 7 and 10, and secondary schools 15, 17, 18 and 19, the heads delegated role and tasks but retained control of significant decision making in the early phase. In the other schools, distribution with responsibility and power came earlier, and by the later phase the distribution in all schools represented a much broader spread of power throughout the organization.

> He shares responsibilities with people and he trusts. He trusted every-
> body. If he asked anyone to do something, he trusts that they will do
> it. He doesn't chase their tail, saying have you done this, have you
> done that? He just trusts that we will do it.
>
> (Primary Key Stage Co-ordinator)

The increased distribution of leadership throughout the school was associated
with an increase in trust.

> And he's been here quite a while now, but there were more people
> on the edge, on the periphery, am I in or not? Whereas if we
> drew a diagram now, like a target board, and if you feel part of the
> process, part of the leadership and management of the school deci-
> sion making, even if you weren't a leader designate, you would be
> nearer to the centre of the target board. And before, most people
> would have been on the outside of it. The balance has been tipped and
> most people would now be hitting the target board and not on the
> periphery.
>
> (Primary Key Stage Co-ordinator)

> So I've learned that here about distributive leadership but I don't
> think the head teacher would have done that in the early days, and if
> I was a new head in a school I wouldn't do it straight away. I would
> want to know everything that was going on and I think it might be a
> phase of your leadership when distributive leadership comes in. As a
> new head you don't know how good your deputy or the senior leaders
> are, you'd want to be more involved initially until you felt you could
> let the reins go.
>
> (Primary Deputy Head)

Over half of the heads commented that they had adopted a more autocratic
style of leadership in the early stages of headship, and that as trust and confidence between them and their staff had been built, they had (from the middle
phase onwards) increased participation in decision making through forms of
distributed leadership. This is an important finding that relates to the concept
of layered leadership (Chapter 8).

> One of the things that I learned was that my style through the last
> part of the 1990s, even though I had changed, was still quite auto-
> cratic and authoritative. Too much. What I was doing was not
> really allowing people to lead their own aspect. So that's the first thing,
> allowing people to lead. Second giving them opportunities to lead.
>
> (Primary Head)

In the beginning there was a lot of telling. It was not democratic. I was doing most of the decision making and fairly quickly when the SLT was ready they supported me. Also, I was doing a lot of the lesson observations and then alongside me the SLT. Now things have changed. Middle leaders in the second phase and now teachers and pupils participate in the decision making and responsibilities are distributed across the school.

(Secondary Head)

Creating cultures of trust

In order to create an atmosphere where the head feels ready to genuinely distribute leadership responsibility to the staff, and the staff feel comfortable and prepared to take this on, it is essential to develop a culture of trust in the school. In the 20 case study schools this happened gradually throughout the school improvement phases (see Chapter 7).

I think the work of the senior management team has [been] in encouraging staff to be involved, in encouraging them to question and ask, and encouraging them to be involved and to lead certain things, or many aspects of the school development, because of that they are on board, and so when you do have to put something in place quicker or you have to say no, we are going to do it this way, they will come with you, because they trust you. I think trust and ownership are really important. It does not just happen overnight, you have to work very hard at it and you have to invest in your staff, time, trust and energy, all those aspects, and then I think they will come along with you.

(Primary Deputy Head)

The importance of developing this trust over time and based upon knowledge and experience was recognized by all the heads.

First of all you've got to show that you trust people. Nobody is going to grow, nobody is going to make any personal development unless they're in a world where they feel trusted. One of the hardest things to do is to be able to criticize people in a way that doesn't undermine their confidence, because obviously you're going to have to do that because people aren't always going to get things right. So people have got to feel that they're valued, they're trusted, that they're respected, that they can get it wrong and it's not a problem, and that takes longer with some people than with others.

(Secondary Head)

Most of our successful heads had developed well-established cultures of trust. This is illustrated clearly by staff in one primary school where the high-trust environment was commented on from a number of perspectives. The staff recognized the trust the head had in them by virtue of the responsibility and support he gave them as professionals.

> I have given staff the onus themselves to monitor their subject, the subject leaders. It's all about ownership from the staff. And because I had such a good staff, that's why. I leave the staff to teach. That's what they're good at, that's what they have been trained for. And I don't interfere. I trust them 100 per cent, implicitly. If they come up with an idea I will go for it because I trust their judgement. Like the foundation stage unit manager she came to me and she said, 'Look we have reception class and we've got nursery classes, what about a foundation stage unit?' So we looked into it, and I said, 'Right, I will back you 100 per cent.' And that's what you need, you need a staff that are as proactive as that. And that is what I have got.
>
> (Primary Head)

> I think he trusts the staff, I think he trusts us to do the job. I mean, I came back from this conference [and] I said I think this foundation stage idea is a brilliant one and immediately he was behind me, and he was finding money to knock the walls down, to get electricians and to get joiners in, and he was just 100 per cent behind me. And he is the same with the rest of the staff. If there is anything that they want to try or do, he backs them 100 per cent.
>
> (Primary Senior Leader)

> I think he has an awful lot of trust in all of us, he knows what our strengths are, he utilizes our strengths for the benefit of the school. My subject areas [are] literacy and numeracy so those are the subjects he has given me to lead across the school. I think he is a democratic leader as well, I think that is where I get it from since this is the only school I have been in. In some subconscious way I must have modelled my leadership practices on him.
>
> (Primary Key Stage Co-ordinator)

This comment shows the iterative nature of the development of trust. Looking now at the comments from staff about the head teacher of nine years at another primary school, we can identify a clear process, based on trust that develops further over time and grows alongside the increased distribution of leadership. Initially the head took the lead, but she began to give people more responsibility, let people become more independent and feel empowered, which helps them to succeed. Now there is a high-trust environment and leadership is widely distributed to all staff, from senior leadership through to classroom teachers.

> I think initially she was the leader but now it's dispersed in a way. I think when she first came she took the reins but in a way where we were always involved in discussion, but obviously she can't carry on working like that, and now things are delegated down so people are given responsibility which makes her job easier, and the fact that she trusts people in this school to do . . . I mean delegating's fine but you need to be able to trust the person you're delegating to because at the end of the day she's responsible for what happens in the school, and I think she has a respect for everybody who works here.
>
> (Primary Key Stage Co-ordinator)

> Have we talked about empowerment of staff, us becoming more independent, that's not something I've talked about is it? I think when you were asking me about how things have changed, we've become more independent and there's more trust. I think again after Ofsted everyone felt happier, we got that more independent.
>
> (Primary Teacher)

> Going from my last head to this head I felt more empowered here than I did with the last one, and I think it's because this head's quite happy to give me responsibility. She trusts me. She says, 'It won't be a problem to me. I know you can do it.' And lo and behold, I do. So I think that has a big impact on me.
>
> (Primary Deputy Head)

> She's very trusting. There's certain things where you have deadlines to do which every school has but I've spoken to other teachers and there doesn't seem to be as much as other schools. We probably do more but the things that other schools have to hand in every week, every day, that's not there. There's a lot more trust, she knows what we can do and she lets us get on with it.
>
> (Primary Teacher)

Qualitative factors which contribute to the progressive distribution of trust

There are a number of factors identified by staff which had contributed toward a culture of trust. These included: care for well-being, open and honest communication and understanding, modelling behaviour, friendliness, sharing and collaboration, respect and valuing, high expectations, and collective responsibility for progress: involving everyone in evaluation, monitoring and improvement.

Care for well-being

Staff talked about experiencing cultures of caring that promoted safe, working environments.

> I think that people who work in the school as either pupils or staff are very fortunate because it is a culture of caring. I think that comes through when people come in and it underpins everything . . . people know that we have the best interests of children at heart and that is the focus. That comes through the head teacher as much as anything because she doesn't drive all of the things . . . she is the hub of it, if you like, so she is thinking, well, this might work and it might make the school a bit better.
>
> (Primary Teacher)

> He is very good at backing us up and if we have a good reason for doing something he trusts us to do it, and I would say that his strongest thing because I've been to other meetings and I know that some people do not have that.
>
> (Primary Foundation Stage Manager)

The head explained how giving trust and a feeling of safety had helped develop trust in his school.

> I don't think that anyone learns whether they are a child or an adult, they might do what is expected of them, but that you don't learn very much if you are frightened. What you have got to have is a climate of trust. For teachers it is professional trust. I don't pretend I always get things right; quite often I get things wrong. So you have to give credit and praise where it is due, and you've got to be prepared to say, how can you make it better, have you tried such and such?
>
> (Primary Head)

Communication and understanding

Ensuring that communication is open and honest is vital if relational trust is going to develop.

> So we have got a culture of debate, and because of that and because everyone has their different views, that is healthy. It is not a question

of 'Well, the head says let's do this'; a lot of times they probably say 'Oh no, she's come up with another idea!' It is a culture of debate, democracy in the end.

(Primary Head)

I personally think honesty is such an important thing in leading anybody because if you're honest with them, they trust you and then when you ask them to do something even if they don't want to do it, they will, because they know you're asking for a good reason.

(Secondary Head of Department)

But I think by being very honest, by being very open, by trusting people, by giving people responsibility.

(Secondary Head)

And I think by being very open and honest with people, trusting people, philosophically I do believe that people are all right. I don't have a problem believing that.

(Primary Head)

Modelling behaviour

New heads need staff to feel confident that they know what is expected of them and modelling is a common way in which they do this. It relates to creating high expectations and a sense of purpose in the school.

When I started, I had to do a lot of modelling. I knew what I wanted people to do and I could keep writing it in the bulletin, and I could keep standing up at staff briefings and I could do staff training but I needed people to see it, I needed people to understand.

(Secondary Head)

Friendliness

These heads ensured the 'belongingness' needs of the staff, creating a friendly environment and providing opportunities for collaboration.

Friendly, welcoming, equal. Nobody's sitting up there with a chip on their shoulder, everyone is, 'this is my role'. It's all compromising rather than dictating what people need to do.

(Secondary Teacher)

> I think it is a very friendly school. There is an open door; if you have a problem there is always someone you can go and talk to and I think that helps a lot definitely. The head teacher is a nice guy, he is the headmaster that you feel, if you have a problem, you can knock on the door and go and talk to him.
>
> (Secondary Governor)

> One thing I noticed as soon as I came in was how visible the senior management were and how friendly, visible and supportive, nice little touches like sending you cards. It made a big difference to me because I came from a culture where it was a bit more hard-nosed so little touches like that made a big difference to me.
>
> (Secondary Teacher)

Sharing and collaborating

Providing opportunities for sharing and collaboration also contributed to the culture of trust.

> There is a kind of culture of sharing good practice as well. There is a lot of that now and that school we do a lot of lesson observations across departments. There are opportunities to feed back between departments and discuss.
>
> (Secondary Assistant Head)

> I think it's very much a sharing and cooperative approach, you know. With some of the types of students that we have here, you know, you can't go it alone, you know. There are occasions when you need support. I mean we have a classroom teacher . . . we have a sort of timeout system to support classroom teachers, you know, the community structure is designed so there's support for . . . If ever there's a problem, there's someone there to support them is what I'm saying. So I think the culture really is cooperative, collaborative and supportive.
>
> (Secondary Head of Department)

Respect and valuing

Respecting and valuing the staff were seen as being essential when building up a culture of trust.

> The interpersonal is absolutely crucial in how you respect people and how you, you know, I always think, you know, how I speak to people I expect them to speak the same back.
>
> (Secondary Head)

> I think it's the environment, the atmosphere that exists. I think the ethos of the school and the respect both ways between staff and staff, pupils and pupils, and pupils and staff is super.
>
> (Secondary Teacher)

> Teachers can't do it by themselves, pupils can't do it, say we can't do that without you, there's got to be mutual respect and it took time. Now you go to any classroom and there's purposeful teaching taking place, respect.
>
> (Secondary Assistant Head)

When asked whether giving someone trust makes them more trustworthy, this teacher pointed out the importance of feeling involved and how this helped trustworthiness to develop.

> Yes, because I think people can make their own decisions about things and if you respect them and trust them, they honour that by performing. If it is coming from you and you are initiating it, you're quite happy about that. Sometimes if you get someone saying you have to do this and you have to do that, you think to yourself I don't want to do this, I want to do that, whereas if you ask people what they think they should be doing, then they feel involved. So I think everybody is part of the school and nobody is scared to say what they think.
>
> (Primary Teacher)

High expectations

Establishing high expectations was also regarded as a vital part of the cluster of values in action which, together, built trust and motivation.

> Expectations that you should always do your best. High expectations but at the same time a warm and friendly enough institution that if people feel they cannot meet those expectations, they don't feel they're going to be disadvantaged or picked on, I'm talking in terms of staff as well who'd get support there. To some degree it should be a nice place to work. People spend a lot of time here and it's quite

important that they feel valued, that they enjoy their job and that the children enjoy their schooling.

(Secondary Deputy Head)

Collective responsibility and accountability

A sense of participation in decision making also contributed to the creation of high-trust environments.

> Everyone needs to be involved in that process of evaluation and everyone needs to move forward together because of the shared understanding of where the school is, and that's quite difficult to do at the different levels so sometimes you have to filter that information out and you've also got to time it as well with so many innovations coming into schools.
>
> (Primary Deputy Head)

> It's a culture whereby people are free to make suggestions, people are encouraged to think of ways to take the school forward, and from my point of view I can't think of experiences where staff are actually turned down with anything. So, in terms of trying to boost staff confidence, the culture is one of . . . it's an open culture, does that make sense? Yeah? Staff are encouraged to do more but . . . not so they take on too much.
>
> (Primary Teacher)

> Traditionally people see monitoring of something that happens to them by people who are above them. Because the culture here is so, everyone has been here a long time and knows everyone, it's slightly easier, the monitoring, because you don't feel threatened. There is a trust there; people recognize what your expertise is. So when you say 'This would be even better if . . .' they know that you're speaking not about being personally but that you know what you're talking about. We are trying to be self-monitoring. And that's to do with the self-evaluation process.
>
> (Primary Teacher)

> People seem to know what they are doing and I have worked in schools before where everything is laid out for you, you do it like this, this and this, and it was a very different feeling amongst the staff. There is something about being trusted I think; I think it is high accountability, low trust, high trust, low accountability. I think it's the second one: people feel that they can get on with their job and trusted.
>
> (Primary Teacher)

The culture and ethos of the school, I think, is one of its huge strengths, and it's about giving ownership to all of the staff in the school, everyone having responsibility and feeling that they are a vital part and they are going to take a vital part in decision making. So how I lead is by giving that power to other staff to make their decisions.

(Secondary Head)

I think it is impossible to do everything, you either delegate or you have a nervous breakdown. You just cannot keep your finger on every pulse, you've got to trust people and you have to delegate . . . A very important part of the role here as head is to let people take on responsibility, to do things for you. Otherwise I don't think I would last in headship. If you don't trust the people you work with, there is no point in being there.

(Primary Head)

This head of 26 years was very clear about the relationship between trust building and success in the school.

I see my job as being able to enable teachers, enabling them to take on board their viewpoints and have a go at something but as long as the kids are not harmed, I have to have the confidence in them as a school leader not to tell them but to let them find their own way round it. It's the aspiration of trust – I trust you to do your job, I trust you to work with these children and I trust you to work within the ethos of this school and if we do it together, it gets successful.

(Primary Head)

Conclusions

Finally, as we have noted throughout this chapter, trust and distributed leadership are also closely bound up with what Halpern (2009) has termed 'the economy of regard':

The economy of regard, and the fabric of social capital in which it is embedded, is worth more than the real economy in monetary terms (consider, for example, the value of social care) and, perhaps more importantly, matters far more to most of us in our everyday lives than the focus of conventional economics.

(Halpern, 2009: 16)

David Halpern's argument is that social capital – 'the extent to which individuals and communities trust each other, reciprocate helpfully and are connected to other people' (2009: 10) – applies to matters concerned with national wealth. However, he also identifies other benefits to individuals and societies from higher investment in social capital which might go some way to explaining why particular forms of distributed leadership in schools provide powerful drivers for success. For example, Halpern also suggests that there are powerful physical and mental health benefits to individuals and that social capital affects the educational attainment of pupils, although he admits that this relationship is more complex. Investment in social capital may account for the high levels of self-efficacy, low levels of staff (and student) absenteeism and high staff retention rates commonly associated with schools which are judged to be successful. Our own research echoes that of research in other countries in identifying distributed leadership as a key feature of such schools.

Trust is central, in Halpern's terms, to the 'economy of regard', and so defining the meaning of trust as it is enacted in contexts in which heads and staff work and in which children and young people are educated provides an important means of identifying the ways in which school leadership is distributed in practice (its forms), how and over what time periods. This has important implications for the length of time which heads may need to commit themselves to a school as well as the qualities and strategies which they need to possess and enact in order to achieve success which lasts. Our research suggests that heads of schools who continued to improve and sustain success over longer periods of time had stability in leadership. Even more importantly, it enables us, also, to extend our understandings of the ways in which such distribution contribute to staff and pupils' well-being and achievement and, through this, the sustained growth and improvement of schools.

10 Successful leadership
Contexts, claims and qualities

This book has provided a comprehensive analysis of the values and qualities of head teachers, the strategies they use and how they adapt these to their particular school context in order to ensure positive increases in the learning, well-being and achievement of their students. We have explored these aspects of leadership from a variety of angles, based both on the national mixed-methods research study of effective and improved schools (the first of its kind) which we conducted – the School Leadership and Pupil Outcomes Research (IMPACT) Project – and with reference to a range of robust international research literature.

In this book, we have:

• claimed that not only is successful school leadership characterized by robust sets of qualities/practices that travel well across a variety of jurisdictions but that these are always selected and applied in ways that are sensitive to a consideration of personnel, organizational and policy contexts;

• identified, outlined and elaborated a basic set of leadership practices in relation to our empirical findings and the extant literature;

• analysed and described the leadership values, qualities and behaviours related to different phases in schools' improvement journeys;

• described the sample and methodology of our research with particular reference to how we took account of the context of three school improvement groups;

• demonstrated that school leaders adopt different behaviours that relate specifically to the improvement group the school is in;

• explored the particular differences as well as similarities in successful leadership behaviour between primary and secondary schools;

• provided illustrative case studies of a primary and secondary school that highlighted the accumulation, combination and relative intensity of context-sensitive strategies which contribute to general improvement trajectories in practice; and

- focused on the crucial role of 'trust' as being central to the improvement process and the progressive and conditional distribution of leadership beyond the senior leadership group.

In this final chapter these threads of our work are drawn together, in particular, to discuss the challenges that will continue to face successful leaders in the years ahead. In discussing the progress and prospect of school leadership, we do the following:

1 describe briefly the evolving context of school leadership;
2 enumerate the challenges facing school leaders;
3 summarize, against this background, the ten strong evidence-informed claims previously made about associations between successful school leadership and pupil outcomes based on our research (Day et al., 2010);
4 propose a framework in which school successful leadership in individual schools of the kinds described in this book may contribute to knowledge of successful leadership; and
5 identify five key qualities of successful leaders that not only underpin their success but also enable them to continue to be successful in their work in changing and increasingly complex contexts:
   a) vulnerability and risk;
   b) academic optimism;
   c) emotional resilience;
   d) hope; and
   e) moral purpose.

The evolving context of school leadership

School leadership in most European countries, and particularly England, has changed dramatically since the 1990s (Higham et al., 2007). Taking England as an example:

- The somewhat *laissez-faire* and paternalistic culture of leadership in the 1980s changed radically as a direct consequence of the introduction of Local Management of Schools (LMS) in the Education Reform Act (1988), which allowed all schools to be taken out of the direct financial control of LAs.
- By devolving resource allocation and priorities from LAs to governors, heads in one sense *de facto* became considerably more autonomous. This autonomy, however, was tempered by the highly developed national standards framework that held them accountable for school performance and subject to significant areas of national prescription.

- The publication of exam results and a national inspection regime where reports on the performance of individual schools became publicly available put considerable pressure on heads and served to encourage a high degree of competitiveness between schools in the mid-1990s.
- This competitive environment was mitigated somewhat by the establishment of the National College for Leadership of Schools and Children's Services (National College[1]) and the increasing professionalism with which school leadership was being regarded. This trend was enhanced by the significant commitment to collaboration incentivized by a wide range of government initiatives such as Excellence in Cities, the Leadership Incentive Grant and Primary Networks.
- Inevitably the policy challenges for school leaders have increased dramatically over this period, intensified their work and made it more complex. Two critical and current examples are the balance between standards and welfare – the introduction of the 'Every Child Matters' (ECM) agenda in 2006, and the impetus for school diversity and parental choice.
- Whatever the general and specific challenges of policy implementation, the ability to work and lead beyond an individual school is becoming of increasing importance. Nearly all schools in England now are involved in some form of collaborative activity or networking.
- This in turn is leading to a more collaborative approach to schooling where school leaders are having a significantly more substantive engagement with other schools in order to bring about school improvement that leads to system transformation. This is currently termed 'system leadership', where school leaders whose schools are regarded as outstanding by external inspection judgements are now playing both active and explicit roles in implementing system reform across a number of schools in addition to their own.

In short, the years from 1988 to 2010 have seen a remarkable movement from schooling as a 'secret garden' to significantly increased levels of transparency, forms of accountability and 'bounded', all in the pursuit, though not yet always the reality, of higher standards of learning, well-being and achievement of students. And it is the school head who is increasingly in the vanguard of this movement. Given the clarity of this direction of travel, it will be interesting to see how these heads will respond to the increasing degree of autonomy and deregulation proposed by the new coalition government.

---

[1] The National College was established in 2000 as the National College for School Leadership (NCSL), a name which it held until 2010 when it was re-named National College for Leadership of Schools and Children's Services.

The research reported here demonstrates unequivocally that successful heads have deep and abiding moral/ethical purposes and hold and promote educational ideologies that are focused upon achieving academic, aspirational and personal success for every pupil. In order to influence these, to raise expectations or levels of progress and achievements of those who are unambitious for themselves, heads give sustained attention to:

- the policy, social, physical and pedagogical environments of their schools and communities;
- adult as well as pupil motivation, commitment and well-being;
- the engagement of parents and members of their local communities; and
- systemic commitment.

They do so through the values and intra- and interpersonal qualities which they articulate and communicate daily, their wise diagnosis of contextual needs and concerns, their strategic acumen and discernment, the nurturing of individual and collective efficacy, relational and organizational trust, academic optimism through timely capacity-building initiatives based upon their judgement of individual readiness and organizational need, and the progressive distribution of leadership based upon trust and trustworthiness and a belief in the power of individual and collective agency to release the creative energies necessary for improvement.

Underscoring all of these, however, is a potentially disturbing trend. Put simply, heads in the English study exemplify the increasing intensity of the school leadership environment: the increasing complexity of the work that they must carry out if they and their schools, and those they collaborate with, are to succeed. Alongside these is the increase in the sheer number of hours each week that they must work.

At the time of this research (2006–09) heads' pay rose markedly as did the investment of resources in schools, including improvements to teacher pay and conditions, and increases in the number of support staff. There was a major programme of improving school buildings. It is likely that this context played an important supportive role in promoting and facilitating school improvement.

The challenges facing school leaders

If the need to respond proactively to this rapidly changing context was not enough, there are also sets of key (almost timeless) personal and strategic challenges which our research has identified as being at the heart of school leadership. These include ensuring consistently good teaching and learning, integrating a sound grasp of basic knowledge and skills within a broad and balanced curriculum, managing behaviour and attendance, strategically managing resources and the environment, building the school as a professional learning community, and developing partnerships beyond the school to encourage parental support for learning and new learning opportunities.

Within these broad challenge contexts, in England there is also a set of specific contemporary challenges that stem in particular from the scale and complexity of agendas as more specifically from 'the changes associated with the juxtaposition between the ECM agenda, of the learning and standards agendas on the one hand, and the social and inclusion agendas on the other' (PwC, 2007: 161). These include:

- *The balance between standards and welfare.* School leaders are now asked to retain a rigorous focus on raising pupil attainment while at the same time leading improvements in provision that enable children to be safe and healthy, and to enjoy and achieve and make a positive contribution to society. The latter 'welfare agenda' includes the development of extended provision (including before- and after-school clubs) as well as the coorganization of multi-agency children's services. This not only stems from concerns for child safety and protection, but is also an important strand in national approaches to tackle the pervasive impact of social class on educational achievement.

- *The drive to increasingly personalize the learning experience of students.* This demands, among other things, that leaders embed assessment for learning and the use of data on pupil achievement as whole-school professional practices in the design of learning experiences that really stretch individual pupils.

- *The implementation of workforce reform.* From September 2005, under the national workforce agreement, schools were legally bound to introduce for the first time guaranteed professional (preparation) time for teachers at 10 per cent of their teaching time. This is part of a broader reform to devolve administrative tasks from teachers to support staff, limit requirements on teachers to cover absent colleagues and achieve an overall reduction in workload and a reasonable work–life balance. The challenge for school leaders is to ensure that this supports broader school improvement or, at the very least, does not undermine stability.

- *The impetus for school diversity and parental choice.* Particularly in the secondary phase, the New Labour government up to 2010 encouraged schools to diversify away from a common comprehensive school model toward a wide range of school types in terms of both curriculum (specialist status) and governance (Trusts and Federations). This was coupled with an explicit move to provide parents with greater choice in the school(s) they send their children to in terms of both admissions procedures and the construction of new schools (Academies). Both the diversity and choice agendas have been seen by successive governments as drivers of improvement from 1988 onwards. The challenge of school leaders is to make sense of these initiatives at their local level, engaging with the broader system in a meaningful way while protecting their students, staff and school ethos from uncoordinated or even unnecessary change.

- *The progression of particular groups of students.* These include specific minority ethnic and social economic groups (including black boys and white students on free school meals); students with English as an additional Language (EAL), particularly in urban areas; students with the potential for high attainment so as to ensure they are really stretched and engaged; children with special educational needs, particularly where they are moved from special schools into mainstream schools (as part of the government's inclusion agenda).

In addition to these specific challenges, school leaders are also faced with a range of other issues, including: planning their own succession in the face of a potential shortage in the supply of leaders and a declining number of candidates applying for headship, staying abreast of and implementing curriculum and assessment changes across the Key Stages and 14–19, managing potential falls in student numbers in particular local areas, and also leading schools in challenging circumstances. To this must now be added not only increased autonomy and deregulation, but also the prospect of significant reductions in funding, after a decade or more of year-on-year budgetary increases.

Ten strong claims

So what forms of leadership not only can cope with this evolving context and the increasing list of challenges, but still be able to continue to raise the standards of learning and achievement of their students? This is the conundrum that we have attempted to resolve in this book. Elsewhere we have summarized our research into this question as *10 Strong Claims about Successful School Leadership* (Day et al., 2010). As is seen below, these claims build on our previous review of literature *Seven Strong Claims about Successful School Leadership* (Leithwood et al., 2006a) but have been elaborated and deepened as a result of the research reported in this book. As such, the ten claims provide a succinct encapsulation of those values and strategies that enable such a resilient approach to leadership to prevail. In one sentence, these heads improve pupil outcomes through who they are – their values, virtues, dispositions, attributes and competences – as well as what they do in terms of the strategies they select and how they adapt their leadership practices to their unique context.

Claim 1: head teachers are the main source of leadership in their schools

Head teachers are perceived to be the main source of leadership by key school staff. Their educational values, reflective strategies and leadership practices shape the internal processes and pedagogies that result in improved pupil outcomes. The leadership of the head has a direct effect on teachers' expectations and standards. This includes the way they think about, plan and conduct their teaching and learning practices, their self-efficacy, commitment and sense of well-being, and their organizational loyalty and trust – all of which indirectly influence pupil outcomes.

Leaders in improving schools diagnose individual and organizational needs, and place the needs of pupils first. They then select improvement strategies in well thought-out combinations and sequences so that they reinforce and support each other. There is a strong link between setting the direction and restructuring the organization and between reculturing the organization and improving school conditions.

Claim 2: there are eight key dimensions of successful leadership

Our research identifies eight key dimensions of successful leadership – all centred on student learning, well-being and achievement. Successful leaders:

- define their values and vision to raise expectations, set direction and build trust;
- reshape the conditions for teaching and learning;
- restructure parts of the organization and redesign leadership roles and responsibilities;
- enrich the curriculum;
- enhance teacher quality;
- enhance the quality of teaching and learning;
- build collaboration internally; and
- build strong relationships outside the school community.

Although the sequence, timing, order and combination of these strategies vary from school to school, the visions and values are strikingly similar.

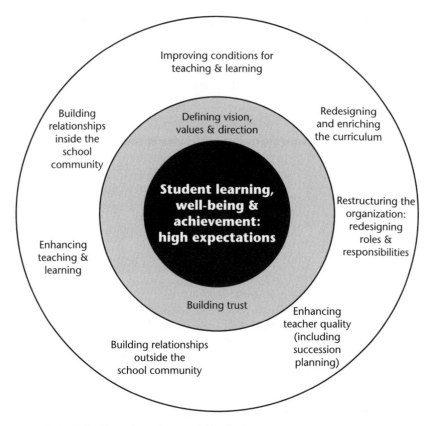

Figure 10.1 Eight dimensions of successful leadership

In Figure 10.1, the inner ring illustrates the core focus of leaders' attention, the middle ring their core strategies, and the outer ring the actions they take in support of these strategies.

Claim 3: head teachers' values are key components in their success

In the earlier review, we argued that variation in the effectiveness of leaders is often explained by a small number of personal traits. Our claim is that the most successful school leaders are open-minded and ready to learn from others. They are flexible rather than dogmatic within a system of core values. They are persistent in their high expectations of others, and they are emotionally resilient and optimistic. Such traits help explain why successful leaders facing daunting conditions are often able to push forward against the odds. Our research confirms this. Data from across the case studies have provided rich illustrations of these core values.

Successful heads share certain attributes and hold the following common core values:

- a strong sense of moral responsibility and a belief in equal opportunities
- a belief that every pupil deserves the same opportunities to succeed
- respect and value for all people in and connected with the school
- a passion for learning and achievement
- a commitment to pupils and staff

Successful heads see pupil achievement as having behavioural, academic, personal, social and emotional dimensions:

- setting high expectations for staff and students is central to developing teaching and learning programmes.
- care and trust feature highly in achievement-focused cultures that aim to improve student outcomes.
- introducing a whole-school approach to pupil behaviour management is considered a positive step toward improving student outcomes.

Claim 4: successful heads use the same basic leadership practices but there is no single model for achieving success

Since our 2006 review, other studies (e.g. Robinson et al., 2009) have identified significantly larger effects for instructional leadership (relating to teaching and learning) than for transformational leadership (which is more focused on developing teachers). The new evidence described in this book is that successful heads draw equally on elements of both instructional and transformational leadership. They work intuitively and from experience, tailoring their leadership strategies to their particular school context. Their ability to respond to their context and to recognize, acknowledge, understand and attend to the needs and motivations of others defines their level of success.

The heads in our research deployed the same strategic leadership approaches as one another, but the combinations, sequence and timing of the approaches varied. Heads use a combination of leadership strategies according to:

- their judgements about the conditions for teaching and learning in the school;
- the confidence, experience and competence of their staff;
- the behaviour, aspirations and attainment levels of the pupils; and
- the experience of the heads themselves.

Claim 5: differences in context affect the nature, direction and pace of leadership actions

The national sample of highly effective and improving schools used in the research was split into three distinctive improvement groups – Low Start, Moderate Start and High Start – and revealed important relationships between school contexts and school improvement profiles. These are evidenced in significant differences in certain leadership practices between each group of schools, particularly in Low Start schools and those serving disadvantaged areas.

Schools that had improved from a low start had experienced the most changes in pupil behaviour, attendance, motivation and engagement. There is strong evidence that schools in the Low Start Group had made greater improvements in changing school culture, climate and addressing teaching and learning and use of performance data during the previous three years – all important precursors and facilitators for raising academic achievement, especially in highly disadvantaged contexts.

Successful heads in disadvantaged contexts make greater efforts to effect improvement across a range of areas – especially pupil behaviour, motivation and engagement, and school culture – because they know that improvements in only one or two areas are unlikely to be enough to secure sustained gains in pupil outcomes. Heads in disadvantaged contexts especially seek to make specific improvements in teaching and assessment, and use performance data to monitor the effectiveness of changes made. Substantial improvements in pupil behaviour, attendance, attitude and motivation are important precursors and facilitators for improvement in students' academic achievement, especially in schools in highly disadvantaged contexts.

Claim 6: heads contribute to student learning and achievement through combinations and accumulations of strategies and actions

Research suggests that within-school variation in pupil outcomes is often considerably greater than variation between schools (for a recent example, see Stringfield et al., 2008). Nonetheless, highly effective and improving schools tend to reduce within-school variation by building common goals and being consistent in their approach. However, although most school-level variables have small effects on pupil outcomes when examined independently, the combination of their impact tends to be stronger.

Heads' accounts indicate that pupil learning and achievement are affected by a combination of leadership strategies which, when taken together, address school culture and staff development, and focus on enhancing the processes of teaching and learning. Among the most powerful variables influencing pupil outcomes are improvements in school conditions, such as emphases on raising academic standards; assessment for learning; collaborative teacher cultures; monitoring of pupil and school performance; coherence of teaching programmes; and the provision of extracurricular activities.

Successful head teachers select leadership strategies according to the context they are in. Of particular note are:

- the role played by heads' trust in teachers, both in relation to the senior leadership team and broader staff leadership;
- the important link between redesigning the organization and setting directions;
- the way redesigning the organization predicts improvement in school conditions;
- the way leadership strategies to develop people link with the teacher collaborative culture, and with high academic standards and positive learner motivation and learning culture; and
- the positive associations between improvement in school conditions for teaching and learning and better outcomes in terms of pupil behaviour, pupil attendance, and positive learner motivation and learning culture.

Claim 7: there are three broad phases of leadership success

Successful heads prioritize combinations of strategies and manage these within and across three broad phases of success. They can be classified under three broad headings – early (foundational), middle (developmental) and later (enrichment).

In the early phase, heads prioritized:

- improving the physical environment of the school to create more positive, supportive conditions for teaching and learning, and for teachers and pupils;
- setting, communicating and implementing school-wide standards for pupil behaviour;
- restructuring the senior leadership team, its roles and responsibilities; and
- implementing performance management systems for all staff – there were differences in timing and emphasis between sectors, but in general this had the effect of distributing leadership more and led to the development of a set of organizational values.

In the middle phase, heads prioritized:

- the wider distribution of leadership roles and responsibilities; and
- a more regular and focused use of data to inform decision making about pupil progress and achievement – learning objectives and target setting were important practices in all case study schools.

In the later phase, heads' key strategies related to personalizing and enriching the curriculum, as well as a wider distribution of leadership.

In schools in more challenging contexts, greater attention and efforts were made in the early phase to establish, maintain and sustain school-wide policies for pupil behaviour, improvements to the physical environment and improvements in the quality of teaching and learning than in other schools.

Claim 8: heads grow and secure success by layering leadership strategies and actions

Effective heads make judgements, according to their context, about the timing, selection, relevance, application and continuation of strategies that create the right conditions for effective teaching, learning and pupil achievement within and across broad development phases.

So although some strategies did not continue through each phase – such as restructuring, which was a particular feature of the early phase – others grew in importance and formed significant foundations on which other strategies could be built. For example, growing confidence in using data, which began in Phase 2, was a necessary step on the way to raising achievement and developing a complex personalized curriculum in later phases. The two strategies then continued to develop in tandem. It was clear that in these later phases a range of strategic actions were being implemented simultaneously. Some had a higher priority than others, but it was the combination of actions – along with gradual broadening and deepening of strategies – that enabled the later strategies to succeed and made it possible for the head's leadership to have such a powerful impact on pupil outcomes.

Claim 9: successful heads distribute leadership progressively

There is a connection between the increased distribution of leadership roles and responsibilities and the improvement of pupil outcomes. The distribution of leadership roles and responsibilities was a developing feature in all schools and was initiated and nurtured by heads over time.

Primary and secondary heads were quick to distribute leadership by sharing new roles and responsibilities across the senior leadership team in the early or middle phase of their tenure. Over half of these heads noted, however, that beyond this small group of staff they had been more autocratic in the early phase, working to build trust and confidence between themselves and a range of staff before moving toward a broader distribution of leadership roles, responsibilities and accountabilities in the middle and later phases of their leadership.

This presents a pattern of progressive and selective leadership distribution over time, determined by four factors:

- the head's judgement of what was right for the school at different phases of its development
- the head's judgement about the readiness and ability of staff to lead
- the extent to which trust had been established
- the head's own training, experience and capabilities

Claim 10: the successful distribution of leadership depends on the establishment of trust

Trust is essential for the progressive and effective distribution of leadership. It is closely associated with a positive school ethos, improved conditions for teaching and learning, enhanced sense of teacher classroom autonomy, and sustained improvement in pupil behaviour, engagement and outcomes. The distribution of leadership over time by heads was a clear expression of the importance they placed on gaining others' trust and extending trust to them. The heads played an active and instrumental role in the distribution of leadership, and this increased the engagement, commitment and self-efficacy of staff.

For these heads, effective distributed leadership depended upon five key factors of trust:

- *Values and attitudes*: beliefs that people cared for their students and would work hard for their benefit if they were allowed to pursue objectives they were committed to.
- *Disposition to trust*: experience of benefits derived from previous trusting relationships.
- *Trustworthiness*: the extent to which others trusted them.
- *Repeated acts of trust*: enabling the increasing distribution of leadership roles, responsibilities and accountabilities and broadening of stakeholder participation.
- *Building and reinforcing individual, relational and organization trust*: through interactions, structures and strategies that demonstrated consistency in values and vision and resulted in success.

Building and sustaining trust and trustworthiness played a key part in the longer-term success. Having trust made it more possible to achieve changes over a range of aspirations, expectations and practices, and heads were prepared to take informed risks as a result.

So to return to the original theme of this section, it would appear that it is the cognitive, emotional and practical capacities of heads that enable them both to achieve success and meet the increasing range of challenges in a significantly more demanding and complex context than heads have ever been required to work in.

The focus of the research on which this book is based has been the improvement of individual schools and the ways school improvement fostered better outcomes for pupils. However, it is clear from the testimony of the heads themselves that as their schools move toward excellence they wish to share these successful practices with other schools. The move toward distributed leadership clearly noted in the preceding pages is partially to support their increasing efforts to collaborate with other schools. In many ways distributed and system leadership need to be seen as the opposite sides of the same coin. The theme of collaboration and increased systemic involvement provides the focus of the discussion in the following section.

Toward system leadership

Collaboration is at the forefront of leadership development. The General Secretary of the Association of School and College Leaders, in an address to the National Conference of the Specialist Schools and Academies Trust (SSAT), argued that:

> The greatest challenge on our leadership journey is how we can bring about system improvement. How can we contribute to the raising of standards, not only in our own school, but in others and colleges too? What types of leaders are needed for this task? What style of leadership is required if we are to achieve the sea change in performance that is demanded of us?
>
> (Dunford, 2005: 4)

This implies a significantly more substantive engagement with other schools in order to bring about system transformation. In England this is termed 'system leadership'. Specifically, a system leader may be defined as a school leader who is willing and able to shoulder wider system roles, and in doing so is almost as concerned with the success and attainment of students in other schools as they are with their own (Hopkins and Higham, 2007).

The concept of system leadership was endorsed by the government in the White Paper, *Higher Standards, Better Schools for All* (DfES, 2005). Although at the time of writing this policy proposal is now five years old, it does give a clear indication of how the landscape of system leadership has evolved in the recent past. Specifically, the White Paper set out the government's intention:

- to develop better career paths for: school leaders who have the talent and experience to be considered as national leaders of education; those with the ability to run our most challenging schools; and those with the talent to be school leaders of the future
- to ask the National College for School leadership (NCSL), working in partnership with the National Strategies, to develop the leaders of our most complex schools – those facing multiple disadvantage, and federations
- to encourage the growth of federations and other partnership arrangements which ensure our most successful school leaders are used to best effect and are able to support our less successful schools.

Following research to map the emerging territory of system leadership, Hopkins and Higham (2007) proposed five key categories of innovative leadership practice.

- First are the heads who are developing and *leading successful educational improvement partnerships* between several schools. These partnerships are most usually focused on a set of specific themes that have clear outcomes and reach beyond the capacity of any one single institution.
- Second are heads who are choosing to 'change contexts' by choosing to *lead and improve low-achieving schools in challenging circumstances* and then sustain them as high-valued-added institutions over a significant period of time.
- Third are those heads who are *partnering another school facing difficulties in order to improve it*. Executive heads provide an example. They are responsible for two or more schools that have entered into either a Federation or a local (often time-bound) agreement focused on a lead school working to improve a partner.
- Fourth, there are heads who act as *community leaders* to broker and shape partnerships or networks of wider relationships across local communities to support children's welfare and potential. Such leadership is firmly rooted within the context of both the national Every Child Matters and Extended School agendas.
- Fifth are heads who are working as *change agents* or *expert leaders*. The focus here is on providing practical knowledge and guidance as well as the transfer of best practice within a formalized school-improvement programme. There are, also, in England, at least three emerging change agent roles within the system whose remit

is specifically school improvement – consultant leaders, school improvement partners (SIPs) and the newly created national leaders and local leaders of education (NLEs and LLEs).

The collective sharing of skills, expertise and experience creates much richer and more sustainable opportunities for rigorous transformation than can ever be provided by isolated institutions. This is the canvas on which system leadership is exercised. The evidence of preceding chapters is illustrative of how our most successful leaders are building such capacity and capital in their schools. This is why in the concluding section we return again to a final reflection on these qualities.

Five qualities of successful leaders

There are five qualities that successful heads in particular seem to possess:

1 a willingness to take (calculated) risks based upon clear educational values despite the vulnerability of doing so;
2 academic optimism;
3 emotional resilience;
4 hope; and,
5 moral purpose.

Vulnerability and risk

Pat Thomson, in her recent book, *School Leadership: Heads on the Block?* (2009) characterizes principalship as a risky business and cites Beck and colleagues, who argue that the growth of a risk society has caused three practices to be integral to the everyday life of principals:

> Risk assessment – the development of calculative practices which anticipate possible risks;
> Risk avoidance – taking decisions based on the potential for adverse consequences;
> Risk management planning – the development of rational plans to be used when risks become reality to deal with effects and prevent them spreading.
>
> (Thomson, 2009: 4)

She juxtaposes these practices, however, with what Shulman (1998) once called the exercise of judgement under conditions of unavoidable uncertainty in which, for example, 'an overemphasis on regurgitation of prescribed materials leads to failure to experiment, to dream of possibilities, to explore potential avenues and to face the reality of making a mistake' (Thomson, 2009: 8). Successful classrooms in successful schools are those in which some teaching and learning risks occur. We have shown in the research reported in this book that among the qualities of successful principals are those associated with risk taking in the interests of challenging the boundaries of teaching and learning. We know also, however, that the creative management of ambiguities – an essential feature of leadership lives in schools – is both stimulating and stressful. Moreover, as well as risk, heads emphasized clear and consistent structures and systems to support and emphasize student achievement and well-being, and reduce the risk of educational failure.

Academic optimism

Academic optimism in teachers has been defined as teachers' individual and collective beliefs, 'that they can teach effectively, their students can learn, and parents will support them so that the teacher can press hard for learning' (Beard et al., 2010). It includes 'cognitive, affective, and behavioural components of optimism merging into a single integrated construct' (Beard et al., 2010: 1142) and is associated with relational and organizational trust (Bryk and Schneider, 2002; Seashore Louis, 2007). It is claimed to be 'one of the few organizational characteristics of schools in the United States that influences student achievement when socio-economic status and previous achievements are controlled' (Beard et al., 2010: 1136) '[it] influences student achievement directly through at least two mechanisms: motivation with high, challenging goals and co-operation among parents and teachers to improve student performance' (Beard et al., 2010: 1143). Finally, the authors theorize from their data that, 'schools and teachers with strong academic optimism have students who are highly motivated because of challenging goals, strong effort, persistence, resilience, and constructive feedback' (Beard et al., 2010: 1143). Our research has found that these qualities also characterize the work of successful principals.

While it follows that academic optimism is a necessary constituent for success for teachers it is not unreasonable to argue, and can be evidenced from the empirical data in this book, that academic optimism is a characteristic which is common to all successful heads too. Indeed, Beard et al. (2010) also associate academic optimism with 'enabling' school cultures, defined by Hoy and Miskel (2005) as hierarchies that help rather than hinder and systems of rules and regulations which guide problem solving rather than punish failure.

Emotional resilience: a necessary but insufficient condition for success

Resilience in the traditional psychological literature is almost always associated with the capacity to 'bounce back'; to recover strength or sprint quickly in the face of adverse circumstances. Certainly (though little is written about the personal costs), successful heads in our study and teachers worldwide seemed able to do this, however bumpy their journey had been at times.

To lead at one's best over time requires resilience. It is an essential quality and a necessary capacity to exercise both for principals and teachers. While the concept of resilience elaborated in the discipline of psychology helps clarify the personal characteristics of trait-resilient people, it fails to address the capacity to be resilient in different sets of negative circumstances, whether these are connected to personal or professional factors, or can be enhanced or inhibited by the nature of the settings in which we work, the people with whom we work and the strength of our beliefs or aspirations.

Resilient qualities can be learned or acquired (Higgins, 1994), and can be achieved through providing relevant and practical protective factors, such as caring and attentive educational settings, positive and high expectations, positive learning environments, a strong supportive social community, and supportive peer relationships (see, for example, Rutter et al., 1979; Johnson et al., 1999). Resilience, therefore, is not a quality that is innate. Rather, it is a construct that is relative, developmental and dynamic (Rutter, 1990). It is thus both a product of personal and professional dispositions and values influenced by organizational and personal factors, and determined by individuals' capacities to manage context-specific factors. For example, teachers may respond positively or negatively in the presence of challenging circumstances, and this will depend on the quality of organizational or colleague leadership as well as the strength of their own commitment. The social construction of leadership resilience acknowledges, as the psychological construction does not, the importance of such combinations of personal, professional and situated factors and, as for teachers, on the capacities of heads to sustain their emotional well-being and professional commitment.

Yet resilience itself is not enough. Poor leaders (and teachers) may be resilient. They may survive without changing, without improving. Resilience without moral purpose, without a willingness to be self-reflective and learn in order to change in order to continue to improve is not enough. Resilience, then, cannot be considered in isolation from these and other constructs of commitment, competence, agency, vocation, and individual and collective academic optimism and hope. Moreover, the head's responsibility is to ensure that the nature, environment and management of teachers' work is, as far as possible, designed to reduce negative experiences of stress and increase capacities for resilience. Resilience, from this perspective, describes 'what arises in a dynamic or dialectic between person and practices that reflects the evidence that the person is acting on and reshaping challenging circumstances in their lives so that they can propel themselves forward' (Edwards, 2010).

Hope

Teaching, and thus leadership, are a values-led profession concerned, at its heart, with change for the betterment of pupils and, ultimately, for society as a whole. Indeed, a world without hope would be 'a world of resignation to the status quo' (Simecka, 1984: 175).

Vision is an expression of hope, as Sockett suggests: 'an affirmation that despite the heartbreak and trials that we face daily . . . we can see that our actions can be purposeful and significant' (1993: 85). For school leaders, vision and hope need to be revisited regularly through daily acts of aspiration and trust and not just the end- or beginning-of-year staff meeting or workshop. The expression of hope through visioning is a dynamic process. It involves:

> A complex blend of evolving themes of the change programme. Visioning is a dynamic process, no more a one-time-event that has a beginning and an end than is planning. Visions are developed and reinforced from action, although they may have a seed that is based simply on hope.
>
> (Seashore Louis and Miles, 1990: 237)

Good leadership, like good teaching, is, by definition, a journey of hope based upon a set of ideals. Arguably, it is our ideals that sustain us through difficult times and changing personnel and professional environments. They are an essential part of resilience:

> Having hope means that one will not give in to overwhelming anxiety . . . Indeed, people who are hopeful evidence less depression than others as they manoeuvre through life in pursuit of their goals, are less anxious in general, and have fewer emotional distresses.
>
> (Goleman, 1995: 87)

The evidence from our research is that successful leaders, especially heads, are always beacons of hope in their schools and communities.

Moral purpose

There is a striking quality about fine teachers and school leaders – they care deeply about their students and want to improve their life chances, seeing high-quality education as a crucial factor that can be seen as an effective intervention to help to reduce inequality and the adverse impact of social disadvantage. Most teachers and heads come into teaching because they want to make a difference. A key characteristic of those outstanding teachers in the OECD 'Quality of Teaching' study was their 'love of children' (Hopkins,

1994). It may well be that, for various reasons, many of which may be to do with the context within which teachers currently work, a degree of cynicism and weariness may dull this initial enthusiasm. But as Michael Fullan commented long ago (1993: 10), 'scratch a good teacher and you find a moral purpose'.

In October 2006 one of us convened a group of 100 principals from 14 vastly different countries (the G100) at the National Academy of Education Administration (NAEA) in Beijing, China, to discuss the transformation of and innovation in the world's education systems. During the final session of the workshop the whole group collaborated in preparing a communiqué about their conclusions (Hopkins, 2008). The final paragraphs read thus:

> We need to ensure that moral purpose is at the fore of all educational debates with our parents, our students, our teachers, our partners, our policy makers and our wider community.
>
> We define moral purpose as a compelling drive to do right for and by students, serving them through professional behaviours that 'raise the bar and narrow the gap' and through so doing demonstrate an intent, to learn with and from each other as we live together in this world.
>
> (Hopkins, 2008: 127)

That such a diverse – in terms of context, yet homogenous, in terms of values – group of heads could unanimously say that speaks volumes of the moral purpose that drives our outstanding heads, both nationally and globally.

Moral purpose for successful heads is not high-blown idealism; it is simply the commitment to provide a high-quality education for all students regardless of background, to ensure that the conditions are in place to enable every student to reach their potential. This moral purpose is usually reflected in a small number of tangible but ambitious objectives for student learning and achievement that are being vigorously pursued. Through setting such goals and establishing the processes to achieve them, they intend, as we have seen in this book, to achieve a step change in the quality of education for their students. If these are the goals, then the means of achieving them are the values, behaviours and strategies that we have described and discussed in the preceding pages.

Finally, it is important to remember that, ultimately, the challenge of leadership, particularly within a systemic context, has great moral depth to it. It directly addresses the learning needs of students and the professional growth of teachers, and enhances the role of the school as an agent of social change. As we have seen, moral purpose in education is best defined as a resolute failure to accept context as a determinant of academic and social success – acting on context and not accepting poverty and social background as necessary determinants of success in schooling, exercising wise and timely judgements about what to do, when and with whom, refusing to accept uncritically external policy mandates and guidelines, committing themselves to the school and its community and being prepared to communicate this and build trust, capacities and influence by staying, are at the heart of successful school improvement.

Appendices

Appendix 3.1 Selected examples of questions from head teacher survey

1. To what extent do you believe your leadership practice and actions have changed in relation to the following over the past _three years_?

	Not at all	Very little	Little	Partially	A lot	Very significantly
a) Giving staff a sense of overall purpose	1	2	3	4	5	6
b) Helping clarify the reasons for our school's improvement initiatives	1	2	3	4	5	6
c) Providing assistance to staff in setting short-term goals for teaching and learning	1	2	3	4	5	6
d) Demonstrating high expectations for staff's work with pupils	1	2	3	4	5	6
e) Demonstrating high expectations for pupil behaviour	1	2	3	4	5	6
f) Demonstrating high expectations for pupil achievement	1	2	3	4	5	6
g) Working collaboratively with the Governing Body	1	2	3	4	5	6
h) Working collaboratively with the Local Authority (LA)	1	2	3	4	5	6
i) Working collaboratively with the SMT/SLT	1	2	3	4	5	6
j) Integrating school priorities with the National Government's policy agenda	1	2	3	4	5	6

2. To what extent do you believe your actions have changed in relation to the following over the past _three years_?

	Not at all	Very little	Little	Partially	A lot	Very significantly
a) Giving staff individual support to help them improve their teaching practices	1	2	3	4	5	6
b) Encouraging them to consider new ideas for their teaching	1	2	3	4	5	6
c) Modeling a high level of professional practice	1	2	3	4	5	6
d) Developing an atmosphere of caring and trust	1	2	3	4	5	6
e) Promoting leadership development among teachers	1	2	3	4	5	6
f) Promoting a range of CPD experiences among all staff	1	2	3	4	5	6
g) Encouraging staff to think of learning beyond the academic curriculum (e.g. personal, emotional and social education, citizenship, etc.)	1	2	3	4	5	6

(Continued)

3. To what extent do you believe your actions have *changed in relation to the following* over the past *three years*?

	Not at all	Very little	Little	Partially	A lot	Very significantly
a) Encouraging collaborative work among staff	☐1	☐2	☐3	☐4	☐5	☐6
b) Ensuring wide participation in decisions about school improvement	☐1	☐2	☐3	☐4	☐5	☐6
c) Engaging parents in the school's improvement efforts	☐1	☐2	☐3	☐4	☐5	☐6
d) Increasing dialogue about school improvement between pupils and adults	☐1	☐2	☐3	☐4	☐5	☐6
e) Improving internal review procedures	☐1	☐2	☐3	☐4	☐5	☐6
f) Building community support for the school's improvement efforts	☐1	☐2	☐3	☐4	☐5	☐6
g) Utilising support staff skills for the benefit of pupil learning	☐1	☐2	☐3	☐4	☐5	☐6
h) Allocating resources strategically based on pupil needs	☐1	☐2	☐3	☐4	☐5	☐6
i) Working in collaboration with other schools	☐1	☐2	☐3	☐4	☐5	☐6
j) Structuring the organisation to facilitate work	☐1	☐2	☐3	☐4	☐5	☐6

4. To what extent do you believe your actions have *changed in relation to the following* over the past *three years*?

	Not at all	Very little	Little	Partially	A lot	Very significantly
a) Providing or locating resources to help staff improve their teaching	☐1	☐2	☐3	☐4	☐5	☐6
b) Regularly observing classroom activities	☐1	☐2	☐3	☐4	☐5	☐6
c) After observing classroom activities, working with teachers to improve their teaching	☐1	☐2	☐3	☐4	☐5	☐6
d) Using coaching and mentoring to improve quality of teaching	☐1	☐2	☐3	☐4	☐5	☐6
e) Frequently discussing educational issues with staff	☐1	☐2	☐3	☐4	☐5	☐6
f) Buffering teachers from distractions to their teaching	☐1	☐2	☐3	☐4	☐5	☐6
g) Encouraging staff to use data in their work	☐1	☐2	☐3	☐4	☐5	☐6
h) Encouraging all staff to use data in planning for individual pupil needs	☐1	☐2	☐3	☐4	☐5	☐6
i) Incorporating research evidence into my decision making to inform practice		☐2	☐3	☐4	☐5	☐6
j) Using pupil achievement data to make most decisions about school improvement	☐1	☐2	☐3	☐4	☐5	☐6

Appendix 3.2 Categorized primary head responses to three most important actions/ strategies used to effect improvement over three years

	No. responses	%	No. cases	%
A) Leadership practices				
1) Setting directions				
i) Giving staff a sense of purpose	16	1.3	16	4.2
ii) Improved school improvement planning	43	3.4	39	10.3
iii) Assistance with short-term goal setting for teaching and learning	35	2.8	34	9.0
iv) Demonstrating high expectations for staff	28	2.2	25	6.6
2) Developing people				
i) Giving staff support and ideas to improve teaching practice	29	2.3	27	7.2
ii) Modelling a high level of professional practice	3	0.2	3	0.8
iii) Atmosphere of caring and trust	12	1.0	11	2.9
iv) Promoting leadership development and CPD	63	5.0	60	15.9
v) Improved recruitment and retention of staff	12	1.0	12	3.2
3) Redesigning the organization				
i) Encouraging collaborative work and participation amongst staff	38	3.0	37	9.8
ii) Engaging parents and the community	20	1.6	20	5.3
iii) Improving internal review procedures	6	0.5	6	1.6
iv) Strategic allocation of resources	86	6.8	77	20.4

Appendix 3.3 Categorized secondary head responses to three most important actions/ strategies used to effect improvement over three years

	No. responses	%	No. cases	%
A) Leadership practices				
1) Setting directions				
i) Giving staff a sense of purpose	17	1.5	17	4.7
ii) Improved school improvement planning	24	2.1	23	6.3
iii) Assistance with short-term goal setting for teaching and learning	53	4.5	51	14.0
iv) Demonstrating high expectations for staff	40	3.4	38	10.4
2) Developing people				
i) Giving staff support and ideas to improve teaching practice	18	1.5	18	4.9

(Continued)

	No. responses	%	No. cases	%
ii) Modelling a high level of professional practice	6	0.5	6	1.6
iii) Atmosphere of caring and trust	7	0.6	7	1.9
iv) Promoting leadership development and CPD	58	5.0	55	15.1
v) Improved recruitment and retention of staff	9	0.8	9	2.5
3) Redesigning the organization				
i) Encouraging collaborative work and participation amongst staff	23	2.0	21	5.8
ii) Engaging parents and the community	20	1.7	19	5.2
iii) Improving internal review procedures	36	3.1	36	9.9
iv) Strategic allocation of resources	31	2.7	29	7.9
v) Working in collaboration with other schools	12	1.0	12	3.3
vi) Restructuring the organization to facilitate work	57	4.9	52	14.2
4) Improving teaching practices				
i) Providing and allocating resources	73	6.3	71	19.5
ii) Classroom observation	25	2.1	25	6.8
iii) Coaching and mentoring	20	1.7	20	5.5
iv) Buffering teachers from distractions	5	0.4	5	1.4
v) Encouraging the use of data and research	130	11.1	124	34.0
vi) Focus on teaching policies and practices	105	9.0	101	27.7
B) Leader self-efficacy	6	0.5	6	1.6
C) Leadership distribution	15	1.3	15	4.1
D) Persuasion tactics	5	0.4	5	1.4
E) School conditions				
1) The school	41	3.5	40	11.0
2) Disciplinary climate	36	3.1	35	9.6
3) Academic press or emphasis				
i) Teachers/school have high standards	14	1.2	14	3.8
ii) Monitoring of departments and teachers	61	5.2	58	15.9
iii) Improved assessment procedures	69	5.9	68	18.6
iv) Changes to pupil target setting	44	3.8	43	11.8
4) School culture	85	7.3	77	21.1
5) Co-curricular programmes	6	0.5	6	1.6
6) Extended services	4	0.3	4	1.1
F) Classroom conditions				
1) Workload volume	9	0.8	9	2.5
2) Workload complexity	4	0.3	4	1.1
Missing	–	–	16	4.4
Total	1168		365	

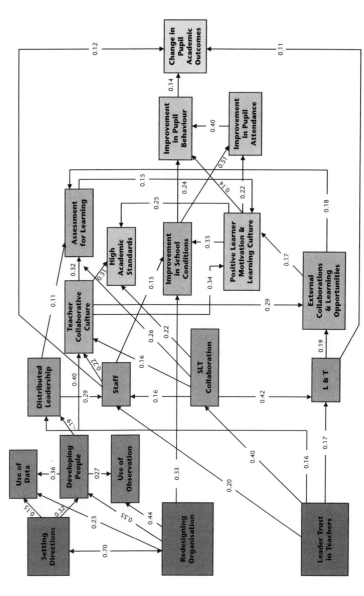

N = 309 Predicting change in pupil academic outcomes % GCSE 5A*-C: Secondary School Heads (standardised solution displayed LISREL SEM model)

Appendix 3.4 SEM model for Secondary Schools

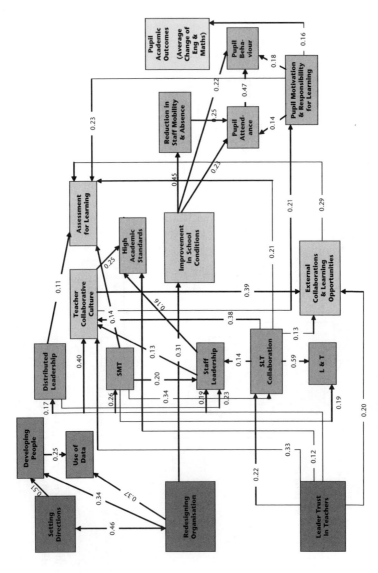

Appendix 4.1 Head teacher perceptions of leadership practices and changes in pupil outcomes over three years (2003–05): primary

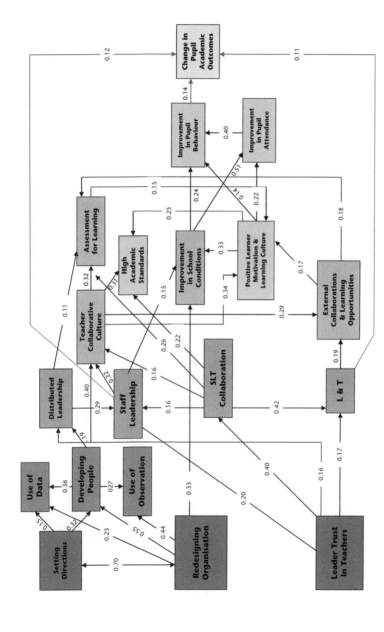

Appendix 4.2 Example of leadership practices and changes in secondary pupil outcomes over three years: a structural equation model (N = 309)

Appendix 5.1 Definitions of FFT improvement flags

Based on three years of data, FFT classified schools' raw and contextual and simple VA results according to the statistical significance of the differences. The results are 'flagged' if there has been a significant change (95% Confidence Limits, 1.96 SD; $p < 0.05$) over the three-year period: Trend 3 flags.

Thus, 'Improving' over a three-year period could be any one of:

a) significant improvement Year 1–Year 2 and then no significant change Year 2–Year 3;
b) no significant change Year 1–Year 2 and significant improvement Year 2–Year 3; and
c) significant improvement Year 1–Year 3.

Similar criteria apply to 'Declining'. 'Varying' is significant improvement ($p < 0.05$) and decline (or vice versa), whereas 'Steady' suggests no significant change over the three-year period.

Improvement flags are derived by counting how many Trend 3 flags are 'Improving' – based upon the definition above – for two indicators per Key Stage combination: Level 5+ in English, maths and science, and Mean NC Level (English, maths, science) at KS2–3; 5A*–C and PTC at KS2–4 and KS3–4. Thus, the maximum possible is six improvement flags.

In sum, schools with one to six improvement flags are those which have seen significant improvement based on raw, simple and contextual value added results between 2003 and 2005. The more improvement flags, the greater levels of significant improvement of the school.

Appendix 5.2 FFT improving and effective schools by FSM Band

	Secondary Potential Sample		Secondary National		Primary Potential Sample		Primary National	
	Frequency	(%)	Frequency	(%)	Frequency	(%)	Frequency	(%)
FSM1	401	35	1159	37	1852	37	6150	42
FSM2	393	34	1097	35	1366	27	3896	27
FSM3	191	17	520	17	870	17	2359	16
FSM4	156	14	339	11	915	18	2267	15
Total	1141	100	3115	100	5003	100	14672	100

Appendix 5.3   Survey response rate

	Returned questionnaires (N)	Overall response rate School sample size (N)	Response rate (%)
Table A: Survey response rate (head teachers)			
Primary	378	1550	24
Secondary	362	1140	32
Table B: Survey response rate (key staff at school level)			
	No. of schools with returned questionnaires		
Primary	409	1550	26
Secondary	393	1140	34
Table C: Survey response rate (key staff at questionnaire level)			
		Overall response rate Questionnaire sample size* (N)	
Primary	608	3100	20
Secondary	1167	5700	20

* Schools were sent two forms for key staff in primary schools and five for head of department in secondary schools.

References

Anderson, N. (2010) Supportive leadership helps retain top teachers, *The Washington Post*. www.washingtonpost.com/wpdyn/content/article/2010/03/02/AR2010030204203.html.

Avolio, B.J. (1994) The alliance of total quality and the full range of leadership, in *Improving Organizational Effectiveness through Transformational Leadership*, B.M. Bass and B.J. Avolio (eds), Sage, Thousand Oaks, CA.

Avolio, B.J. and W. Gardner (2005) Authentic leadership development: Getting to the root of positive forms of leadership, *Leadership Quarterly*, 16 (3): 315–38.

Ball, S.J. (1993) Education markets, choice and social class: The market as a class strategy in the UK and the USA, *British Journal of Sociology of Education*, 14 (1): 3–19.

Bandura, A. (1986) *Social Foundations of Thought and Action*, Prentice-Hall, Englewood Cliffs, NJ.

Bass, B.M. (1985) *Leadership and Performance beyond Expectations*, Free Press, New York.

Bass, B.M. and B.J. Avolio (1994) *Improving Organizational Effectiveness through Transformational Leadership*, Sage, Thousand Oaks, CA.

Beard, K.S., W.K. Hoy and A.W. Hoy (2010) Academic optimism of individual teachers: Confirming a new construct, *Teaching and Teacher Education*, 26: 1136–44.

Bennis, W. and B. Nanus (1985) *Leaders: The Strategies for Taking Charge*, Harper & Row, New York.

Braukmann, S. and P. Pashiardis (2009) From PISA to LISA New Educational Governance and School Leadership: exploring the foundations of a new relationship in an international context, paper presented to the AERA annual meeting, San Diego, April.

Brooks, J.S., G. Jean-Marie, A.H. Normore and D. Hodgins (2007) Distributed leadership for social justice: Equity and influence in an urban school, *Journal of School Leadership*, 17 (4): 378–408.

Bryk, A.S. and B. Schneider (2002) *Trust in Schools: A Core Resource for Improvement*, Russell Sage Foundation, New York.

Bush, T. and G. Oduro (2006) New principals in Africa: Preparation, induction and practice, *Journal of Educational Administration*, 44 (4): 359–75.

Cameron, D.H. (2010) Working with secondary school leadership in a large-scale reform in London, UK: Consultants' perspectives of their role as agents of school change and improvement, *Educational Management and Administration*, 38 (3): 341–59.

Clarke, S. and H. Wildy (2004) Context counts: Viewing small school leadership from the inside out, *Journal of Educational Administration*, 42 (5): 555–72.

Coleman, J.S. (1966) *Equality of Educational Opportunity*, Government Printing Office, Washington, DC.

Connolly, M. and C. James (2006) Collaboration for school improvement: A resource dependency and institutional framework of analysis, *Educational Management Administration and Leadership*, 34 (1): 69–87.

Creemers, B.P.M. and L. Kyriakides (2008) *The Dynamics of Educational Effectiveness*, Routledge, London.

Davies, L. (1987) The role of the primary school head, *Educational Management and Administration*, 15: 43–7.

Day, C. and Q. Gu (2010) *The New Lives of Teachers*, Routledge, London.

Day, C. and K. Leithwood (2007) *Successful School Principal Leadership in Times of Change: International Perspectives*, Springer, Dordrecht.

Day, C., P. Sammons and Q. Gu (2008) Combining qualitative and quantitative methodologies in research on teachers' lives, work and effectiveness: From integration to synergy, *Educational Researcher*, 37 (6): 330–42.

Day, C., A. Harris, M. Hadfield, H. Tolley and J. Beresford (2000) *Successful Leadership in Times of Change*, Open University Press, Buckingham.

Day, C., P. Sammons, D. Hopkins, A. Harris, K. Leithwood, Q. Gu, C. Penlington, P. Mehta and A. Kington (2007) *The Impact of Leadership on Pupil Outcomes: Interim report*, DSCF Research Report RR018, Department of Children, Families and Schools/National College of School Leadership, Nottingham.

Day, C., P. Sammons, D. Hopkins, A. Harris, K. Leithwood, Q. Gu, C. Penlington, P. Mehta, E. Brown and A. Kington (2009) *The Impact of Leadership on Pupil Outcomes: Final Report to DSCF*, Department of Children, Families and Schools/National College of School Leadership, Nottingham.

Day, C., P. Sammons, D. Hopkins, A. Harris, K. Leithwood, Q. Gu and E. Brown (2010) *10 Strong Claims about Successful School Leadership*, National College for Leadership of Schools and Children's Services, Nottingham.

De Maeyer, S., R. Rymenans, P. Van Petegem, H. van der Bergh and G. Rijlaarsdam (2006) Educational leadership and pupil achievement: The choice of a valid conceptual model to test effects in school effectiveness research, unpublished manuscript: University of Antwerp, Belgium.

DfES (Department for Education and Skills) (2005) *Higher Standards, Better Schools for All*, DfES, London.

Dunford, J. (2005) *Watering the Plants: Leading Schools and Improving the System*. Address to the National Conference of the Specialist Schools and Academies Trust.

Edwards, A. (2010) Resilience as a concept from a cultural historical perspective. Paper presented to ESRC Seminar Series, *An Interdisciplinary Inquiry into the Nature of Resilience in Teachers*, 16 June, 2010, University of Oxford.

Evans, A. (2009) No Child Left Behind and the quest for educational equity: The role of teachers' collective sense of efficacy, *Leadership and Policy in Schools* 8 (1): 64–91.

Fink, D. and C. Brayman (2006) School leadership succession and the challenges of change, *Education Administration Quarterly*, 42: 62–89.

Finn, J.D. (1989) Withdrawing from school, *Review of Educational Research*, 59 (2): 117–43.

Finnigan, K. and T. Stewart (2009) Leading change under pressure: An examination of principal leadership in low-performing schools, *Journal of School Leadership*, 19 (5): 586–618.

Foster, R. and B. St Hilaire (2004) The who, how, why, and what of leadership in secondary school improvement: Lessons learned in England, *Alberta Journal of Educational Research*, 50 (4): 354–69.

Fullan, M. (1993) *Change Forces: Probing the Depths of Educational Reform*, Falmer Press, London.

Fullan, M. (2003) *The Moral Imperative of School Leadership*, Corwin Press, Thousand Oaks, CA.

Goddard, R.D., W.K. Hoy and A.W. Hoy (2000) Collective teacher efficacy: Its meaning, measure, and impact on student achievement, *American Educational Research Journal*, 37 (2): 479–507.

Goddard, R.D., S.R. Sweetland and W.K. Hoy (2000) Academic emphasis of urban elementary schools and student achievement: A multi-level analysis, *Educational Administration Quarterly*, 36: 683–702.

Goldring, E.B. (1990) Elementary school principals as boundary spanners: Their engagement with parents, *Journal of Educational Administration*, 1: 53–62.

Goldring, E., J. Huff, H. May and E. Camburn (2008) School context and individual characteristics: What influences principal practice, *Journal of Educational Administration*, 46 (3): 332–52.

Goldring, E. and S. Rallis (1993) *Principals of Dynamic Schools*, Corwin Press, Newbury Park, CA.

Goldstein, H. (1995) *Multilevel Statistical Models*, Edward Arnold, London, and Halsted Press, New York.

Goleman, D.P. (1995) *Emotional Intelligence: Why It Can Matter More Than IQ for Character, Health and Lifelong Achievement*, New York, Bantam Books.

Goodson, I.F. and A. Hargreaves (eds) (1996) *Teachers' Professional Lives*, Falmer Press, London.

Gordon, J. and J.A. Patterson (2006) School leadership in context: Narratives of practice and possibility, *International Journal of Leadership in Education*, 9 (3): 205–28.

Grace, G. (1995) *School Leadership: Beyond Education Management. An Essay in Policy Scholarship*, Falmer Press, London and Washington.

Graen, G.B. and M. Uhl-Bien (1995) Relationship-based approach to leadership: Development of leader-member exchange (LMX) theory of leadership over 25 years: Applying a multi-level multi-domain perspective, *Leadership Quarterly*, 6: 219–47.

Gray, J. (2000) *Causing Concern but Improving: A Review of Schools' Experience*, Department for Education and Skills, London.

Gray, J., D. Hopkins, D. Reynolds, B. Wilcox, S. Farrel and D. Jesson (1999) *Improving Schools: Performance and Potential*, Open University Press, Buckingham.

Gronn, P. (2008) Hybrid leadership, in *Distributed Leadership According to the Evidence*, K. Leithwood, B. Mascall and T. Strauss (eds), Routledge, London.

Gu, Q., P. Sammons and P. Mehta (2008) Leadership characteristics and practices in schools with different effectiveness and improvement profiles, *School Leadership and Management*, 28 (1): 43–63.

Hadfield, M. (2003) Building capacity versus growing schools, in *Effective Leadership for School Improvement*, A. Harris, C. Day, D. Hopkins, M. Hadfield, A. Hargreaves and C. Chapman (eds), Routledge Falmer, New York.

Hallinger, P. (2001) The principal's role as instructional leader: A review of studies using the 'Principal Instructional Management Scale'. Paper presented at the annual meeting of the American Educational Research Association, Seattle, WA.

Hallinger, P. (2003) Leading educational change: Reflections on the practice of instructional and transformational leadership, *Cambridge Journal of Education*, 33 (3): 329–51.

Hallinger, P. (2005) Instructional leadership and the school principal: A passing fancy that refuses to fade away, *Leadership and Policy in Schools*, 4 (3): 1–20.

Hallinger, P., L. Bickman and K. Davis (1996) School context, principal leadership, and student reading achievement, *The Elementary School Journal*, 96 (5): 527–49.

Hallinger, P. and R. Heck (1996) The principal's role in school effectiveness: An assessment of methodological progress, 1980–1995, in *International Handbook of Educational Leadership and Administration*, K. Leithwood and P. Hallinger (eds), Kluwer, Dordrecht.

Hallinger, P. and R. Heck (1998) Exploring the principal's contribution to school effectiveness: 1980–1995, *School Effectiveness and School Improvement*, 9 (2): 157–91.

Hallinger, P. and R. Heck (1999) Next generation methods for the study of leadership and school improvement, in *Handbook of Research on Educational Administration*, J. Murphy and K. Louis (eds), Jossey-Bass, San Francisco, CA.

Hallinger, P. and R. Heck (2009) Assessing the contribution of distributed leadership to school improvement and growth in math achievement, *American Educational Research Journal*, 46 (3): 659–89.

Hallinger, P. and R. Heck (2010) Collaborative leadership and school improvement: Understanding the impact on school capacity and student learning, *School Leadership and Management*, 30 (2): 95–110.

Halpern, D. (2009) Capital gains, *Royal Society of Arts Journal* (Autumn): 10–15.

Hardin, R. (2006) *Trust*, Polity Press, Malden, MA.

Hargreaves, A. and D. Fink (2006) *Sustainable Leadership*, Wiley and Sons, San Francisco, CA.

Harris, A. (2008) Distributed leadership: The evidence, in *Distributed School Leadership: Developing Tomorrow's Leaders*, Routledge, London.

Harris, A. and C. Chapman (2002) *Effective Leadership in Schools Facing Challenging Circumstances*, National College for School Leadership, Nottingham.

Harris, A., P. Clarke, S. James, B. Harris and J. Gunraj (2006) *Improving Schools in Difficulty*, Continuum Press, London.

Harris, A., I. Jamieson and J. Russ (1995) A study of effective departments in secondary schools, *School Organisation*, 15 (3): 283–99.

Harris, A. and D. Muijs (2004) *Improving Schools through Teacher Leadership*, Oxford University Press, London.

Haydn, T. (2001) From a very peculiar department to a very successful school: Transference issues arising out of a study of an improving school, *School Leadership and Management*, 21 (4): 415–39.

Henchey, N. (2001) *Schools that Make a Difference: Final Report, Twelve Canadian Secondary Schools in Low Income Settings*, Society for the Advancement of Excellence in Education, Kelowna, BC.

Higgins, G. (1994) *Resilient Adults: Overcoming a Cruel Past*, Jossey-Bass, San Francisco, CA.

Higham, R., D. Hopkins and E. Ahtaridou (2007) *Improving School Leadership: Country Background Report for England*, available from www.oecd.org/data-oecd/33/45/39279379.pdf (accessed on 23 November 2007).

Highfield, C. (2010) Disparity in student achievement within and across secondary schools: An analysis of department results in English, maths and science in New Zealand. *School Leadership and Management*, 30 (2): 171–90.

Hofstede, G. (2001) *Culture's Consequences: Comparing Values, Behaviors, Institutions, and Organizations Across Nations*, Sage, Thousand Oaks, CA.

Hopkins, D. (1994) *Quality in Teaching*, OECD, Paris.

Hopkins, D. (2008) *Transformation and Innovation: System Leaders in the Global Age*, Specialist Schools and Academies Trust, London.

Hopkins, D. and R. Higham (2007) System leadership: Mapping the landscape, *School Leadership and Management*, 27 (2): 147–66.

Horn, I.S. and J.W. Little (2010) Attending to problems of practice: Routines and resources for professional learning in teachers' workplace interactions, *American Educational Research Journal*, 47 (1): 181–217.

House, R.J., P.J. Hanges, M. Javidan, P.W. Dorfman and V. Gupta (2004) *Culture, Leadership, and Organizations: The GLOBE Study of 62 Societies*, Sage, Thousand Oaks, CA.

Hoy, A.W., W.K. Hoy and N.M. Kurtz (2008) Teachers' academic optimism: The development and test of a new construct, *Teaching and Teaching Education*, 24: 821–32.

Hoy, W.K. and C.G. Miskel (2005) *Educational Administration: Theory, Research and Practice*, McGraw-Hill, New York.

Jackson, D. (2002) The creation of knowledge networks: Collaborative enquiry for school and system improvement, paper presented at the CERI/OECD/DfES/

QCA ESRC forum 'Knowledge Management in Education and Learning', 18–19 March, Oxford.

James, C., M. Connolly, G. Dunning and T. Elliott (2006) *How Very Effective Primary Schools Work*, Paul Chapman, London.

Johnson, B., S. Howard and M. Oswald (1999) Quantifying and prioritising resilience-promoting factors: Teachers' views, paper presented at the Australian Association for Research in Education and New Zealand Association for Research in Education conference, Melbourne, 29 November–2 December.

Kelly, C. and J. Shaw (2010) *Learning First! A School Leaders' Guide to Closing the Achievement Gap*, Corwin Press, Thousand Oaks, CA.

Kerr, S. and J.M. Jermier (1978) Substitutes for leadership: Their meaning and measurement, *Journal of Organisational Behaviour and Human Performance*, 22 (3): 375–403.

Kmetz, J. (1982) Elementary school principals' work behavior, *Educational Administration Quarterly*,18 (4): 62–78.

Kruger, M., B. Witziers and P. Sleegers (2007) The impact of school leadership on school level factors: Validation of a causal model, *School Effectiveness and School Improvement*, 18 (1): 1–20.

Kythreotis, A., P. Pashiardis and L. Kyriakides (2010) The influence of school leadership styles and culture on students' achievement in Cyprus primary schools, *Journal of Educational Administration*, 48 (2): 218–40.

Lee, V. and R. Croninger (1994) The relative importance of home and school in the development of literacy skills for middle-grade students, *American Journal of Education*, 102 (3) (May): 286–329.

Leithwood, K., P.T. Begley and J.B. Cousins (1992) *Developing Expert Leadership for Future Schools*, Falmer Press, London.

Leithwood, K. and C. Day (2007) Starting with what we know, in *Successful Principal Leadership in Times of Change*, C. Day and K. Leithwood (eds), Springer, Dordrecht.

Leithwood, K., C. Day, P. Sammons, A. Harris and D. Hopkins (2006a) *Seven Strong Claims about Successful School Leadership*, DfES, London, and NCSL, Nottingham.

Leithwood, K., C. Day, P. Sammons, A. Harris and D. Hopkins (2006b) *Successful School Leadership: What it Is and How it Influences Pupil Learning*, DfES, London, available at www.dfes.gov.uk/research/data/uploadfiles/RR800.pdf.

Leithwood, K., A. Harris and D. Hopkins (2008) Seven strong claims about successful school leadership, *School Leadership and Management*, 28 (1): 27–42.

Leithwood, K., A. Harris and T. Strauss (2010) *School Turnaround Leadership*, Jossey-Bass, San Francisco, CA.

Leithwood, K. and D. Jantzi (1999) The relative effects of principal and teacher sources of leadership on student engagement with school, *Educational Administration Quarterly*, 35 (supplemental): 679–706.

Leithwood, K. and D. Jantzi (2000) *The Transformational School Leadership Survey* OISE/University of Toronto, Toronto, ON.

Leithwood, K. and D. Jantzi (2005) A review of transformational school leadership research: 1996–2005, *Leadership and Policy in Schools*, 4 (3): 177–99.

Leithwood, K. and D. Jantzi (2006) Transformational school leadership for large-scale reform: Effects on students, teachers, and their classroom practices, *School Effectiveness and School Improvement*, 17 (2): 201–27.

Leithwood, K. and D. Jantzi (2009) 'A review of empirical evidence about school size effects: a policy perspective', *Review of Educational Research* 79 (1): 464–90.

Leithwood, K., D. Jantzi and R. Steinback (2009) *Changing Leadership for Changing Times*, Open University Press, Maidenhead.

Leithwood, K. and B. Mascall (2008) Collective leadership effects on student learning, *Educational Administration Quarterly*, 44 (4): 529–61.

Leithwood, K., B. Mascall and T. Strauss (eds) (2008) *Distributed Leadership According to the Evidence*, Routledge, London.

Leithwood, K. and C. Riehl (2005) What we know about successful school leadership, in *A New Agenda: Directions for Research on Educational Leadership*, W. Firestone and C. Riehl (eds), Teachers College Press, New York.

Leithwood, K. and R. Steinbach (1995) *Expert Principal Problem Solving: Evidence from School and District Leaders*, SUNY Press, New York.

Leithwood, K. and J. Sun (2009) Transformational school leadership effects on schools, teachers and students, in *School improvement*, W. Hoy, and M. DiPaola (eds), Information Age Publishers, Charlotte, NC.

Leithwood, K., K. Louis, S. Anderson and K. Wahlstrom (2004) *The Learning from Leadership Project (2004–2009)*, Wallace Foundation, New York.

Little, J. (1982) Norms of collegiality and experimentation: Workplace conditions of school success, *American Educational Research Journal*, 19: 325–40.

Locke, E.A. (2002) The leaders as integrator: The case of Jack Welch at General Electric, in *Leadership*, L.L. Neider and C. Schriesheim (eds), Information Age Publishing, Greenwich, CT.

Lord, R. and K. Maher (1993) *Leadership and Information Processing: Linking Perceptions to Performance*, Routledge, New York.

Lowe, K.B., K.G. Kroeck and N. Sivasubramaniam (1996) Effectiveness correlates of transformational and transactional leadership: A meta-analytical review of the MLQ literature, *Leadership Quarterly*, 7 (3): 385–425.

Lutyen, H. and P. Sammons (2010) Multilevel modelling, in *Methodological Advances in Educational Effectiveness Research*, ed. B.P.M. Creemers, L. Kyriakides and P. Sammon, Routledge, London.

Lytton, H. and M. Pyryt (1998) Predictors of achievement in basic skills: A Canadian effective schools study, *Canadian Journal of Education*, 23 (3): 281–301.

Ma, X. and D.A. Klinger (2000) Hierarchical linear modeling of student and school effects on academic achievement, *Canadian journal of Education*, 25 (1): 41–55.

MacBeath, J. (2008) Distributed leadership: Paradigms, policy and paradox, in *Distributed Leadership According to the Evidence*, K. Leithwood, B. Mascall and T. Strauss (eds), Routledge, London.

MacGregor, D. (1960) *The Human Side of Enterprise*, McGraw-Hill, New York.

Marks, H. and S. Printy (2003) Principal leadership and school performance: An integration of transformational and instructional leadership, *Educational Administration Quarterly*, 39 (3): 370–97.

Marzano, R.J., T. Waters and B.A. McNulty (2005) *School Leadership that Works: From Research to Results*, Association for Supervision and Curricula Development, Alexandria, VA.

Mascall, B., K. Leithwood, T. Strauss and R. Sacks (2008) The relationship between distributed leadership and teachers' academic optimism, *Journal of Educational Administration*, 46 (2): 214–28.

Mascall, B., S. Moore and D. Jantzi (2008) *The Impact of Leadership Turnover on School Success*, final report of research to the Wallace Foundation, New York.

Mattessich, P.W. and B.R. Monsey (1992) *Collaboration: What Makes it Work?*, Amherst H. Wilder Foundation, St Paul, MN.

Matthews, P. and P. Sammons (2004) *Improvement through Inspection: An Evaluation of the Impact of Ofsted's Work*, Ofsted/Institute of Education, London, available at www.ofsted.gov.uk/publications/index.cfm?fuseaction=pubs.displayfilean did=3696andtype=pdf.

Matthews, P. and P. Sammons (2005) Survival of the weakest: The differential improvement of schools causing concern in England, *London Review of Education*, 3 (2): 159–76.

McGuigan, L. and W.K. Hoy (2006) Principal leadership: Creating a culture of academic optimism to improve achievement for all students, *Leadership and Policy in Schools* 5: 203–29.

Mintrop, H. (2004) *Schools on Probation: How Accountability Works (and Doesn't Work)*, Teachers College Press, New York.

Mortimore, P., P. Sammons, L. Stoll, D. Lewis and R. Ecob (1988) *School Matters: The Junior Years*, Open Books, Wells.

Muijs, D., A. Harris, C. Chapman, L. Stoll and J. Russ (2004) Improving schools in socioeconomically disadvantaged areas: A review of research evidence, *School Effectiveness and School Improvement*, 15 (2): 149–75.

Mulford, B. (2007) *Overview of Research on Australian Educational Leadership 2001–2005*, Australian Council for Educational Leaders Monograph No. 40, Australian Council for Educational Leaders, Melbourne.

Mulford, B. (2008) *The Leadership Challenge: Improving Learning in Schools*, Australian Education Review Number 53, Australian Council for Educational Research, Camberwell.

Murphy, J. and L. Beck (1995) *School-Based Management as School Reform*, Corwin Press, Thousand Oaks, CA.

Northouse, P. (2007) *Leadership: Theory and Practice*, Sage, Thousand Oaks, CA.

O'Day, J. (1996) Incentives and student performance, in *Rewards and Reform: Creating Educational Incentives that Work*, S. Fuhrman and J. O'Day (eds), Jossey-Bass, San Francisco, CA.

Ofsted (2000) *Improving City Schools*, Ofsted, London.

Ofsted (2009) *Twelve Outstanding Secondary Schools Excelling Against the Odds*, Ofsted, London.

O'Neill, O. (2002) *A Question of Trust: The BBC Reith Lectures 2002*, Cambridge University Press, Cambridge.

Pashiardis, P. and P. Ribbins (2003) On Cyprus: The making of secondary school principals, *International Studies in Educational Administration*, 31 (2): 13–34.

Penlington, C., A. Kington and C. Day (2008) Leadership in improving schools: A qualitative perspective, *School Leadership and Management*, 28 (1) (February): 65–82.

Podsakoff, P., S. MacKenzie, R. Moorman and R. Fetter (1990) Transformational leader behaviours and their effects on followers' trust in leader satisfaction and organizational citizenship behaviours, *Leadership Quarterly*, 1 (2): 107–42.

Printy, S. (2010) Principals' influence on instructional quality: Insights from US schools, *School Leadership and Management*, 30 (2): 111–26.

PWC (2007) *Independent Study into School Leadership*, a report for the DfES, RR818A, DfES, London.

Reeves, J. (2000) Tracking the links between pupil attainment and development planning, *School Leadership and Management*, 20 (3): 315–32.

Reynolds, A.J., S. Stringfield and D. Muijs (n.d.) Results for the High Reliability Schools Project, unpublished manuscript.

Reynolds, D. (1998) The study and remediation of ineffective schools: Some further reflections, in *No Quick Fixes: Perspectives on Schools in Difficulties*, L. Stoll and K. Myers (eds), Falmer Press, London.

Reynolds, D., D. Hopkins, D. Potter and C. Chapman (2001) *School Improvement for Schools Facing Challenging Circumstances: A Review of Research and Practice*, Department for Education and Skills, London.

Rizvi, F. (1989) In defence of organisational democracy, in *Critical Perspectives on Educational Leadership*, J. Smyth (ed.), Falmer Press, London.

Robinson, V. (2007) The impact of leadership on student outcomes: Making sense of the evidence, in *The Leadership Challenge: Improving Learning in Schools. Proceedings of the Australian Council for Educational Research Conference*, Melbourne, 12–16.

Robinson, V. (2008) Forging the links between distributed leadership and educational outcomes, *Journal of Educational Administration*, 46 (2): 241–56.

Robinson, V., M. Hohepa and C. Lloyd (2009) *School Leadership and Student Outcomes: Identifying What Works and Why. Best Evidence Syntheses Iteration (BES)*, Ministry of Education, New Zealand, available from http://educationcounts.govt.nz/goto/BES.

Robinson, V., C. Lloyd and K. Rowe (2008) The impact of leadership on student outcomes: An analysis of the differential effects of leadership types, *Educational Administration Quarterly*, 44: 635–74.

Rosenholtz, S.J. (1989) *Teachers' Workplace: The Social Organization of Schools*, Longman, New York.

Rowan, B. (1996) Standards as incentives for instructional reform, in *Rewards and Reform: Creating Educational Incentives that Work*, S.H. Fuhrman and J.J. O'Day (eds), Jossey-Bass, San Francisco, CA.

Rutter, M. (1990) Psychosocial resilience and protective mechanisms, in *Risk and Protective Factors in the Development of Psychopathology*, J. Rolf, A. Mastern, D. Cicchetti, K. Neuchterlein and S. Weintraub (eds), Cambridge University Press, New York.

Rutter, M., B. Maughan, P. Mortimer and J. Ousten (1979) *Fifteen-thousand Hours: Secondary Schools and Their Effects on Children*, Harvard University Press, Cambridge, MA.

Sammons, P. (2007) *School Effectiveness Research and Equity: Making Connections*, CfBT, London.

Sammons, P. (2008) Zero tolerance of failure and New Labour approaches to school improvement in England, *Oxford Review of Education*, 34 (6): 651–64.

Sammons, P., Gu, Q., Day, C., and Ko, J. (2011) "Exploring the impact of school leadership on pupil outcomes: Results from a study of academically improved and effective schools in England", *International Journal of Educational Management*, 25 (1): 83–101.

Sammons, P., T. Mujtaba, L. Earl and Q. Gu (2007) Participation in network learning community programmes and standards of pupil achievement: Does it make a difference?, *School Leadership and Management*, 27 (3) (July): 213–38.

Sammons, P., S. Thomas and P. Mortimore (1997) *Forging Links: Effective Schools and Effective Departments*, Paul Chapman, London.

Sarason, S. B. (1996) *Revisiting 'The Culture of the School and the Problem of Change'*, Teachers College Press, New York.

Scheerens, J. and R. Bosker (1997) *The Foundations of Educational Effectiveness*, Pergamon, Oxford.

Schussler, D.L. and A. Collins (2006) An empirical exploration of the who, what and how of school care, *Teachers College Record*, 108 (7): 1460–95.

Seashore Louis, K. (2007) Trust and improvement in schools, *Journal of Educational Change*, 8: 1–24.

Seashore Louis, K. and S.D. Kruse (1995) *Professionalism and Community: Perspectives on Reforming Urban Schools*, Corwin Press, Newbury Park, CA.

Seashore Louis, K. and S.D. Kruse (1998) Creating community in reform: Images of organizational learning in inner-city schools, in *Organizational Learning in Schools*, K. Leithwood and K. Seashore Louis (eds), Swets & Zeitlinger, Lisse.

Seashore Louis, K. and M.B. Miles (1990) *Improving the Urban High School: What Works and Why?*, Teachers College Press, New York.

Seashore Louis, K. and K. Wahlstrom (in press) Introduction, in *Learning from Leadership: Investigating the Links between Leadership and Student Learning*, K. Leithwood and K. Seashore Louis (eds), Jossey-Bass, San Francisco, CA.

Seldon, A. (2004) *Blair Unbound*, Simon and Schuster, London.

Seldon, A. (2009) *Trust: How We Lost it and How to Get it Back*, Biteback Publishing, London.

Shulman, L.S. (1998) Teaching and teacher education among the professions, 38th Charles W. Hunt Memorial Lecture, AACTE 50th Annual Meeting, New Orleans, Louisiana, 25 February 1998.

Silins, H. and W. Mulford (2002) Leadership and school results, in *Second International Handbook of Educational Leadership and Administration*, K. Leithwood and P. Hallinger (eds), Kluwer, Dordrecht.

Silins, H. and B. Mulford (2004) Schools as learning organisations: Effects on teacher leadership and student outcomes, *School Effectiveness and School Improvement*, 15 (4): 443–66.

Simecka, M. (1984) A world with utopias or without them?, in *Utopias*, P. Alexander and R. Gill (eds), Duckworth, London.

Smith, P.A. and W.K. Hoy (2007) Academic optimism and student achievement in urban elementary schools, *Journal of Educational Administration*, 45 (5): 556–68.

Sockett, H. (1993) *The Moral Base for Teacher Professionalism*, Teachers College Press, New York.

Solomon, R.C. and F. Flores (2001) *Building Trust: In Business, Politics, Relationships, and Life*, Oxford University Press, Oxford.

Southworth, G. (2008) Primary school leadership today and tomorrow, *School Leadership and Management*, 28 (5): 413–34.

Spillane, J. (2005) Primary school leadership practice: How the subject matters, *School Leadership and Management*, 25 (4): 383–97.

Spillane, J.P. (2006) *Distributed Leadership*, Jossey-Bass, San Francisco, CA.

Spillane, J.P., E.C. Camburn and A.S. Pareja (2008) School principals at work: a distributed perspective, in *Distributed Leadership According to the Evidence*, K. Leithwood, B. Mascall and T. Strauss (eds), Routledge, London.

Spillane, J.P., E. Camburn, J. Pustejovsky, A. Pareja and G. Lewis (2008) Taking a distributed perspective: Epistemological and methodological tradeoffs in operationalizing the leader-plus aspect, *Journal of Educational Administration*, 46 (2): 189–213.

Stein, M. and J. Spillane (2005) What can researchers on educational leadership learn from research on teaching?: Building a bridge, in *A New Agenda for Research in Educational Leadership*, W. Firestone and C. Riehl (eds), Teachers College Press, New York.

Stringfield, S., D. Reynolds and E.C. Schaffer (2008) *Improving Secondary Students' Academic Achievement through a Focus on Reform Reliability: Four and Nine Year Findings from the High Reliability Schools Project*, CfBT, London.

Sun, J. (2010) A review of transformational leadership research, University of Toronto, unpublished doctoral thesis.

Supovitz, J., P. Sirindides and H. May (2010) How principals and peers influence teaching and learning, *Educational Administration Quarterly*, 46 (1): 31–56.

Tashakkori, A. and C. Teddlie (2003) *Handbook of Mixed Methods in Social and Behavioural Research*, Sage, Thousand Oaks, CA.

Tschannen-Moran, M. (2001) Collaboration and the need for trust, *Journal of Educational Administration*, 39 (4): 308–31.

Tschannen-Moran, M. (2004) *Trust Matters: Leadership for Successful Schools*, Jossey-Bass, San Francisco, CA.

Tschannen-Moran, M. and M. Barr (2004) Fostering student achievement: The relationship between collective self-efficacy and student achievement, *Leadership and Policy in Schools*, 3 (3): 189–210.

Teddlie, C. and D. Reynolds (2000) *The International Handbook of School Effectiveness Research*, Falmer, London.

Teddlie, C. and P. Sammons (2010) Applications of mixed methods to the field of educational effectiveness research, in *Methodological Advances in Educational Effectiveness Research*, B.P.M. Creemers, L. Kyriakides and P. Sammons (eds), Routledge, London.

Thomson, P. (2009) *School Leadership: Heads on the Block?*, Routledge, London.

Wahlstrom, K. and K. Louis (2008) How teachers experience principal leadership: The roles of professional community, trust, efficacy and shared responsibility, *Educational Administration Quarterly*, 44 (4): 458–97.

Walberg, H. (1984) Improving the productivity of America's schools, *Educational Leadership*, 41 (8): 19–27.

Wallace, M. and L. Huckman (1999) *Senior Management Teams in Primary Schools*, Routledge, London.

Waters, T., R.J. Marzano and B. McNulty (2003) *Balanced Leadership: What 30 Years of Research Tells us about the Effect of Leadership on Pupil Achievement. A Working Paper*. Mid-continent Research for Education and Learning (McREL), Denver, CO.

Weindling, D. and C. Dimmock (2006) Sitting in the 'hot seat': new headteachers in the UK, *Journal of Educational Administration*, 44 (4): 326–40.

Wendell, T. (2000) *Creating Equity and Quality: A Literature Review*, Society for the Advancement of Excellence in Education, Kelowna, BC.

West, M., M. Ainscow and J. Stanford (2005) Sustaining improvement in schools in challenging circumstances: A study of successful practice, *School Leadership and Management*, 25 (1): 77–93.

Whitaker, P. (1993) *Managing Change in Schools*, Open University Press, Buckingham.

Wohlstetter, P., A. Datnow and P. Park (2008) Creating a system for data driven decision making: Applying the principal-agent framework, *School Effectiveness and School Improvement*, 19 (3): 239–59.

Woods, P.A., G.J. Woods and M. Cowie (2009) 'Tears, laughter, camaraderie': Professional development for headteachers, *School Leadership and Management*, 29 (3): 253–75.

Yukl, G. (1994) *Leadership in Organizations*, Prentice-Hall, Englewood Cliffs, NJ.

Index

SYSTEM LEADERSHIP IN PRACTICE

Rob Higham, David Hopkins
and Peter Matthews

978-0-335-23611-4 (Paperback)
2009

eBook also available

System leadership is a new, exciting and growing phenomenon in education. It refers to leadership that goes beyond a single school, where leaders work directly for the success and welfare of students in other institutions as well as their own.

In this inspirational book, the authors offer you new perspectives, support and guidance – whether you are a school leader, policy-maker or advisor – and show how working collaboratively and leading networks can bring about positive change. They encourage you to innovate, develop rigorous partnerships, take managed risks and deploy resources creatively in order to build sustained improvements in student learning and well-being.

Key features:

- Reference to real cases of system leadership in practice
- Reference to recent legislation
- Notes on relevant literature

www.openup.co.uk

NEW KINDS OF SMART
How the Science of Learnable
Intelligence is Changing Education

Bill Lucas and Guy Claxton

9780335236183 (Paperback)
2010

20th Century schools presumed that students' intelligence was largely fixed. 21st century science says that intelligence is expandable – and in a variety of ways. *New Kinds of Smart* argues that this shift in the way we think about young minds opens up hitherto unexplored possibilities for education.

Each chapter presents:

- Practical examples
- Tools and templates so that each new strand of thinking can be woven into your work as teachers and into your lives as learners

www.openup.co.uk

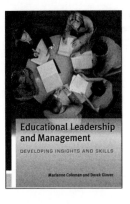

**EDUCATIONAL LEADERSHIP
AND MANAGEMENT**
Developing Insights and Skills

Marianne Coleman and Derek Glover

9780335236084 (Paperback)
2010

This accessible book demonstrates the insights and skills needed by leaders in education in an increasingly diverse society. It integrates theory with practice by presenting a real life scenario in each chapter. Drawing on literature and examples from both the UK and international sources, it takes a stance on equity, and offers a fresh look at what it means to be a leader in education today.

Key features:

- Theory and practice are brought together in a clear and accessible way
- It promotes an ethical stance based on values of social justice and equity
- Strong focus on cultural diversity
- The authors draw on their own extensive research to provide authentic and informed views

www.openup.co.uk

OPEN UNIVERSITY PRESS
McGraw - Hill Education

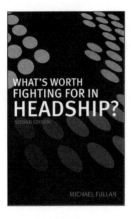

WHAT'S WORTH FIGHTING FOR IN HEADSHIP?

Michael Fullan

9780335235384 (Paperback)
2008

In the exciting new edition of this bestselling book, Michael Fullan looks at how much has changed in the world of headship and school improvement in recent decades, and offers key guidelines for being a successful head teacher in the 21st century.

This new edition provides:

- Six action guidelines for heads
- Six systems to enable Heads to make dramatic improvements in schools
- Ways to help incumbent and would-be head teachers to leverage action that will positively change the system in both small and large ways

www.openup.co.uk

 **OPEN UNIVERSITY PRESS**
McGraw - Hill Education